CHRISTMAS ON THE SCREEN

CHRISTMAS ON THE SCREEN

REVIEWING THE EVOLUTION OF AMERICAN SPIRITUALITY

JOHN A. ZUKOWSKI

The Pilgrim Press, 700 Prospect Avenue East
Cleveland, Ohio 44115-1100
thepilgrimpress.com

Published 2021.

In-text artwork and photographs used by permission. Scripture quotations, unless otherwise noted, are from the New Revised Standard Version of the Bible, © 1989 by the Division of Christian Education of the National Council of Churches of Christ in the United States of America. Used by permission. Changes have been made for inclusivity.

Printed on acid-free paper.

25 24 23 22 21 1 2 3 4 5

Library of Congress Cataloging-in-Publication Data on file
Library of Congress Control Number: 2021932642

ISBN 978-0-8298-2122-2 (alk. paper)
ISBN 978-0-8298-2176-5 (ebook)

Printed in The United States of America.

To

Virginia Zukowski

and

Ann Zukowski

for teaching me how to

live the Christmas spirit

all year round.

CONTENTS

1

What Is a Christmas Movie?

Even at a young age, I felt Christmas was connected to pop culture.

In an era before home video, I marked the *TV Guide* so I wouldn't miss *A Charlie Brown Christmas*, *Rudolph The Red-Nosed Reindeer*, and *How the Grinch Stole Christmas*. After I discovered classic Hollywood cinema, I also watched *It's a Wonderful Life*, *The Bishop's Wife*, and *Remember the Night*. Christmas wasn't the same if I didn't see them. Recently, when loading them up for another annual viewing, I wanted to figure out why.

It was more than nostalgia. The Hollywood war-era Christmas classics and the TV specials of the 1960s and 1970s portray spiritual awakenings and redemption stories. I saw three common elements in these spiritual conversions: validation of the transcendental, a rejection of materialism, and a move toward community.

But when watching more recent Christmas films I saw a startling difference. Beginning with the Christmas films of the 1980s, instead of spiritual and moral realizations, Christmas movies largely depict how to navigate dysfunctional families during the holiday. And many recent films subvert the traditional Christmas film themes by ignoring the transcendental, embracing materialism, and limiting community to immediate family.

When I researched the Christmas movie genre, I discovered this was largely unnoticed. And there were few serious studies of the Christmas movie genre. So I decided to explore the genre and track its changes over the years.

But first I had to define a Christmas film. By one estimate at least a quarter of the top-grossing films feature Christmas scenes.[1] So how much time must a movie devote to Christmas to be a Christmas movie? About half an hour of *Meet Me in St. Louis* takes place during the Christmas season. Does that make it a Christmas film? *It's a Wonderful Life* features most of its action in a flashback that doesn't take place during the Christmas season. So if the standard is the amount of time set during the Christmas season, *The Apartment*—a movie not usually associated with Christmas—has more time devoted to the Christmas season than *It's a Wonderful Life*. And what about movies such as *The Bells of St. Mary's* and *When Harry Met Sally*, with key scenes set around Christmas but most of the film not taking place at Christmas?

Movies with Christmas scenes aren't full-fledged Christmas films—even if important scenes or climactic scenes are set during Christmas. A significant portion of a movie must be set during the Christmas season to be a Christmas film. So *Meet Me in St. Louis*, with a quarter of its running time set on Christmas Eve, is a Christmas film, while *The Bells of St. Mary's*, with just a few Christmas scenes, isn't.

But are all films that devote considerable screen time to the Christmas season actually Christmas movies? Not necessarily. Some movies utilize the Christmas season for the imagery of Christmas, the emotional context associated with it, or simply a plot device to gather characters together. For example, *Diner* and *Just Friends* use the Christmas season as a reason for characters to return to their hometown. But the holiday itself isn't adequately integrated into the narrative. Other movies, such as *The Thin Man*, the film noir *Lady in the Lake*, and the neo noir *Kiss Kiss Bang Bang*, use Christmas as an ironic device to contrast associations of home and family with crime or detachment from community.

To be a true Christmas film it's necessary that a movie integrate Christmas into the story so the Christmas season affects plot and character development. This means assessing on a case-by-case basis how much impact Christmas has on the characters.[2] In the comedy *Diner*, Christmas doesn't have a transformative impact. Yet Christmas is transformative to characters in a black comedy such as *The Ref* and the existentialist crime drama *The Ice Harvest*. In films such as *Lethal Weapon* and *In Bruges*, Christmas is lodged somewhere between being a transformative and non-transformative influence.

The next question is how to define the genre in general. Every year a debate recirculates on the internet about whether *Die Hard* is a Christmas movie or not. Can an action film be a Christmas film? Despite

Is the action film *Lethal Weapon* (1987) a Christmas film? In some ways, yes, in some ways, no; this shows the difficulty sometimes in defining a Christmas movie. Courtesy Warner Brothers/Everett Collection.

the consistent iconography of Christmas music, decorations, and imagery used in Christmas films, the Christmas movie genre isn't a separate genre. Christmas films integrate into other genres. Christmas films can be musicals, Westerns, film noir, stoner comedies, crime stories, coming-of-age stories, action moves, as well as comedies and dramas. So, yes, *Die Hard* is a Christmas film.

A Charlie Brown Christmas **(1965) is part of the genre's Second Wave, which are Christmas TV shows from the 1960s and 1970s. The Christmas film genre is divided into three distinct eras, the first of which started in the World War II years.** Courtesy United Features Syndicate/Everett Collection.

Another distinctive feature of Christmas movies is that they are largely grouped together in three specific eras. That's because Christmas acts as a vehicle to respond to cultural anxieties of those time periods.

This is such a significant element to the genre that this book is organized by these three eras. The First Wave of Christmas movies appeared during the turmoil of the World War II era. The Second Wave emerged on television in the 1960s in the midst of civil unrest and generational clashes. And the Third Wave began in the 1980s in an era of growing materialism.

After doing research into the history of the holiday, I found out the major themes in First and Second Wave Christmas movies (validation of the transcendental, rejection of materialism, and movement toward community) emerged long before the advent of cinema.

Washington Irving's collection *The Sketch Book* (1819), describing an English country Christmas in an estate called Bracebridge Hall, is the first major influence. It's a romanticized journey to an idealized home where a somewhat world-weary but curious traveler gains insight about shortcomings, connects with community, and experiences nostalgia. The Christmas celebration restores a sense of well-being damaged by modern living.[3] This theme later manifests in Christmas films in journeys to homes associated with tradition, simpler living, and nostalgia that produce both a stronger sense of community and an inner transformation. The first major movie to use this convention was the 1940 film *Remember the Night*, which showed a drive from New York City to an idyllic Midwest country home. But it continued into the Third Wave era with busy affluent professionals returning to suburban family homesteads in films such as *The Family Stone*.

The second major pop culture influence occurred in 1823 with a redefinition of the figure that came to be known as Santa Claus when Clement Clarke Moore published the poem "A Visit from St. Nicholas" (also known by its first line "'Twas the Night Before Christmas"). In it, a "chubby and plump" man enters a home through the chimney to fill stockings with gifts. This jovial image of Saint Nicholas—soon to be renamed Santa Claus—became so widespread it replaced traditional stories of St. Nicholas and folklore legends of gift givers from other nationalities.[4] Moore's St. Nicholas softens St. Nicholas's enactment of Christmas as a "mini-version of the Day of Judgment."[5] In stories about St. Nicholas, good children are rewarded. Those who aren't sometimes are taken away by a punishing entity such as the folk figure Krampus. This mini-judgment is expressed in the 1934 song

"Santa Claus Is Coming to Town" where children are told "you better watch out," that Santa has omnipotent powers to know what children are doing, and that he divides children into the "naughty" and the "nice."[6] However, Moore's poem was significant because it changed St. Nicholas from a judgmental moral agent to a jovial working-class character.[7]

Moore's poem and Thomas Nast's widespread illustrations of this new Santa Claus a few decades later solved a growing concern about the commercialism of the holiday. The conflict between the nonmaterialism of a religious holy day and consumer materialism in the Christmas season creates what Russell Belk calls "the paradox of Christmas."[8] But instead of condemning materialism, these new works assimilated the sacred and secular. Images of elves in Santa's workshop producing toys by hand and Santa distributing them for free removes gifts from the commercial marketplace.[9] This embodies a highly romantic version of capitalism.[10] It focuses on material rewards without the commercial processes of mass manufacturing, marketing, and sales. To accomplish this, Santa uses his supernatural powers to mediate between the sacred and material worlds.[11] He is a sacred character because he becomes a Jesus-like figure who through the promise of reward or punishment encourages children to pursue a moral path.[12] He is in the realm of materialism, however, because he rewards children with material objects for their good behavior.

So Santa represents both secularized excess and an assessor of morality. Belk argues that Santa is a full-fledged hedonistic and materialist substitute for Jesus, with Santa providing toys and luxuries in contrast to Jesus, who offers health and necessities.[13] Santa brings items that are not everyday necessities, but exciting toys and games, while other activities such as office parties, family feasts, and candy encourage gluttony and self-indulgence.[14] The Christ figure analogies also come through other devices, including miracles such as flying reindeer, elves as apostles, letters to Santa as secular prayers, and Christmas carols as surrogate hymns.[15]

Yet even with Santa's emphasis on materialism as a reward, Santa's supernatural abilities still equate him with faith.[16] In the Christmas movie genre, Santa Claus sometimes becomes a symbol of the supernatural in films such as *Miracle on 34th Street* and *The Polar Express*. In recent years some films subverted this image of divine benevolence. In *Bad Santa* and in Christmas horror films, characters who dress as Santa instill fear or shatter the conception of trust children associate with Santa. These films show the tension between the Santa outfit and the personality inside it.[17] The connection between Santa and religion still prevailed in the early 2000s when some communities banned Santa Claus from holiday celebrations because organizers felt Santa was too associated with Christianity.[18]

Two other works enlarged the concept of Santa as a symbol of faith. The first was *Wizard of Oz* author Frank L. Baum's 1902 book *The Life and Adventures of Santa Claus*. It mythologized Santa Claus by creating a backstory for Santa where Santa becomes immortal because of his good deeds of giving toys to children.

The second came from an unlikely source. In 1897, eight-year-old Virginia O'Hanlon wrote a letter to *The New York Sun* asking if there was a Santa Claus. Editor Frank Church's widely reprinted reply with the famous first line "Yes, Virginia, there is a Santa Claus" argues against skepticism and rationality. At times sounding like a religious mystic, Church says a "veil" covers an "unseen world" temporarily experienced through sensations such as faith, poetry, love, and romance. Connecting Santa to transcendental spiritual experiences makes him not only the figure of supernatural power that Baum created but constructs Santa as a symbol of a broader spirituality that is personally experienced.

Although Santa was an important character who served sometimes as a deity figure or as an intermediary to solve the tension between spirituality and consumerism, one other figure became the most important influence on the Christmas movie genre.

Charles Dickens's 1843 novella *A Christmas Carol* featured the character of Ebenezer Scrooge undergoing a dramatic conversion experience from misanthropic miser to someone who is generous, charitable, and focused on community. Protagonists in Christmas films often become variations on Dickens's Scrooge who undergo spiritual awakenings. One writer termed this the Dickens Model.[19] The conversion experiences that characters undergo in Christmas films and TV shows, from George Bailey in *It's a Wonderful Life* to *How the Grinch Stole Christmas*, became a dominant narrative in First and Second Wave films but was minimized, ignored, and even subverted in many Third Wave films.

So the question I asked about the yearly ritual of watching Christmas movies and TV specials in the end led to something far bigger than just a summary of Christmas films. The images of Christmas on the screen over the history of the genre reflect the changing nature of American spirituality.

2

The Birth Narrative of Jesus on Film

For all of the Christmas movie genre's focus on the transcendental, Christmas movies have little direct connection to the birth of Christ. The films that depict Jesus's birth are the so-called "Jesus films," based on the gospels, as well as some films that update the nativity story to the present day.

The greatest constraint on the *Christ Film* is the theological issue of Christ's divinity.[20] To make the gospel film more accessible to nonbelievers, filmmakers downplay supernatural elements such as a virgin birth in the nativity story. Overall, gospel-based films emphasize Jesus's teachings rather than miracles or supernatural events.[21]

As a result, filmmakers depicting the Christmas origin story avoid or alter the supernatural elements and the theological implications surrounding the virgin birth. They insert extraneous material, exclude biblical material, and merge divergent material from the two gospels containing accounts of Jesus's birth. Over time, selecting, deleting, and combining material from the gospels created pop culture's own variation on the birth of Jesus.

From the Gospel of Matthew filmmakers take two key elements. The first is the account of the Judean ruler Herod, who orders the killing of babies in Bethlehem under the age of two so the prophecy of a newborn messiah won't be fulfilled. This forces Joseph, Mary, and Jesus to flee into exile in Egypt until Herod dies. Matthew's gospel sets up a tension between Herod and Jesus, with Herod encompassing worldly power and Jesus embodying spiritual power.[22] This contrast would often be the focus of the reworked nativity story in movies with an expanded role for Herod as a tyrant. The second element from Matthew's gospel is a visit to the holy couple from men often referred to as wise men or magi, who follow a star and are not named or numbered. Because they bring three gifts, it's often believed there were three of them.

The most popular components from the Gospel of Luke for filmmakers were the shepherds. Rather than the contrast and tension of power between Jesus and Herod, the Gospel of Luke shows how characters are spiritually transformed by the birth of Jesus. In Luke, the spiritual transformation is apparent in Mary's blessing and prayer (often called "The Magnificat") and Simeon's statements in the Jerusalem temple that Jesus will bring widespread change and a reversal of fortune in the world.

The selective blending of these elements from separate gospels is the "harmonizing" structure of gospel movies, which means combining elements from the gospels together.[23] In movies that feature the birth narrative, the most common four harmonized components are the Star of Bethlehem, the magi, the scene of Jesus's birth in a manger, and the shepherds. This is largely Luke's account, with the magi from Matthew. Gospel movies that devote more screen time to the virgin birth add the fifth component of Herod's character from Matthew.

However, the most pervasive image is putting the magi and the shepherds together at the place of Jesus's birth even though there is no indication in the gospels they were there together. This nonbiblical harmonized account conveys that Christ is—as a character in the movie *The Nativity Story* says—"for the highest of kings and the lowest of men." This serves as a vehicle to erase class tension and economic divide, with affluent noblemen and humble shepherds honoring the child together. It is different from what some scholars believe, which is that the magi represent scholars, not kings, and the shepherds symbolize sinners more than humility.[24]

This convention representing the social harmony of star, magi, shepherds, and manger in a stable became so standardized that the Bible-era epic *Ben Hur* (1959) presents a nativity scene in about three minutes with music and no dialogue. Nativity stories use these four components so often that the beginning of Monty Python's gospel satire *The Life of Brian* (1979)—with choral music, magi traveling across a desert on camels, and a trip through narrow streets to a stable with straw and animals—is indistinguishable from conventional nativity depictions. By the time of *Son of God* (2014), the birth narrative is just part of the opening credits and is reduced to ninety seconds. Mary and Joseph, the holy couple, say a total of four words between them.

Movies about the life of Jesus frequently emphasize this harmonized manger scene and avoid the subject of a virgin birth and physical appearances by angels announcing the birth to Mary. Because of this, Mary is marginalized and often reduced to a motherly figure holding a baby.

Another way the gospel movies handle the birth narrative dilemma is to focus on the ruler Herod, who in some gospel-based films receives more screen time than Mary, Joseph, and the infant Jesus. This places some gospel films more in the genre of the Roman-era historical film.[25] In gospel-based movies, Herod often becomes a stock character of an oppressive autocrat.

DOWNPLAYING THE SUPERNATURAL

The gospel-based movie with the most angels and supernatural elements is the first significant one to feature the birth narrative: the nineteen-minute silent film *The Life and Passion of Christ* (1902). It features numerous angels throughout the film, including angels appearing in the sky to the shepherds, a group of angels serenading the baby Jesus, and an angel protecting the holy couple on their way to Egypt. However, the next significant gospel movie, *From the Manger to the Cross* (1912), filmed on location in the Middle East with a running time of an hour, already shows a shift away from the virgin birth and angels. There are no physical representations of angels. Instead, the actors respond as if they see an angel, and Mary looks more like an adult nun than a young girl. The silent version of *Ben Hur* (1925) features a spectacular color sequence after the birth, with the shepherds and the wise men making separate visits to the nativity scene; however, the annunciation is not shown. Cecil B. Demille's blockbuster *King of Kings* (1927) shows no birth narrative at all.

In Nicholas Ray's *King of Kings* (1961), there are no annunciation, no angels, and probably the least harrowing journey and divine birth of any movie depicting the nativity story. Mary is a flat figure who shows no vulnerability, apprehension, or fear. Herod receives more screen time than Joseph, Mary, and Jesus during the movie's infancy narrative—which takes about seven minutes of the nearly three-hour running time. In the stiff and formal *The Greatest Story Ever Told* (1965), Joseph, Mary, and Jesus receive much less screen time during the birth narrative than Herod. As in *King of Kings*, no angelic visitations are shown. The birth narrative largely focuses on Matthew's emphasis on the birth as fulfilling prophecy, with many shots of oppressed Jewish people chanting and praying for a messiah. Similar is *Son of God* (2014), where the birth narrative is almost a footnote punctuated by a voice-over quoting the Gospel of John that "the Word became flesh and lived among us."[26] It's a quick declaration to emphasize, as in *The Greatest Story Ever Told*, that the messiah is born.

Even when the birth narrative receives more screen time, angels are absent and Mary's role is minimized. *Jesus of Nazareth* (1977) adds nonbiblical material to fill in the gaps in the gospel narrative. The birth story stretches to more than an hour, which makes it the lengthiest birth sequence in a major film until the 2006 film *The Nativity Story*. Real locations are used instead of sets, but the largely English cast still plays the characters as if trapped in a formal theater presentation. The film also includes awkward nonbiblical material, including engagement and wedding ceremonies for Joseph and Mary. The movie adds so much extraneous background it becomes a work of fiction more than gospel.[27] The annunciation happens not with an angel but with a ray of light coming in through a window that Mary (Olivia Hussey) responds to even though there is no voice or image.

The Nativity Story **(2006) accomplishes what nativity stories in the "Jesus film" couldn't do. It broadens and deepens the journey to Bethlehem, making it a period of spiritual awakening for Joseph (Oscar Isaac) and Mary (Keisha Castle-Hughes).** Photo courtesy New Line Cinema/Everett Collection.

So, since the first major silent movie about Jesus's life featuring the birth narrative, there isn't a physical angel shown in the major gospel movies with the exception of Pasolini's *The Gospel According to St. Matthew* (1964). However, in keeping with many gospel movies, Herod is an important figure. Instead of being a stock character repurposed from a Bible epic film, in Pasolini's film there is a disturbing contrast between

Herod's court and the helpless peasants who inhabit the village where Joseph and Mary live. Jesus is born into brutal oppression, and the presence of the angels at crucial moments emphasizes the divine guidance necessary for the holy couple to navigate this dangerous world.

The Nativity Story (2006) reversed the trend of de-emphasizing or eliminating the supernatural element of the birth narrative. It expanded Mary's storyline to the most complex narrative of Mary in the major films based on the gospels.

The movie humanizes Mary and Joseph, showing the faith and effort required to fulfill their mission. Keisha Castle-Hughes's realistic and vulnerable Mary portrays what is an important element to the story, which is Mary's spiritual progress. She starts in uncertainty and bewilderment and ends in faith and courage. During her spiritual development, she must convince her skeptical family about an impending supernatural birth, find a way to make an arranged marriage work when she is already pregnant, and take a perilous journey to Bethlehem with a man she has doubts about. "How do you get inside a leap of faith?" is how the film's director Katherine Harwicke described Mary's story.[28]

In *The Nativity Story*, Nazareth looks like a dystopian world, with its desert landscape and the weight of oppression from an imperialist and savage Roman army. Mary's stoic face, her mannerisms, and her outlook already contain a world-weariness from her bleak surroundings. She is a teenager with both vulnerabilities and determination. The shots of Castle-Hughes riding on a donkey are reminiscent of the compelling shots of the young Mary riding to Egypt from Pasolini's *Gospel According to Matthew*. She doesn't say a word, but her expressions contain a world of meaning about how young and vulnerable she is. That's far different from the spacey mystic Mary of *Jesus of Nazareth* or the overly self-assured Mary in *King of Kings*. Instead, *The Nativity Story* is about a young girl leaving her small community who must confront her doubts.[29]

In most birth narrative movies, there's little growth in Mary's relationship with Joseph, who is often portrayed as nondescript, a far older man, or, in the case of *Jesus of Nazareth,* a kind of English businessman in Middle Eastern clothing. In *The Nativity Story*, their mutual mission and purpose deepens Mary's relationship with Joseph (Oscar Isaac). Joseph learns to trust her and view her as not an idealized person but someone with whom to share a dangerous but necessary journey. And Mary must overcome her reluctance and uncertainty about marrying Joseph.

Mary and Joseph's relationship is not a romantic cliché or an icy obligation. Their relationship grows because they learn to trust each other and share a divine sense of mission. The movie also humanizes the magi, who disagree about whether to take the journey or not, worry about not having their usual comforts, and exhibit a crisis of faith about whether the signs about a new messiah are accurate. The wise men don't simply just arrive in exotic clothes with camels to bow down and deposit the three famous gifts of gold, frankincense, and myrrh. In *Nativity Story* they are given a backstory. They too are on a spiritual journey.

Mary and Joseph are outcasts far from home who grow increasingly desperate as the birth approaches. The familiar harmonized nativity imagery of star, straw, shepherds, and magi often makes the birth seem pastoral and serene. But in *The Nativity Story*, the holy couple are distraught outsiders on the run experiencing a birth shown as a struggle far beyond the cliché of a group of shepherds and magi together with a proud mother.

NATIVITY PLAYS AS SPIRITUAL AWAKENING

The second category of films directly influenced by the birth narrative of Jesus updates the story in various ways to the present day. One technique is having characters put on a nativity play, which transforms their perspectives from preoccupation with the self to focusing on community and spirituality.

A Charlie Brown Christmas (1965) shows a dysfunctional community corrupted by an emphasis on materialism, commercialism, and a loss of community. These things obscure the real meaning of Christmas, which

Linus corrects with a gospel reading of the nativity story. *A Charlie Brown Christmas* is the most radical of the 1960s Christmas TV specials for its condemnation of materialism and critique of the absence of religion in the modern Christmas celebration.

Charlie Brown's examination of the commercialism of Christmas produces an emptiness that appears to have no solution and creates a level of almost constant despair. He's alone in his deep questioning. And he's bullied by many of the other characters because he doesn't combat them with the same posturing or threat of violence other characters use. Many of the other characters are adept at defending their egos and insecurities—or in the case of Lucy, even using the threat of violence to get her brother Linus to be compliant. Charlie Brown is ruthlessly picked on, which he seems to accept as his fate. This is the burden the moral and examining person must endure.

Charlie Brown is acutely aware of the world's moral flaws and the pain of isolation that comes from social ostracization. Most of the other children don't have his sensitivity. The community is dysfunctional because characters are too much a product of their egos and insecurities. They also exhibit rampant materialism.

Many of the characters emphasize money, along with a crass glitz and spectacle—which Charlie Brown loathes—including Snoopy outfitting his doghouse with a garish spectacle of lights to win a contest. Charlie Brown and some of the other characters call this "commercialism." Some of them are aware of its pitfalls, yet they engage in it. They want money and the material objects of Christmas gifts. At Lucy's psychiatrist's booth, she wants her payment from Charlie Brown up front and loves "that beautiful sound of clinking nickels" after Charlie Brown gives her money. For Christmas, Lucy wants real estate, not "stupid toys, or a bicycle or clothes." When Charlie Brown's younger sister Sally asks him to write a letter to Santa, she says she has "a long list of presents that I want" but to make it easier she suggests sending cash. "All I want is what's coming to me; all I want is my fair share," she adds with a sense of entitlement.

After Lucy advises Charlie Brown to get involved in something to combat his Christmas blues, she names him director of a Christmas play. He insists his play won't be commercial but he's largely ignored by apathetic characters who can't focus on the meaning of the nativity story. Sensing Charlie Brown's frustration, Lucy seems resigned that Christmas is co-opted into commercialism that can't be stopped. The characters aren't motivated to play their parts. Their only enthusiasm comes with the idea of getting a Christmas tree. They suggest Charlie Brown and Linus select the biggest aluminum tree they can find. Instead, Charlie Brown is drawn to the smallest and sparsest Christmas tree. He selects a Christmas tree from a spirit of nurturing when the other children want an aluminum tree in the spirit of artificial showmanship. The children scold Charlie Brown and laugh at him when he brings the Christmas tree back. Something he was so sure of now puts him in a state of confusion. "Isn't there anyone who knows what Christmas is all about?" he asks.

Linus then recites a section of the birth narrative of Jesus from the Gospel of Luke. Reassured that he's done the right thing by selecting the Christmas tree and stirred by the gospel message, Charlie Brown takes the tree to Snoopy's doghouse to decorate it. The tree represents helping the neediest and focusing on what one can give instead of what one can receive. Community is restored after a transcendental experience, which is the children being moved by the message of the gospel birth narrative. The nativity play transforms the perspective of the largely self-centered characters when they have a collective conversion experience after hearing Linus read from the Gospel of Luke.

Similar to *A Charlie Brown Christmas*, in *Nativity!* (2009) a group of students are spiritually rejuvenated by putting on a nativity play. The play's director, Paul Maddens (Martin Freeman), is sullen and irritable after a painful breakup with his girlfriend, Jennifer (Ashley Jensen), who has left for Hollywood, and his rivalry with his friend Gordon Shakespeare (Jason Watkins), who takes a job at an elite private school and stages critically praised nativity plays.

Like many loners in Christmas movies, Maddens doesn't like Christmas. While putting together his variation of a nativity play, Maddens sheds his loner qualities and comes out of his deadened routine. The play creates community, repairs troubled relationships at the school, restores a romantic relationship, and even reunites the friends. When the play finally happens, it's a marvelous blend of fun, joy, and heartfelt emotion with an appealing element of self-consciousness and satire. Once they launch their creativity by injecting their own emotions into the story through original songs, that sincerity leads to manifestation of community.

THE NATIVITY STORY AS A WESTERN

In another variation of updating the nativity story to the present day, a newborn baby becomes a surrogate Jesus figure of vulnerability, purity, and redemption that transforms cynical and hardened characters.

The most popular subject in this subgenre is Peter B. Kyne's 1913 Western novel *Three Godfathers.* In the story, while three criminals are hiding out in the desert after a robbery, they promise a dying woman they will care for her newborn child. *Three Godfathers* modernizes the nativity story with variations on the Virgin Mary (the dying woman), the infant Jesus (the newborn baby), and the magi (the three criminals). One by one, the three men are spiritually transformed by their devotion to a Mary figure and the child.[30]

Aside from *A Christmas Carol, Three Godfathers* is the novel with the most major movie adaptations of any Christmas story. Both stories are about transformations of hardened characters from self-focus to self-sacrifice. In *A Christmas Carol,* Ebenezer Scrooge is a misanthropic loner who lives and conducts business within society. *Three Godfathers* is about drifters who are not only disconnected from society but don't follow society's rules of law. In the desert where they reach their core true selves, they find redemption through their mission of bringing a newborn child to safety.

The three men cast off their outlaw personas after deprivation of food and water, a nonvoluntary fasting that helps give them spiritual insights.

It's a deeply American story that shows the identity crisis that comes from disconnection from community, the necessity for individual redemption, and the transcendence that occurs in a bleak landscape when stripped to one's core spiritual self.

The first sound version of *The Three Godfathers*, retitled *Hell's Heroes* (1929), is the grittiest of the three, with the cowboys as hardened outlaws against harrowing and bleak desert photography. The second sound version of *Three Godfathers* (1936) humanizes the cowboys more by giving them backstories, a tactic John Ford also uses in his 1948 version, which is the definitive version. An early scene when they interact with a sheriff and his family before the robbery shows they possess nurturing and self-sacrificing qualities. Those traits are subjugated because of their wandering and aimless life of crime and disconnection from community. But after the robbery, like the other film versions of *Three Godfathers*, those traits are restored in the desert, which becomes a transformative spiritual location of an unplanned religious pilgrimage.[31] To be outside of society wandering in the wilderness with no grounding in civilization is to be spiritually lost. And these three men are spiritually drifting until they commit to saving the child by bringing it back into civilization.

Initially, Robert (John Wayne) is a hardened cynic about religion. While the Abeline Kid (Harry Carey Jr.) and Pedro (Pedro Armendáriz) both hold reverence for religion as their situation worsens, Robert remains skeptical. However, the Kid believes God is working on them through a divine plan. Just before he dies, he tells Pedro to read from Psalm 137, which contains the line "how shall we sing the Lord's song in a strange land?" Like the psalmist, he too seems in exile far from his home. It takes Robert much longer to undergo a spiritual transformation. But after singing "Streets of Laredo," he hears voices from the Kid and Pedro, who appear to him as a version of the communion of saints.[32] The two dead men appear as ghostly figures behind him, encouraging him to go on even though he says it's "the end of the trail." By the end of the movie he's morally and spiritually transformed and integrated into the community instead of being outside of it.

In the Japanese anime film *Tokyo Godfathers* (2003), the *Three Godfathers* story is modified to three homeless people in Tokyo: Gin, a gambler and alcoholic; Hana, a transgender woman with fantasies of being a mother; and a high school-age runaway girl named Miyuki. They find an abandoned baby in a trash pile on Christmas Eve with a note with instructions to care for the child. On a journey from Christmas Eve to New Year's Eve, they find redemption after a series of coincidences, some of which they feel are miracles. Rather than the barrenness of the desert away from human contact as in the other versions of *The Three Godfathers*, they journey through the streets of Tokyo. They encounter gangsters, immigrant families, and street gangs.

Most of the people they meet have dysfunctional or broken family relationships. Separation from family is a major theme in the film, reflecting the emphasis on family in the Third Wave era of Christmas films. The infant brings out the nurturing side of the three main characters and their humanity emerges. The journey also enables them to face the painful truths about their past that have brought them to homelessness. During this journey they act as a surrogate family with Gin as father, Hana as mother, and Miyuki as teenage child. There are a series of coincidences of family members seeing each other again, which are somewhat like miracles. The movie suggests that if one takes the spiritual journey toward redemption, supernatural events and favorable coincidences will occur. This is dramatically shown in one scene when the baby falls, but a gust of wind with a beam of sunlight in the background miraculously brings Hana and the baby to safety. The wind is reminiscent of the howling winds in the desert scenes in all of the *Three Godfathers* films, symbolizing the presence of God.[33]

BABIES AS REDEEMERS

The narrative from *Three Godfathers* of hardened and bitter characters in the desert redeemed by caring for a child was changed into an urban setting during the Great Depression in the Christmas-based films *Bachelor*

Mother (1939) and *Miracle on Main Street* (1939). Both movies show characters changing from their excessive self-focus by caretaking for a child. In these films, the effect of a newborn child is a contemporary version of the nativity story, with the infant offering redemption to flawed characters. The 1945 Academy-Award-winning short *Star in the Night* modernizes the nativity story to an inn at the edge of a desert. Like *Three Godfathers*, the innocence and vulnerability of a newborn child changes characters from being self-focused to other-focused.

Black Nativity **is one of several films in the subgenre of films updating the nativity story to modern times. The movie reimagines the nativity story in an urban setting while presenting Langston Hughes's "Black Nativity" in a church.** Photo courtesy Fox Searchlight Pictures/Everett Collection.

The highlight of the erratic musical *Black Nativity* (2013) is a fantasy sequence with the nativity birth transported to an urban setting where unwed parents Joseph and Mary join other characters to express their longing to know if God is there. But this idea and these characters aren't explored enough and instead sit on the periphery of the story subordinate to the family anxieties of a Harlem pastor.

UNCONVENTIONAL VARIATIONS AND THE ONGOING INFLUENCE

The most unorthodox cinematic updating of the nativity story to contemporary times is Jean-Luc Godard's *Hail Mary* (1985). In his controversial film, Mary is a teenager in Switzerland whose boyfriend Joseph is an aloof taxi driver committed to Mary despite her virginity. A contemporary virgin birth and an abundance of nudity may have been what led Pope John Paul II to condemn the film, saying it "deeply wounds the religious sentiments of believers."[34] However, once one gets past the nudity and unconventional approach and structure, it's a movie that doesn't subvert the birth narrative but is a vehicle for addressing the clash between spirituality and fleshly desires. To resolve this, Mary insists on a spiritual component to both love and life.

Hail Mary centers on Mary's pregnancy rather than the convention in modern nativity stories of building toward the climax of a child being born who becomes a figure of redemption. *Hail Mary* uses a modern virgin birth as a basis for Mary's exploration of why a relationship must contain a spiritual component. The film explores how sexuality affects relationships and challenges the demands of faith.[35] This leads to many discussions between Mary and Joseph about the duality between body and spirit. There are numerous cutaway shots of water, sunsets, and stars, with Mary's voice-overs about her burgeoning ideas about the link between soul and spirit. Although *Hail Mary* contains themes of obedience and uses the nativity story as a basis on which to build the movie, the movie is mostly about a young woman confronting her growing sexuality and her desire to overcome doubt with faith in the supernatural.

A more obscure but interesting homage to the nativity story is in the Christmas home-for-the-holidays dramedy *The Family Stone* (2005). An affluent Connecticut home is the setting for a family of white upscale liberals gathering for Christmas. The tension comes not from the family members interacting among themselves but from the presence of workaholic conservative Meredith (Sarah Jessica Parker), the girlfriend of Everett (Dermot Mulroney). Everett plans on asking Meredith to marry him. This troubles the family matriarch Sybil (Diane Keaton), who wants to spend a happy Christmas with her children because it will be her last one. She has an undefined major health problem she's not telling her children about. She doesn't want her final Christmas clouded by what she feels will be a disastrous marriage partner for her son.

The characters only reach equilibrium when Meredith passes out her Christmas gifts, which are framed prints of a young pregnant Sybil that she made from some film negatives. When they look at the photos, the family, who by this point know about their mother's health problem, is silenced into a near mystical reverie. With death hovering, for them this is a stirring moment of impending life. When the movie later shows Christmas the following year, the camera lingers on the photograph of the pregnant Sybil hanging on a wall. Motherhood itself becomes the spiritual essence of Christmas. Unlike the nativity story, there's no special child; the act of motherhood itself is transcendental.

3

How *A Christmas Carol* Shaped the Christmas Movie Genre

In 1843 at the age of thirty-one, Charles Dickens walked the London streets at night, sometimes ten or fifteen miles at a time, reflecting on what to do next with his life.[36]

He'd seen much in the last year. He had visited America for the first time and had, overall, been disappointed. In observations that perhaps influenced the creation of Ebenezer Scrooge, he disdained the "prevailing seriousness and melancholy air of business" of America that affected family ties, made people less humorous, limited their appreciation of beauty, and created a "coarseness" in their manners.[37]

If his ideals about America were shattered, he also was discouraged by conditions in his native country. The Children's Employment Commission released a disturbing report about children working in mines and factories. It received widespread coverage, and many of the country's most influential writers called for political and social reform. Dickens told one of the report's commissioners he wanted to write a pamphlet that would be a "sledgehammer" on behalf of the oppressed.[38]

At the same time, Dickens's career was in a slump. His seventh novel, *Martin Chuzzlewit*, being published in serial form, wasn't selling well. His publisher was considering cutting his salary.[39] And his promised pamphlet remained unwritten more than six months after the report's release. But a trip north to Manchester gave him new direction. His sister Fanny, who lived in the industrial city, persuaded him to speak at the Athenaeum to benefit the institution, which was a place of education and recreation for the working class. Perhaps the enthusiastic reception he received there made him realize he was a storyteller, not a pamphlet writer.

At some point he likely thought back to a character from his first novel, *The Pickwick Papers*,[40] Gabriel Grubb, a "morose and lonely man, who consorted with nobody but himself." On Christmas Eve a host of goblins show him stories of poor people on a cave wall. Grubb tells the goblins he's a wiser person after seeing the images. Dickens appears to use the character of Grubb as somewhat of a prototype for Scrooge in *A Christmas Carol.*

In *A Christmas Carol*, Dickens added contemporary social commentary in the Ghost of Christmas Present, a psychological and spiritual examination of Scrooge's background through the Ghost of Christmas Past, and a longing for redemption through the Ghost of Christmas Yet to Come. He also inserted his feelings about the dangers of misusing money, social conditions, and the isolation he'd felt as a child. Rather than tackling another long serial like *Martin Chuzzlewit*, Dickens wrote a shorter piece published in one volume. He wrote *A Christmas Carol* in a frenzied six weeks so it would be published before Christmas.

And Christmas would never be the same.

A Christmas Carol created a moral and spiritual context to Christmas in popular culture. Dickens transformed the holiday by giving it a supernatural element, combining religious mysticism through Christian references and images but also incorporating ghosts from popular folk tales.[41]

What makes it the most influential story in the Christmas movie genre, however, is its portrayal of Scrooge, who is redeemed through a supernatural experience. At the time of its release, readers didn't view the story as Scrooge-centered. For Victorian audiences, the center of the story was the Ghost of Christmas Present section and the struggling Cratchit family.[42] But over time *A Christmas Carol* became Ebenezer Scrooge's story. The name Scrooge became synonymous with an antisocial individual who shunned Christmas. Some film adaptations of *A Christmas Carol* are even retitled after the main character.

Scrooge's conversion experience influenced the Christmas movie genre by establishing a pattern of protagonists in Christmas films who undergo a Scrooge-style alteration that occurs either through external intervention by supernatural visitations or internally by a spiritual awakening. The transformation of Ebenezer Scrooge gave pop culture Christmas a spiritual depth through innocence, empathy, and fear represented by three different spiritual entities.

Through the Ghost of Christmas Past, Scrooge rediscovers his innocent and authentic self before he submits to living for the "golden idol" of making money. From the Ghost of Christmas Present, Scrooge learns empathy through seeing the Cratchit family and wanting connection to his family through his nephew Fred. Through the Ghost of Christmas Yet to Come, Scrooge undergoes fear of dying unrecognized and unloved as well as fear of consequences in the afterlife for his earthly actions.

The initial warnings come from another spirit, that of his dead business partner, Marley, who wears chains and unhappily wanders as a spirit in the afterlife. This view of life after death appears to be somewhat modeled after the story in the Gospel of Luke of the rich man in the afterlife who wants to warn others about what will happen if they ignore the poor, but is not able to.[43] In Dickens's variation on the story, Marley, unlike the doomed rich man, can warn Scrooge.

A Christmas Carol was such a popular success that Scrooge became the most influential Christmas pop culture character aside from Santa

Claus. Scrooge has endured for more than 175 years because he represents dangerous universal temptations such as social isolation, economic survivalism, overemphasis on work, and overlooking the needy. The turning point in Dickens's story is when Belle breaks off her engagement to Scrooge. This shows his unhealthy attraction toward the illusion of worldly security that money offers. The disintegration of his relationship with Belle intensifies Scrooge's downward moral trajectory. The reversal is his conversion experience with the Ghost of Christmas Yet to Come. "I am not the man I was," he says, kneeling before the ghost, adding, "Assure me that I yet may change these shadows you have shown me, by an altered life!"[44] This is a desperate plea to an entity with the power to both intercede and enact mercy.

The Christmas film genre has long modeled conversion experiences of protagonists on Scrooge's transformation. In William James's *The Varieties of Religious Experience*, he outlines the qualities of a religious conversion experience, which includes perceiving truths not known before and a sense of newness of life.[45] In Christmas films, instead of a conversion to a religious theology, the experience restores a communion with the divine through a new commitment or behavior.[46] The Christmas film shows how an individual possesses the freedom to shape his or her own salvation through a decision to change.[47] But the films almost always adhere to Scrooge's transformation being a personal one, not a call for widespread social change.[48] Transformative moments similar to Scrooge's conversion occur in supernatural Christmas films.

In *It's a Wonderful Life*, George Bailey pleads with Clarence for his life in Bedford Falls to be restored, as Scrooge pleaded with the spirit to restore his life. In *The Bishop's Wife*, Henry tells the angel Dudley he will sacrifice his life for his wife, which leads Dudley to say his supernatural intervention is complete. A conversion experience also occurs in the Christmas TV special *How the Grinch Stole Christmas* when the Grinch realizes Christmas is more than materialism and his heart literally enlarges.

In other Christmas films, a conversion experience occurs when skeptical characters witness validation of their faith. In *Tenth Avenue Angel*, Flavia sees what she believes to be a Christmas Eve miracle. In *The Polar Express*, the Hero Boy receives Santa's sleigh bell as a Christmas gift, validating his supernatural experience. Other times the Christmas revelation is a conversion in perspective from a worldly frame of mind to a more spiritual one. In *Shop Around the Corner*, the two protagonists convert from their business personas to more authentic identities. In *Remember The Night*, the two antagonists become lovers during the Christmas season after they disassociate themselves from their worldly roles as lawyer and criminal.

A Christmas Carol made the Christmas season and particularly Christmas Eve a time of spiritual possibility.[49] Scrooge's supernatural visitations warning of judgment and consequences leading to Scrooge's conversion experience remain the consistent elements of Dickens's narrative when adapted to film. Major alterations are made, however, to resolve spiritual and social conflicts in the eras when the films were released.[50] This comes through in six time periods of *Carol* adaptations.

THE 1930S: SCROOGE AS BAD CAPITALIST

During the Depression, *Carol* adaptations disregarded the psychological and spiritual development of Scrooge's corruption. In both the 1935 English movie *Scrooge* starring Seymour Hicks and the American film *A Christmas Carol* with Reginald Owen, Scrooge is a stubborn, stingy businessman holding back economic expansion. Ultimately, the films call for staying the course, which in England meant upholding aristocratic standards and in the United States following the New Deal ideology of job growth.[51]

The American *Carol* in particular removes virtually all social commentary.[52] Instead, Scrooge redeems himself partly through materialism by giving Tiny Tim a gift in the ending scene, and by hiring Fred. These Cratchits are the most affluent of the *Carol* film adaptations, with a well-lit and nicely arranged dinner table. They don't eat a meager meal in a

A turning point in *The Christmas Carol* is Scrooge pleading with the Ghost of Christmas Yet to Come for another chance at life. In this Depression-era 1938 version, it's Reginald Owen as Ebenezer Scrooge asking the spirit for mercy. Photo courtesy the Everett Collection.

dark, shadowy home as is shown in many *Carol* films. Both Depression films show family unity as a powerful force to overcome economic oppression.[53] At a time in American history where there could have been the most social commentary derived from Dickens's story, it's the cheeriest version, with the social classes not divided and no one angry or dejected about their economic condition. Never in a *Carol* adaptation has economic struggle seemed so fun.

POST–WORLD WAR II: THE PSYCHOLOGICAL SCROOGE

If the Depression *Carol* movies downplayed Scrooge's past, the adaptation starring Alastair Sim (*Scrooge*, 1951) made up for it. It contains an extended Christmas Past section that is almost a movie within itself and that shows Scrooge's spiritual and moral downfall. It is the longest section of *Scrooge*, taking up nearly thirty of the film's eighty-six minutes. No film adaptation to date has examined Scrooge's past so extensively.

Scrooge is primarily the story of Scrooge's moral and spiritual formation shown in the Ghost of Christmas Past segment. In a major addition not in Dickens's story, Scrooge's mother died giving birth to Scrooge, which makes Scrooge's father reject him. He's a deeply withdrawn person who pressures his sister Fanny to be a figure of redemption. This sets Scrooge up for what will be the catalyst for his downfall: another added scene where Fanny dies (the book mentions she dies, but there is no death scene).

Like many films released during the First Wave era, it contrasts two views of capitalism. Jorkin represents the type of businessman feared after the post–World War II era: the ambitious individualist whose plans for success mean the destruction of small businesses. Fezziwig is the family-oriented, restrained businessman signifying fair and benevolent capitalism.

In a Faust-like moment, Jorkin tempts Scrooge with a new position working for him. Scrooge refuses the offer until after the death of his sister. In the book and nearly every major screen version, the turning point in Scrooge's descent is his breakup with Belle. In *Scrooge*, it's Fanny's death that propels Scrooge into survivalism, greed, and social isolation. Scrooge's downfall comes because his maternal-like connection is gone, not because of an attraction to greed.

THE 1960S/1970S: SCROOGE AS ESTABLISHMENT FIGURE

The first musical screen version of *Scrooge* came just two years after *Oliver!*—based on Dickens's *Oliver Twist*—was a hit. Underneath the studio gloss, Scrooge as played by Albert Finney is radically redefined for another era. He is an uptight establishment figure who needs to cast off his Puritan-like ways and adopt a carpe diem outlook.[54] Scrooge must loosen up to be a lighthearted person who enjoys worldly pleasures and living in the moment. For a movie made at the height of the counterculture movement, this Scrooge is not a figure for political change but someone who accepts happiness and pleasure as worthy personal goals.[55] Although released in 1970 during an era of anti–Vietnam War protests and other political demonstrations, the movie doesn't depict or expand the social commentary of Dickens's story. Instead, it centers on liberating Scrooge through indulgence in sensory gratifications and a focus on enjoying the moment. Scrooge rejects the Puritanism of the business culture and a punishment-centered Christian theology.

The class differences in the book are replaced by tension between Scrooge and the younger generation.[56] Scrooge is the establishment figure, and the younger generation is represented by the street urchins who defy him by teasing and taunting him.[57] Scrooge's oppressed employee Bob Cratchit is the most youthful of any Cratchit in the major *Carol* movies and is another young person whom the establishment figure Scrooge tyrannizes. However, Scrooge once was a young man with a romantic and carefree outlook—as shown in the always pivotal scenes during the Ghost of Christmas Past segment that features his fiancée (named Isabel, and in another change from the book she is Fezziwig's daughter). Isabel sings to Scrooge the film's spiritual philosophy, which is "Happiness is whatever you want it to be," along with "They say happiness is a thing you can't see, a thing you can't touch; I disagree," emphasizing a material source of happiness rather than a spiritual one.

A turning point is when the Ghost of Christmas Present visits Scrooge and pours what he calls "the milk of human kindness" into a golden chalice. Scrooge drinks it, and like a chemical it changes his personality. The ghost is a combination of frat boy and Timothy Leary-style guru.[58] He encourages Scrooge to indulge in what appears to be a mind-altering substance that loosens him up. When he has imbibed, Scrooge adopts a new philosophy, singing, "Life's a pleasure that I deny not" and "I like life, here and now."

Juxtaposed to this ideology is the one offered by Marley (Alec Guinness), which is judgmental Christianity. Marley is a parody of an older generation that unleashes retribution rather than liberation of the self. He represents punishment-based spirituality contrasting with the film's "here and now" philosophy and "happiness is anything you want it to be" viewpoints. Instead of being an agent of regret warning Scrooge, Marley shows Scrooge the ultimate punishment for his wrongs, a solitary surreal version of Scrooge's workplace located in hell. After the spirit shows Scrooge his grave, Scrooge plunges into it and falls through a tunnel with a kaleidoscope of colors that transitions into red the closer he gets to the bottom. Scrooge is forced to take on Cratchit's role of a cold office clerk, this time to Lucifer. In a role reversal, he must endure the suffering he inflicted on Cratchit.

When Scrooge is back home from this bizarre trip to the underworld, instead of accepting the theology of the visit to hell, he embraces the theology of the here and now.[59] He goes on a spending spree, buying presents and singing, "I like living the life of pleasure." In an identification with the secular Christmas, he even puts on a Santa suit.

THE 1980S: SCROOGE AS THATCHERITE; SCROOGE AS BABY BOOMER GONE ASTRAY

As in the Depression era when there were two *Carol* films, the 1980s offered its own English and American adaptations of Dickens's stories that addressed cultural dilemmas. For English audiences, it's Scrooge's danger of overlooking the working class affected by economic policies. For American audiences, Scrooge represents baby boomer anxiety about betraying their counterculture background and joining a yuppie culture of excessive individualism, workaholism, and dependency on the media to define one's identity.

A Christmas Carol (1984) features George C. Scott as a gruff, more controlled, less vulnerable Scrooge. He's the most obstinate and difficult Scrooge to convert in all the major film versions. Scrooge is an extension of a political atmosphere where individualism trumps community.[60] During an era where traditional manufacturing industries are shutting down and the working class is under siege, Scott's Scrooge embodies individualism.[61]

Scott's Scrooge represents the hardened, detached, conservative businessman who must face the reality of the working class and their struggles to regain his humanity. He's later shown as a speculator in corn, which indicates he is a controller of food and has the power to make the poor hungry.[62] He is a financial investor, not a small businessman with just one employee as in Dickens's story. In an added scene (not from Dickens's story) that is the center of the film and Scrooge's turning point toward redemption, the Ghost of Christmas Present takes Scrooge underneath a bridge where he sees a family huddled around a fire. The ghost leaves Scrooge there so he feels the weight of his ignorance about how business transactions affect people. He then pleas for pity and asks, "What have I done to be abandoned like this?" He is alone, a victim of his isolationist economic ideology.[63]

Scrooged (1988), starring Bill Murray as a high-power TV executive (renamed Francis Cross), is the only major version of *Carol* that takes the story out of nineteenth-century London to the present day. The movie is set in the center of New York City business culture, but there isn't the social commentary of the George C. Scott version.

Instead, *Scrooged* depicts the anxiety baby boomers feel about leaving their countercultural past and 1960s idealism to embrace business. It's the only film version of Scrooge where all the ghostly appearances occur at work rather than at the Scrooge character's home. The first ghost shows up not in the middle of night in Cross's home but during an executive lunch at noon in an upscale restaurant. Cross's work is his home. "I'm a widow of business," he says. "It's my life; I've chosen it."

But the Ghost of Christmas Past shows that in the 1960s, he lived with the easygoing Claire (Karen Allen) in Greenwich Village. The 1960s represent a spiritual foundation for baby boomers and also show that their choices about vocation formed identity. This is made clear when Scrooge visits Claire in the present at the homeless shelter where she works and the film contrasts how their jobs have different spiritual outlooks. This is the spiritual conflict so prevalent for the boomer generation.

Can they hold on to their ideals from their youth? Cross's life is a personal de-evolution of values in which he is taken over by a business mentality that can't harmonize with his countercultural past.

THE 1990S: THE VULNERABLE POSTMODERNIST SCROOGE

In *A Muppet Christmas Carol*, Michael Caine plays a vulnerable and tortured Scrooge. He's the most sensitive of the big screen Scrooges. Caine's Scrooge is a regretful man because of Scrooge's usual turning point shown in the Ghost of Christmas Past segment: when Belle breaks off her engagement with Scrooge. Although this is an important part of the story in all *Carol* versions, it's of enormous importance in this film. The movie shows (in its intact unedited version) that Scrooge's bitterness comes from the emotional parting between Scrooge and Belle. Scrooge

Michael Caine is an emo Scrooge in a *Carol* movie defining the force of love as spiritual truth. *The Muppet Christmas Carol* (1992) also shows that the story has entered the postmodern era by including commentary on the action by two narrators.
Photo courtesy Walt Disney Co./Everett Collection.

forsakes his better self by choosing career ambition over love. Of all the major *Carol* films it's the most heartbreaking. That's because in the Muppets' *Carol*, love is a spiritual force. When Scrooge rejects marriage and isolates himself from the power of love embodied in marriage, he deteriorates into regret and despair masquerading as irritability.

The Muppets' *Carol* shows that love elevates the spirit. The Ghost of Christmas Past sings, "wherever you find love, it feels like Christmas." In "Bless Us All," the Cratchits sing, "Let us always love each other; lead us to the light." In Scrooge's post-transformation song "Thankful Heart," Scrooge sings, "Every boy and girl will be nephew and niece to me, will bring love, hope, and peace to me." Scrooge sings "The Love We Found" at the conclusion, showing that he regains his humanity by finding love within community. The two Marleys (played by the two characters who usually play insulting sidemen Statler and Waldorf) tell Scrooge about their fate in the afterlife, that "as freedom comes from giving love, so prison comes with hate."

While Bill Murray's *Carol* version contained an element of postmodernism by placing his ghostly visitations within the context of a TV presentation of *A Christmas Carol* and by having a story within a story, *A Muppet Christmas Carol* takes this further by featuring ongoing postmodernist observations. The Great Gonzo and Rizzo the Rat enact a running commentary on the action, which frequently disrupts the narrative to emphasize the story's status as a cultural artifact.[64] Both characters address the audience directly, and Gonzo identifies so much with Charles Dickens that he never goes out of character. They also sometimes interact with the characters in the story. At one point Rizzo says the story is "scary stuff, should we worry about the kids in the audience?" but Gonzo's reply is "this is culture." Because *A Christmas Carol* is defined as high culture it must be deconstructed, commented on, and dissected to be acceptable in an era that can no longer present a straightforward version of the well-known story.

THE TWENTY-FIRST CENTURY: SCROOGE AS SPECTACLE

After the "*Carol* within a *Carol*" of Bill Murray's radically reframed *Scrooged* and the postmodernist *A Muppet Christmas Carol*, the next step was turning *A Christmas Carol* into a horror movie with dizzying and gratuitous special effects.

Disney's motion capture *A Christmas Carol* (2009) featuring the voice of Jim Carrey as Scrooge shows him nearly always in motion, soaring into the heavens, flying through the air, and even shrinking into a small version of Scrooge that is more Lewis Carroll than Charles Dickens. The movie is so action heavy that Dickens's story becomes a respite between extended action sequences.

Disney's *Carol* isn't the first animated version. The most influential animated *Carol* was the TV special *Mr. Magoo's Christmas Carol* (1962). The play within the film gives *Magoo* a level of artificiality, and the songs and Magoo's humor created a new phase in the *Carol* genre. It largely transforms the "straight" version of *A Christmas Carol* to one that often features animation, songs, and humor. Alistair Sim voiced Scrooge twenty years after his landmark role as Scrooge in the 1951 film version in this twenty-five-minute TV version, whose Gothic imagery may have had an effect on the horror-influenced images in Disney's 2009 *Carol*. The usually reliable production team of Rankin and Bass fell flat with their *Carol* variation *The Stingiest Man in Town* (1978) with Walter Matthau voicing Scrooge. Better is *Mickey's Christmas Carol* (1983), a stripped-down version with Scrooge McDuck as the famous miser, Mickey Mouse as Bob Cratchit, and Donald Duck as Scrooge's nephew, Fred. At shorter than thirty minutes, it could have benefitted from being a feature-length film. The eight-minute 1979 Looney Tunes *Carol* adaptation also could have improved from being longer. It's edgy and funny and features Yosemite Sam as Scrooge and a subversive Bugs Bunny who dresses up as a ghost to scare Scrooge by threatening to send him to the "the man in the red suit." Sam thinks this is Santa Claus, but Bugs hints it's the devil.

The animated versions of *A Christmas Carol* continued with a generic and forgettable 1997 version with Tim Curry as Scrooge and a 2001 version with Simon Callow as Scrooge, which features Scrooge's former fiancée reuniting with Scrooge as in the Bill Murray version. Reuniting Scrooge and his lost love in these movies subverts Dickens's story. Instead of spiritual transformation being the catalyst for change, redemption, and ultimate happiness, it is fulfillment primarily through romance.

Although there were previous animated versions, the onslaught of special effects, motion capture, and horror movie imagery makes Disney's 2009 *Carol* a variation in the subgenre of *Carol* animated versions. And the ghosts are more malevolent than in other *Carol* versions. Even the usually jolly Ghost of Christmas Present becomes a frightening spirit. At the end of his segment he unleashes the children called Ignorance and Want, who are not figures for Scrooge to have pity on. Instead they are aggressive threats; one of them wields a knife. The Ghost of Christmas Present maniacally laughs at all of this as he lies down and turns into a skeleton before completely disintegrating.

The horror and surrealism continue in the Christmas Yet to Come segment when a chariot led by black horses with demonic red eyes chases Scrooge through city streets in the fog. Before his conversion, Scrooge sinks into a grave and grabs on to a branch to prevent himself from falling into an abyss with a red-lit casket below. Carrey's post-transformation scene is unconvincing because he's frightened into cheerfulness through a barrage of horrific images rather than spiritually and morally educated.

From there, the adaptations distanced themselves more from Dickens's story. The loosely adapted *Iron Man 3* (2013) is another movie based on spectacle. As in many Shane Black–penned films, from *Lethal Weapon* to *Kiss Kiss Bang Bang*, the movie is set during the Christmas season but includes few overt Christmas rituals. The film, like so many crime films set during the Christmas season, contrasts the domesticity and peace associated with Christmas with the chaos and antifamily tendencies of the criminal life.

If not for Black dropping hints about it during interviews, the connection between Dickens and *Iron Man 3* might not even be apparent. Black told a newspaper that characters in the film are analogous to different ghosts in Dickens's story.[65] A critic from *Slate* connected Dickens's stories to the ghosts with Maya and the boy he visits in Tennessee as the Ghosts of Christmas Past, the bearded Mandarin as the Ghost of Christmas Present, and Aldrich Killian as the Ghost of Christmas Future.[66] Their encounters motivate the protagonist Tony Stark (Robert Downey Jr.) to become less of a self-centered, withdrawn, fearful person to a more altruistic one better able to connect to his girlfriend Pepper (Gwyneth Paltrow).[67]

The Man Who Invented Christmas (2017) took *A Christmas Carol* adaptations in another direction by chronicling how Dickens wrote the story. This movie is not so much a biopic as both a jumbled psychological profile and a mini-enactment of *A Christmas Carol* using magic realism, with the characters from the book invading Dickens's life. The movie's aim is not accurately documenting the story of how Dickens wrote the Christmas novella as much as making Dickens a stereotype of the tortured artist brooding and isolating himself. Scrooge in some way becomes an extension of Dickens's darkness, but this is never effectively presented.

The romantic comedy *The Ghosts of Girlfriends Past* (2009) went further by eliminating any mention of Christmas and instead using winter scenes and transplanting the story to modern-day New England. It's a Scrooge-inspired story of three spirits who force a womanizer to confront his unwillingness to marry. The movie shows that spiritual progress is solely toward a romantic relationship with none of the accompanying themes of materialism, community, and spiritual transformation so critical to Dickens's story.

4

Scroogelike Characters

Grinches, Skeletons, and Surrogate Santas

Scrooge inspired a specific character in Christmas films: the male loner who is either miserly or greedy and often emotionally damaged, unmarried, and childless. Just as film versions of *A Christmas Carol* in different eras revise Scrooge to depict contemporary social conditions, Christmas films adapt Scroogelike characters to express cultural tendencies of their time periods.

SCROOGE RESOLVING RELIGIOUS DIFFERENCES AND MATERIALISM: THE 1960S GRINCH

The best-known character influenced by Scrooge is the Grinch of the Dr. Seuss 1957 children's book *How the Grinch Stole Christmas*. Part of what makes the character so durable is that, like Dickens's Scrooge, it's partly an expression of the author's dark side. "Something had gone wrong with Christmas, I realized, or more likely with me," Seuss (Theodor Geisel) said. "So I wrote the story about my sour friend, the Grinch, to see if I could rediscover something about Christmas that obviously I lost."[68] Geisel wrote the book when he was fifty-three, and the Grinch says in the story, "for 53 years I've put up with it," referring to Christmas.[69]

Unlike Scrooge, the Grinch has no vocational identity or backstory, so readers can identify with him as a symbol of isolation and grumpiness rather than a specific character who is a business owner in a large city. The Grinch serving as a more universal symbol of alienation and misanthropy is one of the reasons the character became so popular that, in 1966, an animated TV special was adapted from the book.

Like Scrooge, the Grinch shuns community. He lives in a cave high outside Whoville, a village inhabited by a peaceful community of people called the Whos. Also like Scrooge, his spiritual state is in peril. As the TV special's song "You're a Mean One, Mr. Grinch" points out, his soul

The best-known Scrooge-based character is Dr. Seuss's the Grinch. Even after two theatrical versions, the 1966 TV show remains closest to both Dr. Seuss's book and the Scrooge-influenced misanthropic male. Photo courtesy/MGM/ Everett Collection.

is "full of gunk." His heart is two sizes too small, making him incapable of generosity. This is important because as the show later demonstrates, the heart is the gateway to spiritual revelation. As a Scrooge-influenced character, he especially dislikes Christmas because community is more pronounced then. His condemnation of singing is a rejection of community, which is strongly linked in *The Grinch* to spirituality.

In contrast to the solitary Grinch, the Whos are so community-based they aren't portrayed as individual characters with names, but are referred to as a collective. The only named Who with a speaking part is young Cindy Lou, who catches the Grinch taking a Christmas tree during his Christmas Eve raid. There's a clear distinction between Whoville—which is depicted as warm, lighted, busy, noisy, and joyous—and the Grinch's cave, which is cold, quiet, and dark.[70]

The only consistent connection the Grinch has to another individual is to his dog Max. But Max is not the Grinch's friend or pet. Instead, Max takes on the role of ill-treated servant. While the Grinch's past is a mystery, so is Max's. How did he come to live with the Grinch? Even though that's never answered, Max is in many ways the spiritual hero of the story. While the Whos have a large and peaceful community as a support system, Max has no one. He must maintain his cheerful attitude without any comfort from anyone else while the Grinch tyrannizes him.

Why the Grinch doesn't just ignore the Christmas celebrations of the Whos exposes something crucial about the Scrooge-influenced character. He wants to inflict misery on others. By ordering his employee Bob Cratchit to report to work extra early after Christmas, erupting at charity workers, and ridiculing his nephew, Fred, the Scrooge character imposes his cantankerous nature on others. For the Grinch, however, it's not enough to grumble about Christmas; he wants to "stop Christmas from coming." He devises a plan to act as Santa Claus in reverse by taking presents instead of giving them in a twist on the poem "'Twas the Night Before Christmas."[71]

But when the Whos sing in a circle to celebrate Christmas without gifts, he can't logically understand it. After the Grinch's rational efforts to understand what happened are exhausted, a nonrational spiritual awakening occurs. "Maybe Christmas, he thought, doesn't come from a store; maybe Christmas perhaps means a little bit more," the narrator says about the Grinch's epiphany. After this realization, the Grinch's heart (literally) enlarges three times.

The Grinch realizes he can steal the material symbols of Christmas, but he can't take the Christmas spirit expressed through community.[72] The Grinch mistakenly believes Christmas is a material event, not a spiritual one.[73] His transformative epiphany about Christmas being "a little bit more" than materialism gives him the physical strength to lift up the huge sled with the stolen Christmas items and return everything. The Grinch's change is a swift transformative experience that can be defined as a conversion experience.[74] It follows the definition in some forms of Christianity as being "born again." It's a process where someone realizes they've lived a sinful life and turns toward a new life centered around worshipping God, followed by social acceptance into a group of believers. The Grinch experiences something similar when the Whos bring him into their community.[75] In this three-step process, the Grinch commits a sin by stealing the Christmas presents, undergoes a conversion experience where he comprehends the true meaning of Christmas, and then joins the community where he makes up for his sin by returning the presents and is forgiven.[76] The resolution is antimaterialist, with a humanitarian view of Christmas that embodies positive feelings toward one's fellow creatures.[77]

However, the "a little bit more" and "true meaning of Christmas" are not connected to a specific theology or religious belief. For the Whos, the spiritual manifestation of their community is a star that forms inside the circle of Whos when they sing on Christmas morning. It rises into the heavens and significantly does not move from the heavens down to the Whos. That would represent a more traditional religious depiction of a spiritual force coming from the heavens to earth. Instead, the force is generated by the Who community and then released into the heavens.

This important component came from Geisel himself. He struggled with the religiosity of the ending of both the book and the TV special because he didn't want to make an overt reference to religion.[78] Instead, connection to community becomes a spiritual experience. "Christmas day will always be, just so long as we have We," the Whos sing in the absence of their Christmas presents. It is a communal song with no references to the religious events that comprise Christmas, only to the celebration of Christmas.[79] This is different from the explicitly Christian *A Charlie Brown Christmas* and its collective conversion experience of the characters after a reading by Linus from the Gospel of Luke. *The Grinch* resolves tension over two differing religious perspectives by showing both as valid: the more conservative individualized conversion experience and the more liberal community-based spirituality, which can be defined as a spiritual but not necessarily religious experience.

And that's not the only spiritually based duality expressed in the show. There's a mixed message about resolving a prominent dilemma in the Christmas movie genre. That's the tension between materialism associated with contemporary Christmas and anti-materialism associated with Jesus's teachings in the gospels. The Grinch realizes Christmas is more than gifts and material displays such as trees, decorations, and meals. However, he still restores them after his conversion experience and the Whos readily accept them and carry on with their customary Christmas celebration. It's significant that the Grinch redistributes the gifts so the Grinch and the Whos don't experience Christmas without material objects.

To resolve anxiety about consumerism associated with Christmas, the story reconciles materialism as acceptable if one can live without it or doesn't place too much emphasis on it. Because the Whos can celebrate Christmas happily without presents, decorations, and a feast, they have the correct outlook. They recognize that the main point of Christmas is based on community, not on the materialism of Christmas. However, if the Christmas presents, decorations, and food are there, they will enjoy them. The Scrooge character embodied in the Grinch not only resolves apprehension about materialism but shows that Christmas presents, decorations, and food are desirable and enjoyable with the correct perspective. It solves the tension between materialism and spirituality by making materialism secondary but nonetheless acceptable.

SCROOGE AS "THE OTHER": RON HOWARD'S BIG SCREEN GRINCH AND A REBOOT

The TV adaptation of *How the Grinch Stole Christmas* successfully expands the book from the twelve minutes it takes to read aloud to twenty-six minutes. In 2000, an hour of new material lengthens the story into a ninety-minute feature film directed by Ron Howard and starring Jim Carrey as the Grinch.

Its extensive Grinch backstory and other alterations use the Scrooge-inspired Grinch character to demonstrate an enormous cultural shift. The Grinch is no longer sinner to be redeemed but a victim of prejudice because he embodies qualities of "the other"—someone outside the dominant culture. In the 1966 version, the Grinch is a misanthropic sinner who liberates himself through a conversion experience, restores what he stole, and joins a spiritual community that forgives him for his transgressions. Nearly thirty-five years later, in Howard's version, the Scrooge-inspired Grinch is a neurotic but sympathetic misfit ostracized from a materialistic and intolerant society.

This film not only marks a radically different Grinch but a reconfiguration of the Whos into a deeply flawed society rather than the idyllic one of Dr. Seuss and the 1966 TV adaptation. In the story and TV special, the Whos are a cooperative unit who put community before materialism. Howard alters the Whos from a benevolent community to a bullying, materialistic, authoritarian one ruled by a despotic mayor.

The Who community is no longer a collective moral and spiritual force. Instead, a young Who child assumes a role as the ethical voice. In the original story, Cindy Lou is a minor character who is two years old, but in Howard's version she is eight years old and, aside from the Grinch, the most important character. She acts as social worker, therapist, and investigative reporter.[80] The movie attempts to give her some gravitas by having her articulate some nebulous emotions about Christmas. She tells the Grinch, "I myself am having some Yuletide doubts." But what are they? She doesn't articulate doubts other characters her age express in Third Wave films such as *The Polar Express* and *Prancer* or in the First Wave *Tenth Avenue Angel.*

In one of the movie's most blatant subversions of the Seuss story, the Grinch isn't completely converted by the Whos singing when they realize they don't have their Christmas presents. The Grinch experiences only a partial conversion experience, evidenced by his saying, "What's happening to me?" What generates a full conversion is the Grinch rescuing Cindy Lou on top of the sled of heisted presents teetering on a steep cliff. Instead of a realization that Christmas contains spiritual meaning rather than material meaning, care for a child becomes a vehicle for his full redemption. This reflects a tremendous narrowing of community from the entire Who village in the TV special to just one young girl.

This radically different take on the Grinch makes him "the other," a sympathetic figure forced to flee an intolerant dominant culture. In a flashback, the Who school children tease the child-age Grinch, so he flees to a cave to escape the bullying. How an eight-year-old survives alone isn't explained. But Howard's Grinch is more a creature cast aside to a Cave of Misfit Toys than a menacing threat.

The Grinch is not an embodiment of evil or sinful behavior but the result of a society that treats him as a misfit. The Grinch refers to himself as a "nonconformist" and, instead of inhabiting the bare bones barren cave from the TV special, lives in an eccentric cave that looks more like the home of a creative mad scientist. It is the Whos who are the villains, not the Grinch. "The story is about prejudice and fear of the other," Jeffrey Tambor, who plays the Who mayor, said in an interview.[81] "He's part of the disenfranchised," Jim Carrey added about the character he played.[82] One review of the film stated the Grinch is "a character driven to isolation by bigots."[83] This appears to be reinforced in one scene after a taxi passes by the Grinch and he says, "It's because I'm green, isn't it?" suggesting he's the victim of discrimination.[84]

Howard's Grinch is both a postmodern alteration of a well-known cultural narrative and an elimination of a character who in many ways represents evil.[85] Howard's Grinch at times even becomes the moral voice of the film, akin to an Old Testament prophet living outside of society who critiques the community, particularly disparaging the Whos for their materialism.[86] So, in a reversal of the Seuss story, it is the Whos that must realize what they've done wrong, and not the Grinch.[87]

The 2018 *Grinch* defangs the Grinch even more than Howard's film. The Grinch is a misunderstood, somewhat grumpy loner, not a sinister character. The Grinch's backstory isn't nearly as long or involved as in Howard's film, but the Grinch is said to be an orphan. Like Carrey's Grinch, he's neurotic because of his outsider status, but he's not a figure of evil. Here, the Grinch is an emotional overeater and in what appears to be a kind of sanitized antibullying alteration, the Grinch does not mistreat Max. The oppressed pooch from Seuss's story doesn't lead the overloaded sled as he did in Seuss' story and the original TV special.

Although less pointed than in Ron Howard's film, the Whos once again are not a peaceful spiritual community as in Dr. Seuss's story but flawed consumerists with a mayor who wants Christmas to be "three times bigger," with ostentatious lighting displays. And like in Howard's version, Cindy Lou becomes the figure of transformation for the loner Grinch. In a new storyline, she's the daughter of an overworked single mother. Cindy Lou invites the Grinch to their home for Christmas because "you've been alone long enough," as she tells the Grinch. The Grinch simply needs to be brought into the fold of a family Christmas to be changed. With the father at the head of the table absent, the Grinch even becomes a surrogate father figure to Cindy Lou. How watered down this story has become since the groundbreaking 1966 TV special.

SCROOGE AS LONER ARTIST: *THE NIGHTMARE BEFORE CHRISTMAS*

The most bizarre variation on the Scrooge character as well as the most fascinating and original is in Tim Burton's *The Nightmare Before Christmas* (1993). Jack "the Pumpkin King" Skellington (voice of Chris Sarandon), a macabre variation on both Scrooge and the Grinch, sabotages the holiday by ordering Santa Claus to be kidnapped. Like the Grinch, he fills in for Santa to disrupt Christmas. However, instead of snatching Christmas gifts, decorations, and food, Jack delivers frightening variations of Christmas gifts. Then, like the Grinch and Scrooge, Jack undergoes a change that's not a full-fledged conversion experience but nonetheless brings some degree of redemption.

Jack is a tall, spider-like skeleton in Halloween Town, a nearly monochromatic world. The residents praise him for another successful Halloween scaring the living on earth, but Jack is bored and restless, and he sings about "an emptiness" and "a longing that I've never known," sounding at times like the disillusioned narrator of Ecclesiastes. Jack doesn't need to be pushed out of his routine, as Scrooge is, by supernatural encounters. He already wants something different. But he longs for the novelty of new experiences rather than inner transformation. Sally (voice of Catherine O'Hara), a rag doll who overhears him, shares his restlessness. Why this mutual restlessness? At this stage of their spiritual journeys, they don't know what they want.

Seemingly on the edge of despair, Jack takes a walk into the woods and sees a tree with a door leading to Christmas Town, a snow-filled colorful world. In an allusion to the TV adaptation of *How the Grinch Stole Christmas*, Jack first sees the town from above, similar to the view the Grinch saw from his mountaintop cave. He sees this new land as something to possess and dominate.

As a Scrooge/Grinch character, Jack doesn't integrate with other people or try to understand them. Rather than Scrooge's hardened isolation because of choosing money and career over marriage, Jack is motivated by his ego. He can't recognize other people's emotions and he's consumed with his own emotions and impulses, whether it's the despondency he feels in Halloween Town or the desire to terrify Christmas Town.

Despite his emotional turmoil in his attempts to understand the outer world, he's a rationalist, not a mystic. He admits he doesn't understand Christmas or the feelings associated with it. After he returns to Halloween Town, he says, "There's got to be a logical way to explain this Christmas thing." One of the books he reads is entitled *The Scientific Method*, showing he's looking for answers to find out "what does it mean?" as he sings about Christmas. But characteristically he doesn't ask questions from people to gain knowledge. He distances himself by reading books (including *A Christmas Carol*), conducting scientific experiments in solitude, and drawing mathematic formulas on a chalkboard. But he still can't comprehend Christmas because science can't explain the good feelings and absence of fear in this Eden-like Christmas Town. Like the Grinch, Jack defines Christmas through the material objects of gifts and decorations. But after a series of experiments, he gives up trying to understand Christmas and proceeds with his plan to subvert the holiday. Jack aims to play a surrogate Santa and enact his own version of a Grinch-like Christmas Eve visitation.

The ghost dog Zero takes over the role of Dr. Seuss's dog Max, who functioned as the spiritual hero of *How the Grinch Stole Christmas*. However, Zero doesn't have enough personality to inhabit the Max character as the figure of conscience. Instead, Sally expands Max's role of representing a figure uncorrupted by the Scroogelike character. She tries to influence Jack, but, like Max, she is in a subservient position. She sews Jack's Santa costume just as Max sewed the Grinch's Santa outfit.

Despite Sally's appeal to stop his raid, Jack is too obsessed with his plan. So, like a satanic figure, Jack injects chaos and disorder into the innocent and joyful Christmas Town, which has been devoid of fear and death, by delivering frightening variations of Christmas presents. After military weapons shoot down his sleigh, Jack plunges below to a graveyard and lands on a statue of an angel holding a book. Then Jack comes to the Christmas movie convention of a transcendental realization. But the epiphany focuses on his identity crisis more than moral and spiritual awareness. He tears off his Santa suit and reaffirms his identity as Jack the Pumpkin King. Jack doesn't desire to drastically alter his life the way Scrooge did. Jack just must accept who he already is. He doesn't possess serious moral flaws but is misguided because he is pulled too far by forces of creativity and passion. As a result, Jack's critical epiphany in *Nightmare* is much like advice in a business-oriented self-help book: be one's authentic self established through best utilizing one's work skills (some may say spiritual gifts) in the most effective marketplace, which for Jack is Halloween Town.

Jack realizes his situation requires some modification, even if it doesn't mean a Scrooge-like complete transformation. And in his most reflective and soul-searching moment he sings, "What have I done; how could I be so blind?" Despite the fear he's enacted on Christmas Town's children, in the end it's benefited him because the experience provided new ideas and techniques about how to scare people next Halloween. Jack's transformation is not just a reaffirmation of self-identity but a professional rejuvenation.

However, Jack's transformational moment isn't all self-centered. He quickly returns to Halloween Town to rescue the kidnapped Santa Claus (and as a result, Sally). Later, seemingly in gratitude, in an attempt to connect, or perhaps out of pity, Santa sends some snow to Halloween Town in an allusion to Rankin/Bass's *Year without a Santa Claus*, where Mother Nature makes it snow in Southtown, USA, where there is never snow.

The movie displays an inconsistent tone of showing Jack as incongruous and ego-driven yet still celebrating his creativity and ingenuity. Overall, the movie is somewhat ambiguous because of the dilemma of the mixed message about Jack. This is most apparent in the movie's conclusion, which shows Jack's lack of reformation. Instead of establishing community as Scrooge and the Grinch do after their conversions, Jack is redeemed not by either building or reestablishing community but by removing himself from the community once again but this time with a romantic partner.

The movie ends as a Christmas romance. And it's a romance where Sally, during the bulk of the film, waits for Jack to regain some sense of his identity and conscience. Sally feels restless at the beginning of the movie, but she doesn't get to enact her own spiritual search. Instead, her existence is vicariously seen through Jack's transformation. Santa reinforces the idea of Sally as a figure of conscience by telling Jack, "I'd listen to her; she's the only one who makes any sense around this insane asylum." But Sally seems resigned to have no other ambition than to escape the clutches of Finklestein and wait for Jack to let his Christmas Eve misadventure run its course. By the end of the film, other than his connection to Sally, Jack doesn't appear to connect with anyone else. But he incorporates one person (Sally) into his loner existence. Jack's propensity to get too carried away with his own creativity requires an obedient partner to monitor him.

One interpretation of *Nightmare* is that it is a warning against cultural appropriation, that Jack imposes his culture on another culture.[88] However, this argument falters somewhat because Jack never outright attempts to change the culture of Christmas Town. A more convincing argument is that Jack is an overactive capitalist. He wants to impose his products on a culture that doesn't want them.

Another interpretation is that Halloween Town and Christmas Town represent different spiritual approaches. The residents of Halloween Town enact fear-based spirituality. The movie never shows their Halloween activities, but because they haunt and correct the powerful, perhaps they scare people into reevaluating their lives. Halloween Town's fear-based strategy contrasts with Christmas Town, which operates on good feeling, giving, and lack of fear. Christmas Town represents an innocent land. Santa Claus notes there weren't that many naughty children that year. By restricting himself to Halloween Land, Jack understands his spiritual place.

SCROOGE AS SELF-LOATHING MISANTHROPE: *BAD SANTA*

The darkest and raunchiest variation on the Scrooge character is *Bad Santa* (2003). Willie Soke (Billy Bob Thornton) plays a department store Santa as part of a crime scheme. His seasonal work as Santa is a cover to infiltrate stores so he can break into their safes to steal money. Like Scrooge, his business pursuits prevent positive human connection. But unlike Scrooge, he works outside the system as a criminal instead of within society as a business owner.

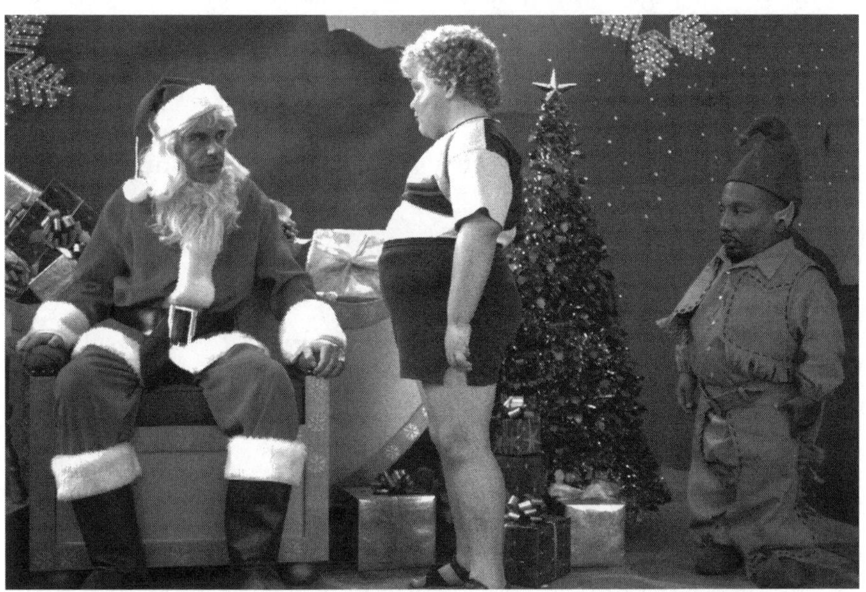

In *Bad Santa* (2003), Willie Soke (Billy Bob Thornton) is the screen's crudest Santa, but with a deep level of despair. Underneath the crassness is a Scroogelike redemption started by caring for the bullied Thurman Merman (Brett Kelly). Photo courtesy Dimension/Everett Collection.

What distinguishes this Scroogelike character is an extreme misanthropy and self-loathing that Willie attributes to the way his father treated him when he was a child. This makes him feel irredeemable. "At this point, it's too late to start over," he laments. At the beginning of the film, Willie sits by himself at a bar in his Santa Claus suit as people around him drink and laugh together in groups. He's a Scrooge-type loner, and this exposition scene is a variation on Scrooge eating alone in a public house on Christmas Eve in *A Christmas Carol.* Willie's dominant association with Christmas is the physical and mental abuse he suffered from his father.

Bad Santa shows a modernized and more severe version of the psychologically damaged Scrooge from the 1951 version of *A Christmas Carol* starring Alastair Sim. That film amended Dickens's story by indicating that Scrooge's father had neglected him because his mother died giving birth to Scrooge. In *Bad Santa,* the father's neglect is so bad it's abusive. As a result, the adult Willie escapes the pain by drinking, crime, and casual sex. Although some of Willie's actions are hedonistic, he doesn't appear to enjoy them. They temporarily distract him from the pain of his self-loathing.

Thornton's character is what makes *Bad Santa* unique in the Christmas movie genre. Beneath the barrage of cursing, sex scenes, and drinking, Willie's character shows a side of Christmas rarely shown in Christmas movies, which is life-threatening despair. In some ways the closest character to share Willie's feelings of worthlessness is George Bailey from *It's a Wonderful Life,* who also is driven to the verge of suicide. While George is frustrated with unrealized dreams and lack of freedom, Willie feels despair because of lack of connection and too much freedom. If George suffers internally because of too much commitment at the expense of his own ambition, Willie suffers from a lack of commitment and too much focus on himself. Willie is lodged in a spiritual state of disillusionment and despair much more than hedonism.

To transform himself, Willie must overcome the negative influence his father has on his life by becoming a father figure himself to a neglected child. This creates a new purpose and self-image. Willie is a mentor to Thurman (Brett Kelly), whom he cons into letting him stay at Thurman's home. Along with being a vehicle for Willie's redemption, Thurman is the one character linked to religious belief. When Willie asks him where his mother is, he tells her she's in heaven. The only sign of religion at Christmas is an Advent candy calendar Thurman has. At his lowest point, Willie sits inside a car in a garage planning to kill himself (which links him again to George Bailey, who also tried to end his life). When Thurman interrupts his plan, he notices Thurman has a black eye from being bullied, and Willie tracks down the culprits. Willie is rescued from death because he cares about someone else. That leads to an epiphany, which he explains to his accomplice Marcus after defending Thurman: "It was like I did something constructive with my life, like I accomplished something."

In Victor Frankl's seminal book *Man's Search for Meaning*, Frankl says despair comes from a lack of purpose.[89] This manifests in what Frankl calls an existential vacuum, which leads to what Frankl calls a primitive will to power. This often produces a magnified libido.[90] Willie's sexual activities are born out of this existential frustration. But as Frankl says, the way out of the existential vacuum is through responsibility.[91] Willie accomplishes this through a commitment to forming a surrogate family with Thurman and bartender Sue. Willie shifts from nihilism to meaning when he realizes he possesses the ability to choose a new identity as surrogate father figure. This also eradicates the pain of his past. Like Scrooge finding something of his alienated child identity in Tiny Tim, Willie finds something similar in his connection to Thurman.

SCROOGE AS SLACKER MAN-CHILD: *FRED CLAUS*

Like Billy Bob Thornton's *Bad Santa*, Vince Vaughn's *Fred Claus* (2007) is irresponsible. However, Fred doesn't possess the darkness, self-loathing, or despair of Thornton's Scroogelike character. Instead, Fred Claus battles immaturity and an inability to commit to adult responsibilities. As in *Bad Santa*, a friendship with a young boy is the catalyst for redemption.

For much of the film, Fred is another version of a phenomenon in recent films described as a "man-child," an adult male who avoids cultural expectations of maturity. In these films, there is an evasion of responsibility by an extended retreat into boyhood-type behavior.[92] One manifestation is avoiding the responsibility of serious relationships with women, who are viewed as limiting male freedom.[93] As with many man-child films, the narrative moves toward the protagonist becoming an adult by conquering the fears preventing him from transitioning into adulthood.[94] That's achieved partly through the influence of psychology (by Fred going to therapy), which replaces the spiritual awakening that is the usual vehicle for traditional Christmas film transformations.

5

The First Wave

During World War II, sixteen million soldiers went to war, many others who were enlisted relocated to other parts of the country, women entered the workforce, and numerous civilians relocated to other areas because of the wartime economy.[95] In the largest mass movement of Americans ever, more than thirty million civilians migrated. Between the Pearl Harbor bombing and the end of the war more than fifteen million Americans moved.[96] This led to a loss of community through both family connections and local culture.[97]

Depictions of Christmas in cinema helped a nation recreate the idea of home after war disrupted it. So the Christmas movie genre is inextricably connected to World War II.

This is expressed in a popular song featured in the film *Holiday Inn*, which helped solidify the Christmas film genre through a desire for a sense of home. Bing Crosby's "White Christmas" became the best-selling song of all time.[98] It dominated the charts for much of 1942, the first full year the United States entered the war. The lyrics contain a sense of nostalgia and bittersweet longing.[99] Lines such as "I'm dreaming of a white Christmas, just like the ones I used to know" resonated with soldiers overseas and families who missed them. The song, and subsequently, the Christmas movie genre, linked Christmas with the yearning for return to a physical or emotional home.

The initial First Wave Christmas films released from 1940 to 1945 anticipate the end of war by instilling hope for a postwar sense of family and home.[100] They venerate community-based small town values as a moral compass in the midst of war-related uncertainty. This also alleviated anxiety that the war was altering small-town America as a growing number of Americans fled to cities.[101] Small towns provide a moral anecdote to urban living, which is associated with workaholism, excessive materialism, and hedonism.

These movies look toward reintegrating returning male soldiers as well as working women. During the war, the percentage of women employed outside the home grew by more than 50 percent, from approximately twelve million to nineteen million working women, representing about 36 percent of the total civilian workforce.[102] Many First Wave Christmas films feature working women who are either protagonists or important characters. *Christmas in Connecticut*, *The Man Who Came to Dinner*, and *I'll Be Seeing You* show independent women protagonists who don't have home and family and instead are working.[103] However, these women face danger, unfulfillment, and exploitation in the workplace. In *I'll Be Seeing You*, Mary (Ginger Rogers) is vulnerable to sexual assault; Maggie (Bette Davis) in *The Man Who Came to Dinner* is itinerant and subservient to a temperamental author; and the career of Elizabeth Lane (Barbara Stanwyck) in *Christmas in Connecticut* is based on a false identity. All three women must move out of the workforce, where they are prone to workaholism, danger, and materialism, into the domestic sphere, which offers the concept of home—in these films far valued over career. These movies reverse the migration so women return to small towns rather than leaving small towns for larger cities.[104]

The First Wave also establishes three major themes to alleviate fears that America was fundamentally changing because of the war: the validity of transcendental spiritual experiences, the importance of community, and the condemnation of workaholism and excessive materialism. These three themes formed and matured the Christmas movie genre, which Christmas-related films in the silent era and the Great Depression hadn't done.

THE PRE–FIRST WAVE CHRISTMAS FILM

D. W. Griffith's *A Trap for Santa Claus* (1909) followed the silent film pattern of the social problem film utilizing film as a tool for social reform.[105] Showing the effects of economic hardship on a family, a father deserts his family only to be unexpectedly reunited with them on Christmas. However, the silent Christmas film that was the most influential created the Christmas black comedy. *Big Business* (1929), featuring Laurel and Hardy as two Christmas tree salesmen, shows how underneath a façade of suburban respectability and materialism are anger, dysfunction, and social disharmony. Stan and Ollie ride the California suburbs in their automobile selling Christmas trees door to door, which culminates in a tit-for-tat feud with an irritable homeowner who doesn't want to be disturbed. It escalates with the homeowner demolishing Ollie and Stanley's car and Ollie and Stanley destroying a large section of the home. Underneath the pretense of civilized material objects and comforts such as an automobile and a suburban home is a primal instinct that manifests in violence. The separation of people into sellers and buyers strips them of their humanity. Instead of Christmas leading to moral transformation, *Big Business* exposes a vast moral distance between the ideals of the holiday and the reality of commerce. It's an important forerunner to the dark view of Christmas in Third Wave neo noir films and Christmas black comedies of the 1990s and 2000s.

During the Great Depression, Christmas was largely absent from the cinema. One reason is perhaps because economically ravaged audiences would view depictions of a bountiful Christmas as unrealistic. The most influential film from the Depression era is *The Thin Man* (1934) because it blended comedy with the detective genre.[106] A mixture of comedy and film noir would emerge decades later in Third Wave crime-related Christmas films. However, *The Thin Man*, like many other Depression-era Christmas films, offers no Scroogelike transformation of the protagonists. Nick Charles (William Powell) is a jovial ex-detective married to the wealthy heiress Nora (Myrna Loy), whose matrimony is an extended vacation of martinis, train rides, and visits to nightclubs. There are not one but two Christmas Eve parties that take up much of the film's screen time. The second Christmas Eve party features criminals and a host of neurotic characters. The anti-family Christmas continues on Christmas morning when Nick shoots Christmas ornaments hanging on a Christmas tree. While the tone of the film is often lighthearted, the use of Christmas and Christmas imagery is at times ironic, with a dark undercurrent. The characters are connected to a criminal world far from associations of Christmas with family and home.

MARRIAGE AS MORAL CHOICE

Along with venerating small town values, First Wave Christmas films emphasize marriage, not so much as a romantic pursuit but a moral decision. One doesn't just choose a partner; one chooses the belief system that person represents. Those ideologies present two visions of American society, characterized by two potential spouses with opposing belief systems. One person represents ambition, surface appeal, and materialism. The other rejects worldly values for something more spiritual, humble, and sincere. The choice also signifies two views of the American economy. One partner embodies the ideology of manageable small economies and reasonable jobs that keep small-town life and community intact. The other potential partner is motivated by ambition and a career that doesn't uphold small-town values or community.

***Holiday Inn* (1942) set up a duality in First Wave Christmas films where a woman's choice of a partner is an ethical one. Marjorie Reynolds must not only choose between Bing Crosby and Fred Astaire but between two ways of life.** Photo courtesy the Everett Collection.

This duality is prominent in *Holiday Inn* (1942), the film that solidified the Christmas movie genre even though only about a third of it is set during the Christmas season. The movie set up dichotomies of small-town versus city living and contrasted individualism with community. This is shown in the difference between Jim Hardy (Bing Crosby), a laid-back singer who yearns for a life away from the limelight, and Ted Hanover (Fred Astaire), an individualistic, manipulative, and career-obsessed dancer. The two have a show business act together but represent different ideals. Not one, but two female dancers must decide between the two men. The first one is the diva gold digger Lila Dixon (Virginia Dale), who chooses Hanover over Hardy after Hanover's promise of materialism and fame. But Hardy is tired of the workaholism of show business and moves to a Connecticut farm away from the perils of stress and excessive work. Hardy converts his home into a performance venue for fifteen holidays a year and takes off the rest of the year. It's a manageable workload that conforms to the Christmas movie genre's veneration of small business and small-town life. His business becomes a mixture of home and work that is appealing and sincere, while work that takes one away from home, represented by Hanover, is unattractive, rootless, and superficial.

At his farm the budding dancer and singer Linda Mason (Marjorie Reynolds) tells Hardy her desire is to live a simple life and define success in modest terms. Linda feels comfortable with Hardy because she views him as a continuation of the family life she grew up with. But Hardy makes the same mistake Scrooge makes in *A Christmas Carol* by delaying marriage until he accumulates enough money first. Then he descends into jealousy and insecurity. Because he doesn't trust her, Linda believes he has "selfish plans" and leaves for Hollywood with Hanover.

When Hardy goes to Hollywood to woo her back, there's a set constructed for a movie version of *Holiday Inn* that duplicates his entertainment space. The symbolism is striking. Hollywood creates an artificial version of the Holiday Inn that is unfulfilling to Linda. What Hollywood creates is exploitation because it's mere atmosphere and artifice, and ultimately Linda longs for something real. In an ending dance routine, Hanover admits defeat and reunites with Lila. Although Jim and Ted put their differences aside to patch up their bromance and stage act, the movie clearly comes down clearly on Hardy's side of choosing a manageable business enterprise in a small town and a partner who isn't overly ambitious.

THE WORKPLACE CONSTRUCTS A FALSE IDENTITY

Shop Around the Corner (1940) is the first Christmas movie in the First Wave and one of the most influential. It presents two themes that carry through to many other Christmas films. The first is how false personas constructed through career identity must be transcended. Characters define themselves within the realm of business but are more authentic outside of work.[107] The second major theme is a formula from *A Christmas Carol* where Christmas Eve becomes a day when the transcendental occurs. The movement of the film builds toward Christmas Eve, which represents a motif of rebirth.[108]

Unlike *A Christmas Carol*, a spiritual transformation occurs to not one protagonist, but three characters. Two of them are Alfred Kralik (James Stewart) and Klara Novak (Margaret Sullavan), who are clerks in a department store. They are modernized versions of Bob Cratchit in *A Christmas Carol*, both underpaid and insecure about their positions in the workplace, with the possibility of unemployment looming over them. However, unknown to each other, they are secret correspondents started by an advertisement for pen pals. They exchange letters where they talk about deeper ideas and express their authentic selves. However, their petty, insecure, and manipulative qualities surface through their business identities at the department store. The third character who undergoes a moral transformation is store owner Hugo Matuschek (Frank Morgan), a Scroogelike aloof and moody character whose whims and economic power as store owner make him thorny, intimidating, and unapproachable.

The movie shows how disabling it is when reality does not conform to expectations.[109] Both Matuschek and Klara take to sick beds when confronted with shattered illusions of their romantic partners.[110] They go through a symbolic death and rebirth as they move toward accepting how their romantic worldviews have splintered. These characters endure a period of desolation before finding a new identity that accepts their limitations. That theme—also employed in *It's a Wonderful Life*—emphasizes that romantic longing and adventure produces despair while acceptance of reality and limitations brings contentment.

EPIPHANIES IN SMALL-TOWN AMERICA

Remember the Night (1940) extends the period of moral transformation from Christmas Eve to the "twin-peaked festival" period from Christmas Eve to New Year's Day.[111] Establishing this period of time as a transformative period influenced many Christmas films as well as non-Christmas films in years to come. In *Remember the Night*, this longer period for change is necessary because the protagonists are so entrenched in roles defined by urban ethos and secular views of justice. They must adopt new identities by traveling from New York City into heartland America. After they experience small-town values and rituals, they progress into the transformation essential to First Wave Christmas films.

John Sargent (Fred MacMurray) is a New York district attorney prosecuting jewel thief Lee Leander (Barbara Stanwyck), who rejects the spirit of Christmas in the midst of Christmas carols and the Salvation Army collecting for the poor.[112] Fearing the jury is less likely to convict just before Christmas, Sargent manipulates the proceedings so the case is rescheduled until after New Year's Day. But he arranges for Lee to be released so she won't spend Christmas in jail. Since they're both from Indiana, Sargent tells Lee he'll drop her off in her hometown for the Christmas break and bring her back to New York after the holiday. After not seeing Lee for years, Lee's mother coldly rejects her when she comes to her home on Christmas Eve. So Sargent brings Lee to his family home.

Remember the Night shows that Sargent and Lee had different outcomes in life because of dissimilar parenting styles. Lee grew up with condemnation while Sargent benefited from forgiveness. Sargent's mother (Beulah Bondi) reminds him that he once took some money she was going to buy a new dress with and worked to pay it back. It was only a matter of making him understand through love, she says. But Lee's mother never gave Lee a chance to pay back "mission money" that Lee says she just borrowed. Lee's mother was unmerciful and unforgiving, and gave Lee the label of a criminal, which she appears to have adopted. These two characters' destinies were shaped by different reactions of their parents to similar transgressions.

Like other First Wave Christmas films, the mercy, compassion, and wholesomeness of a small-town family are revered. This contrasts with the individualistic career-driven urban lifestyle Sargent lives. Christmas in *Remember the Night* is associated with small-town life. The characters are not unsophisticated or ignorant; they have common sense and are models of generosity and serenity.[113] In contrast, there are no Christmas decorations in Sargent's New York apartment or in his place of business. Sargent mocks the spirit of good will toward men associated with Christmas and worries that "juries get soft on Christmas." His job is so results-driven it doesn't enable him to comprehend morality outside of legal definitions. In many Christmas movies, business is an oppressive force. In *Remember the Night*, the legal system is oppressive because it instills punishment and not forgiveness. It doesn't encompass compassion or the capacity to recognize the good in people that Sargent's family does.

I'll Be Seeing You (1944) also shows how small-town humanitarian views of justice contrast with a rigid and oppressive legal system. As in *Remember the Night*, the female protagonist is victimized by punitive and unmerciful laws. And similar to *Remember the Night*, the compassion of a small-town family leads to spiritual rejuvenation. It provides the setting for romance, which, like in *Remember the Night*, occurs during the Christmas Eve to New Year's cycle.

Mary Marshall (Ginger Rogers) is a criminal on a Christmas furlough from prison. On a train ride to her uncle's home in a small California town, she meets the highly decorated soldier Zachary Morgan (Joseph Cotten). He's recovering from what he calls "shell shock" and is on Christmas leave from a psychiatric hospital. Mary tells Zach to look her up where she's staying at the home of her Aunt Sarah (Spring Byington) and Uncle Henry (Tom Tully). Mary later reveals to her niece Barbara (Shirley Temple) what sent her to prison. To avoid the aggressive advances of her boss when he entrapped her in his high-rise apartment, she pushed him and he fell out of an open window and died.

Although the comparison isn't strictly made, Mary, like the pregnant Mary of the nativity story, is met with suspicion, doubt, and misunderstanding.[114] The movie shows the dark side of women's independence that the war years brought.[115] However, Mary's aunt and uncle offer a similar type of support and caring that Sargent's family provided for Lee in *Remember the Night*. Mary confesses to her aunt that prison destroyed her dreams for a home, but Sarah gently counsels her on how to turn broken dreams into happiness. Mary dreams of a home, which she defines as encompassing marriage, children, and a house. Sarah recognizes the value of Mary's dreams but tells her true happiness comes from compromising and acceptance of something less than one's ideal dreams. This is the viewpoint of an era where commitment and acceptance bring happiness, not the realization of individualistic dreams or ambitions.

Mary represents women forced into the workplace who look forward to playing a domestic role, while Zach's character addresses a pressing war-era dilemma: the reintegration of the battle-scarred soldier. Their bond created by the small-town protection of Mary's family redeems them in a way the legal system, psychiatry, and the military cannot.[116] Looking forward to the end of the war, Mary and Zach represent the postwar couple who can begin a new life.[117]

A NOIR CHRISTMAS

The genre later known as film noir began during the World War II years and peaked after the war in the late 1940s. The genre's film style features among other characteristics compositional tension over physical action, oblique and vertical lines over horizontal lines, and the proliferation of shadows and scenes that are lit for night.[118] "One always has the suspicion that if the lights were all suddenly flipped on the characters would shriek and shrink from the screen like Count Dracula at sunrise," Paul Schrader wrote in his seminal essay "Notes on Film Noir."[119] The genre's themes are based on war and postwar disillusionment, the realistic movement in film, and hard-boiled detective novels. This creates what Schrader called a cynical way of thinking and acting that separates people from their everyday emotions into what he calls "romanticism with a protective shell."[120] The characters are often unredeemable people existing in a corrupt society.

This is at odds with the Scroogelike redemption of a protagonist in the Christmas film genre. However, noir Christmas films juxtapose the holiday and its associations with good will and redemption against the irredeemable life of crime, including in *Christmas Holiday* (1944), starring Gene Kelly and Deanna Durbin as a troubled married couple. Both actors play against their cheerful personas largely shaped through musicals and comedies. Durbin was usually cast in roles the *New York Times* described as "everyone's intrepid kid sister or spunky daughter, a wholesome, radiant, can-do girl who... was always fixing the problems of unhappy adults."[121]

However, in *Christmas Holiday* she's an unhappy adult herself. After her husband is jailed for murder, she becomes a nightclub singer and apparently a sex worker. Kelly plays the slippery Robert Manette, who is shown in a flashback charming the young, lonely, and vulnerable Abigail Martin (Durbin) into marriage. After a brief period of marital bliss, Abigail realizes her husband is a criminal, which he chronically lies to her about. She dwells in a life of disgrace where she appears to share her husband's shame.[122]

In the Gothic-themed landscape of seedy New Orleans, there are no Christmas decorations or visible signs of the holiday. *Christmas Holiday* is the first definitive anti-Christmas film. The holiday is not centered around home and community and instead is a bleak depiction of deceit and degradation. However, Abigail, who renames herself Jackie, hopes to find some redemption through religion. On Christmas Eve, she asks a soldier to take her to a midnight Christmas mass. But the priests in the mass scenes are distant figures with their backs turned to the audience. She loudly sobs when the church choir begins singing "O Come All Ye Faithful." Afterwards, Jackie tells the soldier it's the most she's cried in her life because she was hoping for a transformative experience. But redemption didn't come in church. As in many noir films, institutions are oppressive forces, not helpful entities. Redemption only comes near the end of the film at a heavy cost, where Jackie can only find peace outside of the influence of the church and marriage—two institutions that America at the time venerated.

Durbin also stars in *Lady on a Train* (1945), which blends comedy and film noir. However, it's a rare film noir comedy that isn't a parody of the genre.[123] Instead, it instills comedy largely through the actions of the protagonist Nicki Collins (Durbin), the wealthy daughter of a San Francisco magnate. The comedy centers on her boldness in taking on a male power structure that doesn't take her seriously. Her self-assurance makes her the most independent of all the women in First Wave Christmas films.

The film is in some ways an anti-Christmas movie. Much of the film takes place on Christmas Eve at a New York nightclub far from the small-town family life associated with Christmas during the war years. But rather than the remorseful tortured character Durbin plays in *Christmas Holiday*, her character in *Lady on a Train* possesses a confidence, fearlessness, and potent sense of humor that make her a brave heroine rather than the victimized wife of *Christmas Holiday*. Nicki's trip to New York under the guise of a visit to her aunt away from what appears to be an overprotective father is a movement into independence. She establishes herself as a real-life version of a detective she reads about in novels and plays the assertive role usually played by men. But she's also a symbol of home and Christmas itself. A stunning scene shows Durbin singing "Silent Night" to her father over the phone in her New York hotel room. Her voice so embodies a gentleness and religious connotation far removed from the lives the characters live that a hardened criminal is moved to tears by hearing her sing. In the entire Christmas movie genre, there may be no greater contrast between the fellowship of family at Christmas and the criminal life.

NOSTALGIA AND COMMUNITY

Unlike most First Wave Christmas films, which emphasize current social situations, *Meet Me in St. Louis* (1944) isn't set during the World War II era. The movie takes place from 1903 to 1904, culminating in the World's Fair in St. Louis. This gives the movie a strong sense of nostalgia. The family is solidly middle class in an idyllic past where three generations of family live together in a large Victorian home and women possess the leisure time to invest in their family and community.

The family's sense of home and identity comes to be threatened by the family's father Alonzo Smith (Leon Ames) agreeing to take a job in

New York City. This sets up the film's conflict between family and ambition.[124] A promotion is not an opportunity to the family but a decision to make money a priority over community. "What about me and my life?" Esther (Judy Garland) asks. "You can take that with you," her father says. For the family's determined patriarch, an individual's life is not connected to community, so one's identity is portable and malleable when opportunity calls.

Christmas Eve produces a catalyst for Smith to undergo an epiphany similar to Scrooge's when he realizes that community, consistency, and a sense of being rooted is more important than individualistic ambition and monetary gain. This occurs after one of the film's most famous scenes where, to comfort her young sibling, Esther sings "Have Yourself a Merry Little Christmas" to Tootie (Margaret O'Brien). While the song reassures Tootie things will be better in the future, it contains a glimpse of impermanence and uncertainty. "Someday soon we all will be together if the fates allow / Until then, we'll have to muddle through somehow," Esther sings. The song doesn't pacifiy Tootie and instead unleashes a torrent of raw emotion. She runs out of the home and decapitates the snowmen the family built in their yard. She says she'd rather destroy them if she can't take them with her. Her father may believe that life is portable, but for Tootie it isn't. Throughout the film, and particularly in the film's Halloween sequence, Tootie has had a fascination with death, but when confronted with a glimpse of impermanence and uncertainty in her own family, she is traumatized. The fear of moving makes Tootie confront the weight of adulthood with all of its transience.[125] As Esther has just sung to her, adulthood comes with the possibility of loss and an unknown future, and Tootie is overwhelmed and devastated by the realization that adulthood with all of its improbability is looming.

However, Tootie's display of anxiety and awareness of transience soon gives way to a comfortable consistency.[126] After seeing this from an upstairs window, Tootie's father wakes up the family and in his rousing epiphany declares he's "not a puppet on a string" and "we're going to stay here 'til we rot." It's reaffirmation of community, connection, and small-town life over ambition, money, and the lure of New York City.

Instead of the family being forced to go into the world to seek opportunity, the world in a sense comes to their town. The last four minutes of the film is set during spring at the World's Fair in St. Louis, where the family joins the crowd that's come to see the spectacle of the fair. The film thus shows nostalgia and progress co-existing.[127] As *It's a Wonderful Life* demonstrated two years later, adventure isn't as valuable as secure roots and community. *Meet Me in St. Louis* validates the American way of life represented by rooted small-town family life during a time when more individuals than ever left their hometowns. The movie also endorses the domestic sphere associated with the women over the more individualistic career-oriented patriarchy. The women have no interest in life beyond their hometown and perceive the world outside of it with a sense of alarm.[128] Although they define their lives outside the status and attraction that money offers, they nonetheless live with the comforts of their era. The movie is far from a condemnation of materialism; it emphasizes manageable opportunity that retains community. While the film endorses the women's sense of community, it also justifies Smith's view that they haven't sacrificed too much by staying in St. Louis, shown by the grandiose world's fair.[129]

ELIMINATING A FALSE SELF

Elizabeth Lane (Barbara Stanwyck) in *Christmas in Connecticut* (1945) must progress through two of the major narrative devices women undergo in First Wave Christmas movies. Like Klara in *Shop Around the Corner*, she must shed the false self she constructs to survive in a male-dominated business environment. And like the female leads in *Holiday Inn*, she chooses between two men representing two opposing sets of ethics.

Lane creates a false self by adopting a false persona. Although living alone in an apartment, she writes stories for a woman's magazine under the guise that she lives in an idyllic Connecticut farmhouse with a husband, a baby, and farm animals. Her sham persona is endangered after her publisher

The war years' First Wave Christmas film looks forward to the type of society Americans wanted after the war. In *Christmas in Connecticut* (1945) Elizabeth Lane (Barbara Stanwyck) must discard gender role expectations to start a life with veteran Jefferson Jones (Dennis Morgan). Photo courtesy the Everett Collection.

Alexander Yardley (Sydney Greenstreet) says she must take in Jefferson Jones (Dennis Morgan), a sailor rescued from sea for Christmas. Believing she will soon be exposed as a fraud and lose her job, Lane agrees to marry architect John Sloan (Reginald Gardiner), since he lives in a Connecticut farmhouse. But before that happens, the sailor arrives and Lane is immediately attracted to him. This intensifies after he surprises her by reversing expected gender roles by knowing how to change a baby's diaper. Now that an alternative has arrived, she detaches herself from Sloan and Yardley, two men preoccupied with consumerism, greed, and materialism.

The movie clearly shows there will be a place for the war veteran Jones in postwar society.[130] *Christmas in Connecticut* begins with Jones adrift at sea alone, starved for food, and ends in affluence in a suburban home filled with food and comforts. The young veteran Jones provides an alternative to the two men who represent an older establishment. While Sloan and Yardley plot business dealings, Jones represents a freedom and liberation from materialism, career fixation, and traditional gender expectations. This enables Lane to make the moral choice for marriage so critical in First Wave movies—choosing someone not materialistic over someone who is. In a Christmas epiphany she declares she will stop living two stereotypes of what a woman is supposed to be. She can no longer be a marketable commodity as a career woman and she can no longer pretend to be more equipped to be a housewife than she really is. She unravels herself from these two cultural expectations. Lane initially describes herself as someone who "gets herself into a mess and hasn't the moral courage to get herself out of it." But in the end, she does.

Christmas in Connecticut is a notable example of a First Wave film during the war years that looks forward to assimilating women back into the domestic sphere and integrating soldiers back into society. The postwar First Wave Christmas films would show the dark side of what happened after the war by addressing social problems such as housing shortages, postwar materialism, and an even deeper fear of the decline of small-town ethics. But no First Wave film uses Christmas to cover as much spiritual and moral territory as the 1946 film *It's a Wonderful Life*, the subject of the next chapter.

6

George Bailey as a Modern-Day Job

The Suffering of an American Dreamer

The alienation and despair of George Bailey (Jimmy Stewart) in *It's a Wonderful Life* reveal a full-blown spiritual and moral crisis that make him a unique character in the Christmas film canon. He is similar to the biblical Job, who doesn't understand why he suffers and wishes he had never been born.[131]

Job and George Bailey are both pillars in their community who become afflicted.[132] Job's anguish over his unjust suffering comes after his children and servants are killed, his wealth is taken away, and he is stricken with sores. Bailey's suffering is caused by his feelings of entrapment and failure because he cannot leave Bedford Falls to follow his dreams of education, career, and travel. His anguish exposes a deep conflict within American culture: the clash between domesticity and adventure.

Despite the life affirming feel-good ending and George's corrective conversion from frustration to gratitude and acceptance, much of the movie emphasizes the tension between George's outlook that the individual is associated with freedom, romanticism, and adventure, which is at odds with the community's requirements for domesticity, stability, and restriction.[133] For most of the film, George Bailey exists in a grueling trap. He can't pursue his dreams, imaginative energy, and desire for mobility but also can't find a way to express it in his everyday life.[134] Duty isn't enough to make him happy.

As with Job, supernatural intercession creates spiritual insight. In the Book of Job, God makes a spectacular appearance in a whirlwind to respond to Job's suffering. In *It's a Wonderful Life*, a heavenly visitation comes from Clarence (Henry Travers), a guardian angel sent to earth by celestial entities that oversee George's life and respond to prayers. Clarence alleviates George's despair by showing George a frightening alternate real-

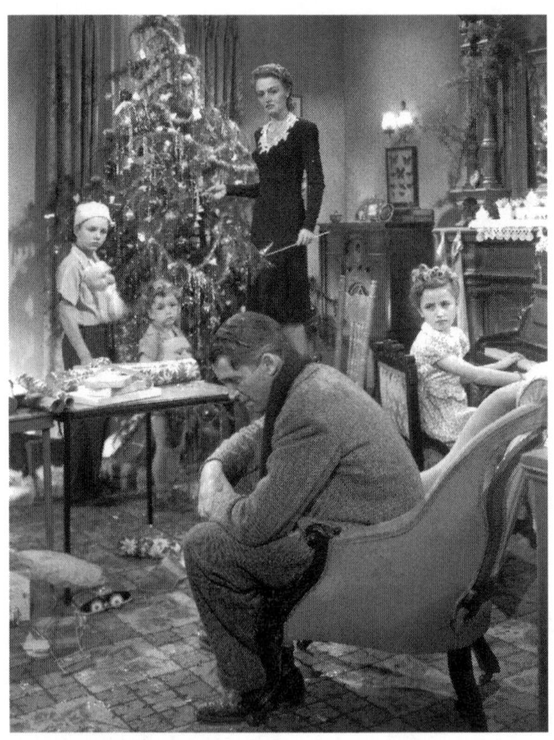

George Bailey in *It's a Wonderful Life* (1946) spends most of his life in spiritual warfare between individual ambition and responsibility to family and community. Despite what many may call a noble life, he lives in a state of near despair after the collapse of his dreams. Photo courtesy the Everett Collection.

ity of George's hometown. George receives a glimpse of what Job also wished for: to have never been born. This alternate reality sequence causes George to submit to his fate just as Job finally submits to God.

However, it is one of American cinema's most harrowing journeys to arrive at that resolution and the Christmas movie genre's most complex and far-reaching film. It contains biblical allusions, a nightmarish film noir–inspired alternative reality, and a penetrating examination of a culture that cannot resolve the conflict between individual achievement and communal responsibility without divine intervention.

ASSESSING A LIFE

The movie begins with a communal plea to the heavens from George's friends and family. Although the theology in the heavens is largely unclear, what is apparent is that sincere and heartfelt prayer is a turning point for supernatural intervention, not conventional religious worship. In a harrowing barroom prayer on Christmas Eve just before he goes to the bridge to end his life, George prays for help. He confesses he's not a "praying man," suggesting he's not a conventionally religious person. It's also revealing that for such a small town there's no church that George attends and church isn't mentioned in the movie. Although George prays on V-E Day and V-J Day, he isn't shown to have a regular prayer life. And when the heavenly beings recount George's life, it is by the deeds he does within the world, not how conventionally devout he is. This is a film that reveres a man of works rather than a man of faith.

With an hour to go before George tries to kill himself, Joseph recounts to Clarence the story of George's life (which actually takes about an hour and a half). The movie follows George Bailey from age twelve to age thirty-eight (1919 to Christmas Eve 1945). Even at the age of twelve, George glamorizes life outside of his town and dreams of exotic places. While working at the pharmacy, he insists the young Mary have her chocolate drink with coconut in it. That's because coconuts are from faraway places such as Tahiti, the Fiji Islands, or the Coral Sea, he says. Even food takes on a romantic nature to George. And he's excited about being up for nomination in the National Geographic Society because George romanticizes distant locations.

George's romanticism comes from being a dreamer. But his dreams to leave town even for college or his honeymoon are later thwarted. His life is a series of dissolving opportunities.[135] This makes George somewhat like the Old Testament character Joseph, about whom his brothers despairingly say, "Here comes this dreamer!"[136] just after they plot to kill him (they throw him into a pit instead). George's version of a confining pit and exile is the small town of Bedford Falls.

Despite what some may regard as a noble life in Bedford Falls, Bailey remains in a state of desperation and anxiety about his inability to fulfill his dreams and sense of adventure.[137] It is the repressiveness of an ordinary life that causes George's frustration.[138] He struggles with a pervasive sense that the essence of life is outside of Bedford Falls, which he views as inert and confining.

The tipping point for George comes on Christmas Eve, when Uncle Billy misplaces $8,000 in a botched bank deposit and George devises a suicide plan as an act of self-sacrifice for his family so they will receive his life insurance money. The bridge where he plans to jump to his death is a symbol of unrealized potential; he has said earlier in the film he wanted to design bridges. And perhaps it is a bridge that leads out of town. Going to the middle of a bridge indicates he's in an agonizing limbo between his responsibilities on one side and his ambitions and adventure on the other. Just before George jumps off the bridge into the river, Clarence appears and dives into the water. As in beginning of George's story where he saved his brother, George once again rescues someone else. George is too busy saving others to kill himself.[139]

After they are out of the water, George (like Job) says he wishes he had never been born. So Clarence grants him his wish. In an alternative reality, Bedford Falls becomes a tyrannical town called "Pottersville." This sequence is shot in the style of film noir that clashes with the iconography of a small-town film, with police sirens, shooting in the streets, darkness, alcoholism, burlesque shows, and the shadows of noir lighting.[140] The noirish Pottersville brings out the worst tendencies in people. They are self-centered, cynical, and following the flawed aspects of their characters. Because George hasn't been there to help them, their lives have changed. The frightened George wants his life restored, which Clarence grants. He returns home to family and friends, who pitch in to give him the money he needs. But this isn't what's important. He's changed internally. He is finally cured of the romantic longing for other places and accomplishments that have consumed him. George realizes he has had a positive effect and his compromises have counted for something.[141] The heavenly induced lesson shows that life is a web of cause and effect, with altruistic and self-sacrificial acts having an especially powerful effect on others.

TWO SCENES OF INNER WARFARE

Two pivotal scenes illustrate George's war between his strong feelings for individualistic goals and communal responsibility, scenes where he radically and intensely vacillates between these two desires.

The first is the courtship scene between George and Mary after she returns home from college. Before he goes to Mary's home, George is already conflicted between responsibilities toward others and living out his personal dreams because his brother Harry returns home from college newly married with a promising job opportunity in Buffalo. Despite his irritability, George is strongly attracted to Mary as they stand close to each other on the telephone when Mary's current suitor, Sam, calls. George seems to sense the limitations marriage will bring. Does he think he has no other choice? Does he see no other way out since he appears reluctant to deny Harry his job opportunity? Does he realize his dreams are once again deferred and that he should at least marry as Harry did?

Whatever the case, he's once again in warfare—this time between his attraction for Mary and his desire to be independent and pursue his ambitions. "I don't want to get married—ever—not to anyone!" he tells

Mary. "You understand that? I want to do what I want to do." But after he passionately declares this, he just as passionately embraces her. As much as he wants independence to pursue his dreams, his attraction to Mary is ultimately stronger. But this scene shows how deeply George is tormented between the domestication that Mary represents and the freedom he longs for.

The second pivotal scene is on Christmas Eve, when George returns home after Uncle Billy misplaces the $8,000 deposit. He sees the money debacle not as an obstacle to overcome but as a representation of everything wrong with his life and his worthlessness. With his dreams to leave town and become an architect abandoned, the only identity he still possesses is his work at the Bailey Building & Loan. But when that is in jeopardy, he feels like a complete failure.

George is a deeply troubled man at war with himself as he alternates between frustration at his family and tender feelings toward them. At first he appears to realize his suicide means he will leave his family behind. So he tearfully embraces his son Tommy. But George becomes angry when Mary reminds him family will be coming over. That creates a litany of complaints to Mary about Bedford Falls, his home, and even that they have too many children.

But once again he seesaws between frustration and tenderness. After Mary tells him that his daughter Zuzu is sick, he suddenly snaps out of his anger into concern for her. He goes upstairs to see her and in a gentle scene pretends to put a flower back together by putting the broken petals in his pocket. He is a caring father, far different from the angry man shown moments earlier. When there is someone for him to help, George will immediately care for other people. However, after this interaction with Zuzu, he goes downstairs and yells at Zuzu's teacher and her husband over the phone. He snaps at his children when they ask questions, further showing how swiftly he can alternate from tenderness to frustration.

He goes to the corner of the living room that still has representations of his architectural ambition, where there are models of buildings, including a bridge with a drafting board. Photographs of key people in his life hang on the wall nearby. This is a physical representation of his inner turmoil. The photographs of people represent duty and domesticity and the building models represent his ambitions. He angrily throws, kicks, and smashes the building models. He destroys his ongoing dream of being an architect. Seeing his family looking at him in fear and bewilderment, he sincerely apologizes. But the calm doesn't last long. He shouts at his children to go back to what they were doing and angrily leaves.

An early version of the movie script featured two George Baileys. There was a "good" George Bailey and a "bad" one who was the wealthy, philandering man he would have been if he hadn't stayed in Bedford Falls. Instead of going through a sequence where he isn't born, he finds a world inhabited by the "bad George."[142] It ends with the good George Bailey killing the bad George Bailey on a bridge.

But in the final version on screen, the good elements and bad elements of George aren't split into separate characters. Instead of being divided into different figures to express different parts of his personality, they are combined into one person. The warfare is within George himself. That's clear in the Christmas Eve scene. He is the "good George" when he calms Zuzu, hugs Tommy, and apologizes for his outburst. That's when he embraces his responsibilities. He is the "bad George" when he lashes out at his family, yells at the teacher and her husband, and kicks and throws his building models in a fit of frustration and anger at his inability to realize his ambitions.

PROGRESSING TO GRATITUDE

Like George Bailey himself, the movie was underappreciated. It lost about $500,000 at the box office.[143] Many critics pounced on it, describing it as close to what Potter declared after one of George's speeches praising the working people of Bedford Falls: "sentimental hogwash." The *New York Times* called it "a figment of simple Pollyanna platitudes." *The New Republic* said it was an attempt to "convince movie audiences that

American life is exactly like the *Saturday Evening Post* covers of Norman Rockwell." *The New Yorker* described it as "so mincing as to border on baby talk."[144] But the film's director Frank Capra defended the film, saying he didn't make it for the critics or literati but for "the weary, the disheartened, and the disillusioned," for those "whose cross is heavy," and "for the Magdalenes stoned by hypocrites and the afflicted Lazaruses with only dogs to lick their sores."[145]

The movie could have been forgotten. But it wasn't. It aired on television, which prompted many viewers to write to Capra about how the movie impacted them. When the film's copyright expired in 1974, it transferred into public domain. TV stations showed it frequently because they could air it for free. The annual airing of the film on TV during the Christmas season turned it into a Christmas pop culture fixture. And over time, the tormented quality of Jimmy Stewart's performance was increasingly praised.

Stewart was at a pivotal moment when he made *It's a Wonderful Life.* It was his first film after returning from World War II. He was by then in his late thirties, and his career was in transition between his prewar romantic lead persona and the next phase of his career where he played a crustier middle-aged man wrestling his own demons in Anthony Mann Westerns such as *Winchester '73* and *The Man from Laramie* and in two key Hitchcock movies, *Rear Window* and *Vertigo.*

It's a Wonderful Life shows him at the crossroads of these two stages of his career, and he embodies both personas in this film. Stewart's acting in *It's a Wonderful Life* may be so convincing because, like George Bailey, Stewart was evaluating whether his own profession had any meaning after all he saw in combat during World War II. Years later in an interview with cast member Jimmy Hawkins, Stewart said he considered retiring from acting after the war. He wondered if acting was important or relevant. He even considered returning to his small hometown of Indiana, Pennsylvania, to run his father's hardware store.[146] It was Lionel Barrymore (who played Potter) who convinced Stewart about the significance of acting: "He reminded me that acting is important. Millions of people see you and it helps shape their lives. . . . Is it more decent to drop a bomb on people or bring a ray of sunshine to them through your acting?"[147]

Stewart added that he liked the movie "because it was about an average guy and there weren't enough stories about average guys."[148] While making the film, Stewart may have thought about the "average guy" he might have been if he had never left his hometown of Indiana, Pennsylvania. But unlike George Bailey, who only dreamed of being an architect, Stewart went to college, attending Princeton University to study architecture. In some ways, George Bailey is the man Stewart might have been if he had never gone to college and had remained in a small town.

The movie also depicts what dominates First Wave Christmas films—the conflict over the post–World War II anxiety about losing small-town values at the expense of financial progress. This manifests in the struggle between Mary's domestic sphere and George's ambition.[149] Mary sees the romance in everyday life. She sees potential in the old home on Sycamore Street, while George says "I wouldn't live there as a ghost." She sees possibility where George sees limitation.

Mary's worldview is romance expressed in family life, stability, and community. For George, romance is in the future in another place through travel, escapist dreams, and accomplishing his own goals.[150] There is an element of George's dreaming that is socially disruptive, individualistic, and idealistic compared to the mildness and rooted qualities of Mary's dreams.[151] Although George is steadfastly responsible, his longing for adventure and career success displays an excessive interest in personal prosperity and impracticality. George has imaginative energy and desire for mobility he cannot actualize.[152] The movie doesn't present a karmic worldview where someone reaps what they sow in terms of tangible self-gaining results. It subverts the American Dream mythology where people attain what they deserve by how ethical they are or how hard they work. For George, material and financial success, and even security, are not returned in exchange for George's virtue.

GEORGE BAILEY AS CHRIST FIGURE

While George is largely a Job figure, he at times becomes a Christ figure. Because of his sense of responsibility and being other-focused, he suffers not in the physical sense but because he is unable to fulfill his passions for adventure and success. Some of his dreams may be escapist, but others aren't. He wants to educate himself and utilize his talents. He is prevented from following his vocational calling.

George also is a Christ-figure because he redeems the lives of several people. In the alternate reality sequence of a Bedford Falls without George, key people in George's life drastically change and even die without George's help. His brother Harry drowns, which means Harry couldn't save many other lives during World War II. Billy is in an insane asylum. George's mother turns hard and bitter in a boarding house. Mary is a frightened spinster. Violet is the town tramp. The taxi driver, Ernie, doesn't live at a home in Bailey Park and is unmarried. Bailey Park doesn't exist, so numerous people never own their own homes. Without Martini's guidance, Nick becomes a cynical, sarcastic, hard personality. These people are rescued and redeemed because of George.[153]

Christ analogies also come through in a few key interactions with other characters, including one with Violet Bick. She becomes a modern version of the adulteress whom Jesus tells to "not sin again."[154] On Christmas Eve, George shows how he views her as a fallen woman who has the opportunity to change her life. He gives her money and writes a letter testifying to her character. Some unknown incident has put her in a position of shame where she must leave town. But like the gospel episode where Jesus forgives the adulteress about to be stoned, George believes Violet deserves a second chance.

Another scene that recalls a key episode in the gospels is when Potter tries to tempt George into taking a job at his bank. Offering him money and the promise of travel, it's a variation of Satan tempting Jesus in the wilderness.[155] Instead of offering the kingdoms of the world, Potter presents financial security and adventure, a benign-sounding piece of the

American Dream. Temptation from evil comes not from deceit, but from a manipulative variation on truth. Potter acutely observes George's situation and describes George's doubts, insecurities, and troubles more than his friends and family do. But when George shakes Potter's hand, he recoils from it. He doesn't politely turn Potter down; he tells him and his staff they are "scurvy spiders." Because George's worldview is so much of entrapment, he sees Potter's job as another form of imprisonment. As confined as George feels in his current situation, the spider imagery suggests he will be prey, stuck even more in a web of confinement if he accepts Potter's job. And to further make Potter a malevolent satanic figure, he never ages or dies; he's a consistent presence of evil.[156]

Another biblical image evoked in the film puts George in the position of a pastor. George and Mary bless Martini's new home in Bailey Park with items representing communion. Mary presents bread and George offers wine. The other item they offer is salt, perhaps recalling Jesus's statement that "you are the salt of the earth."[157] The ending scene when friends and family bring in money to help George is somewhat of a reversal, with the community (congregation) blessing George in his home. An altarlike table is set up in front of George while people bring money and objects to him. Mary calls it a "miracle" and asks Martini if he has some wine, apparently to bless the joyful event.

OPPOSING VIEWS OF CAPITALISM

Some of George's suffering is because he must combat Potter, who, like Satan in the Book of Job, stirs up suffering. Yet Potter has in common with George a passion for ambition. But it's of a different type. Potter wants to possess, destroy, and monopolize to establish power. Being so ruthless in his business practices fits the convention of First Wave Christmas films, which express the fear of ravenous business taking over small businesses. George's father points out that this is not only a cultural hazard, but a spiritual emptiness. Peter Bailey wonders if Potter even has a soul, reinforcing the image of him as a nonhuman, evil figure.

And Potter doesn't reform at the end of the film. He doesn't return the stolen money, and no one finds out he took the money. He is not the Christmas movie convention of a Scrooge-type figure who is ultimately redeemed. The supernatural intervention is to the noble worker George (a substitute Bob Cratchit), not to the cold and heartless businessman as it is in *A Christmas Carol*, where ghosts visit Ebenezer Scrooge to reform him.

Like *A Christmas Carol, It's a Wonderful Life* doesn't condemn business. It supports ethical and community-minded business represented by the small family business Bailey Building & Loan. Bailey and Potter embody opposing views of capitalism. Potter represents greed, while Bailey characterizes modest and honest small business.[158]

Potter dresses in black, has no connection to family or friends, travels in a vehicle that looks like a hearse, and shows no interest in human pleasure. He seems to have given up his body for the sake of accumulation of capital.[159] Potter makes money a tool to dominate, not a tool to help people, which George does with his bank. The view of capitalism in the film is that it's ethical when it's modest in scale.

The heavenly realm operates on different principles by avoiding the economic system altogether. "We don't use money in heaven," Clarence says. Harry reinforces this by saying George is the "richest man in town," as friends and family gather around him. Friendship is the currency most valued, while the world's priority of money is not important.

If Potter is the satanic figure and villain, there are others who in their own way conspire against George by being insensitive to his longings and dreams. Couldn't the bank board have found someone else to take over the business since they knew George planned to go to college? Would his brother Harry follow through with making a new life in Buffalo knowing that George wanted to leave Bedford Falls? Could the townspeople have sacrificed more of their financial needs during a bank run so George would have had enough money to go on his honeymoon? Is it fair for George's father to have said George was "born older" and to have asked him to stay at the Building & Loan even though George desperately wanted to go to college?

Only after an angel shows George Bailey a frightening alternate reality of his hometown can he finally find contentment. He submits to enjoying his friends and family in Bedford Falls as the biblical Job ultimately submitted to God. Photo courtesy the Everett Collection.

Recognition of George's work and sacrifices comes at the end of the film when his friends and family arrive at his home, but before that, although people are always friendly to George, do favors for him, and express gratitude, they can't understand his deepest passions. This makes George a lonely figure. He never has anyone to talk to about his dreams. So his dreams and ambitions often surface in lively fantasy or in frustration when they don't materialize. Mary saves her "George lassoes the moon" illustration of George, but it hangs on the wall almost as a mockery. In this context, George's image of possibility is simply something to be framed and placed in the domestic sphere.[160] It's on the wall in Mary's domestic space as a sentiment, not actualized in the outside world through George's ambitions.

Ultimately, the movie is not critical of the shortcomings of other people in the town. Instead, it champions George's realization that duty supersedes ambition. After his epiphany during the alternate reality sequence, George no longer wants his freedom through escape but finds meaning in connections to community as well as an acceptance of the sense of responsibility that maintains the community.[161]

American literature generally reveres the achievements of the individual adventurer, but *It's a Wonderful Life* alters this ideology by honoring domesticity above adventure.[162] It also advocates that the community's interests are superior to the needs of the individual and individuals must sacrifice self-interest for family and community.[163] Not only is self-sacrifice necessary, but an individual's primary identity is achieved through family and community rather than individualistic goals.[164] This reinforces the nostalgia in many First Wave Christmas films for the vanishing community of small-town American life.[165]

As Job acquiesces to God's unknowable ways, George Bailey succumbs to the postwar era's ideal of sacred duties: family life, ties to community, and ethical capitalism. The supernatural intervention in *It's a Wonderful Life* leads to a metaphysical journey inward for George to a destination and home that has been there all along, which he learns to finally embrace.[166]

7

The Christmas Film at Its Most Probing

The Postwar Years

The veteran in *Mr. Soft Touch* (1949) returns home to find his business run by gangsters. In *It Happened on 5th Avenue* (1947), a veteran is left homeless after being evicted from an apartment building that is to be converted into corporate offices. The rugged ex-soldier in *Holiday Affair* (1948) feels misplaced in a culture that demands conformity and emphasizes materialism.

These Christmas movies with damaged and outsider veterans reflect a postwar disillusionment matching themes occurring during this time in the film noir genre. During the postwar years, noir films featured discouraged veterans. These veterans encountered difficulty fitting into a society that not only seems to work against their well-being, but appears in some ways to no longer be the kind of society they thought they were fighting for.[167]

The ideal of personal sacrifice during the war years dissipated as unbridled consumerism came into vogue and soldiers returned home to start families, sometimes in new suburban homes.[168] There was unprecedented prosperity centered on a large manufacturing-based economy. By the late 1940s, the United States had 7 percent of the world's population but half the world's manufacturing output.[169] Housing was in demand, unemployment was low, and returning veterans could take advantage of the G.I. Bill to receive money for housing and education.

But for some in a generation that experienced the depravation of the Great Depression and the anxiety of the war years, the new materialism and continuing exodus from farms to suburbs and cities didn't feel right. It felt like something of the American character was eroding. The small-business economy perceived to be the bedrock of the American capitalist system was under siege by corporate power in an economic boom. And the frugality and humility that for many defined the American everyman appeared to be shifting to a more materialistic culture.

In somewhat of a subgenre, some film noir movies, while not full-blown Christmas films, incorporate Christmas to reinforce how lost characters were in the postwar world. These films show the reverse of the American dream: characters are unable to find their place in society.[170] In the noir *Lady in a Lake* (1946), Christmas illustrates this unease when detective Phillip Marlowe spends Christmas Eve and Christmas in the home of a troublesome woman while he nurses wounds after he's been shot. A radio production of *A Christmas Carol* plays as the characters sit apart from each other, but the story has no effect on them. Their silence shows how they are fallen characters far from the redemptive quality the *Carol* story carries with it.

Whether noir-influenced or not, postwar Christmas films are far-reaching and profound, and three of the postwar films (*It's a Wonderful Life*, *Miracle on 34th Street*, and *The Bishop's Wife*) are arguably the high-point of the genre.

FAITH ON TRIAL: MIRACLE ON 34TH STREET

In *Miracle on 34th Street*, a man named Kris Kringle who claims he is the real Santa Claus resolves the postwar dual anxiety about materialism and doubts about religious faith. Kringle is both a symbol of belief in the transcendental and a voice for correcting the commercialism of Christmas and the excesses of postwar capitalism. Like *It's a Wonderful Life*, *Miracle on 34th Street* warns of greed in business. However, that isn't embodied in a solitary satanic figure such as Potter in *It's a Wonderful Life*, but by a business system fueled by self-interest and deceit. It's also the return on the screen for Santa Claus.[171] The character hadn't been seen on the screen in a significant role since the silent film era.

Macy's executive Doris (Maureen O'Hara) hires Kris Kringle (Edmund Gwenn) to fill in for a drunk Santa at the Macy's Thanksgiving Parade in New York and later hires him in the Macy's flagship department store. The pressure for excessive consumerism begins when the head of Macy's toy department instructs Kringle to recommend overstocked toys to children who are undecided about what they want. The practice is giving a child something they don't need, Kringle believes. Later, Kringle says he's worried about commercialism ruining Christmas, which he believes to be not just a day but "a frame of mind." He encourages business competition by referring customers to other stores if Macy's doesn't have what a customer wants.

Kringle's actions show that the economic system is ethical when it is public-focused and based on necessity, not on excess or unwanted goods. This reassures a postwar audience that capitalism can still be moral despite a potential for greed and unnecessary consumerism. Santa discerns not good and bad behavior of children, but good and bad business practices. The presence of Santa in a department store enthrones him within the center of commerce to hand down judgments to correct consumer culture.[172] Business ultimately capitulates to Santa's anti-monopolisitic, pro-competition, anti-excess ideology. The values of the department store and Santa become compatible.[173] However, this means the tenets of giving, charity, reciprocity, and public service are channeled into a commercial definition of Christmas.[174]

With business accepting Kringle's definition of ethical consumerism, the main conflict is psychology, which is portrayed as the opponent of faith. This is embodied in Macy's store psychologist Granville Sawyer, who disavows the supernatural and views the impulse for good as neurotic. This clashes with the worldview of religious faith personified by Kringle. Sawyer tells the young janitor Alfred that he plays Santa Claus in Brooklyn because he's suffering from a guilt complex. Kringle confronts Sawyer about this, and, like Jesus using a whip at the temple because he's incensed about the moneychangers,[175] Kris uses his cane to lightly hit Sawyer on his forehead. Kringle is then taken for psychiatric evaluation.

The legal system must resolve the conflict between psychology and faith. Although it's a legal hearing and not a case for a jury to decide, in many ways it's putting faith on trial. Kringle possesses traits of a Christ figure because he's misunderstood when trying to do good. The film alludes to the gospels when the political boss Halloran warns the judge he'll be "a regular Pontius Pilate" if he declares there is no Santa Claus.[176] Sawyer in his role as psychologist is the film's version of Caiaphas, the religious leader who worked to condemn Jesus.[177]

And the hearing shows how faith is childlike. While on the witness stand, executive R. H. Macy imagines the faces of happy children when asked if he believes in Santa Claus. And the film presents Kringle's attorney, Fred Gailey (John Payne), as the most faith-filled character because he possesses a childlike faith that does not question or doubt. The legal system can't integrate this childlike view. However, it doesn't make ultimate decisions about whether faith can be proven. The court concedes that belief in Santa Claus (representing belief in religious faith or the supernatural) is a "matter of opinion." But because Kringle is at a hearing to assess his sanity, the legal system can't leave faith as personal opinion. District Attorney Mara demands that Gailey show that Kringle is the "one and only Santa Claus." This is a desire to prove a single belief system and a clear manifestation of faith, not just the acknowledgement of the possibility of faith/God. Because Gailey is a childlike believer, he doesn't require the verifiable scientific proof the legal system demands. However, the film reassures audiences that belief is already embedded within the legal system.

Kringle as an agent of faith affects the three main characters, who initially represent faith, agnosticism, and atheism.

In *Miracle on 34th Street* (1947), Doris (Maureen O'Hara) is the film's atheist, Susan (Natalie Wood) an agnostic, and Fred (John Payne) the true believer. With Santa Claus representing and agitating for faith itself, the three characters clash because of their belief systems. Photo courtesy 20th Century-Fox/Everett Collection.

Macy's executive and divorced mother Doris Walker (Maureen O'Hara) dismisses faith, fantasy, fairy tales, and even the imagination as dangerous. She places her faith in common sense, pragmatism, and psychology. She demystifies Christmas by viewing it solely through commercialism and pragmatism.[178] In a sense she is the film's atheist. For her, faith is irrational. She is a nervous, hypervigilant, career-oriented survivalist. Doris is especially fearful of anything that threatens her job because it's linked to her survival as a single mother. Doris's hardened pragmatism creates serious doubts for her even when she begins to grow fond of Kris. Her heightened sense of defining reality through pragmatism is a defense against emotional wounds.[179] She escapes the pain of being hurt from her divorce by being overly self-reliant, with a focus on achieving security. She values what can be seen, not an unseen hope or belief. Both Kringle and Gailey say Doris's and her daughter Susan's lack of belief is a kind of atheistic nihilism. "Those two are a couple of lost souls," Kringle says. "She hasn't really believed in anything for years," Gailey adds.

Although Doris indoctrinates her daughter Susan (Natalie Wood) with her atheistic ideas about faith as irrational and dangerous, Susan is the film's agnostic. When she feels that Kringle's beard is real and sees him speaking to a girl in Dutch, she can no longer dismiss Kringle's claim to really be Santa Claus. But to make a conclusion about faith, Susan, a skeptic like District Attorney Thomas Mara, requires proof. She gives Kringle an illustration of a home she wants to live in. This is her Christmas wish (a form of making a prayer) and her test to see if Kringle is who he says he is. Even on Christmas morning after Susan doesn't receive her wish, she repeats "I believe," hoping her wish will come true. After she sees the house for sale she says it's her house and declares she believes in Kringle. The skeptic is convinced through a realization of her wish/prayer. Susan's test of faith relies upon a material outcome.

By Susan having her desire fulfilled, the film suggests a link between spiritual well-being and material well-being.[180] That sends a mixed message about consumerism. Despite Kringle's condemnation of unbridled consumerism, Susan receives the largest of all material goods: the suburban home. But the home for Susan represents not so much physical comfort as restoring a traditional family. Gailey says to Doris, "We can't let her down," implying he and Doris will marry. Susan's fulfillment of a home pushes Gailey and Doris into commitment. It's not a material object but a sacred space for a more family-oriented life away from the city, which is the center of commercialism.

Lawyer Fred Gailey is the true believer of the three main characters. He lives his life by ideals and beliefs that clash with Doris's worldview. Gailey recognizes Kringle as a faith figure and someone important to encourage. He supports Kringle from the beginning, invites him into his home, and defends him in court. He quits his job to defend Kringle because his law firm disapproves of him taking the case. Unlike Doris, he makes decisions based on ideals, not survival. Gailey defends people who are getting "pushed around," which for him is the "only fun in the law." For Doris, fun isn't what a job should be about. She tells him during a heated clash about their differing perspectives on faith that his defending Kris is a "sentimental whim" and an "ideological binge." "Faith is believing in things when common sense tells you not to," Gailey says.

Gailey leaves, and it looks like the relationship is over. But Doris experiences an unseen revelation and is transformed to a believer. If there's a weakness in the film, it's that Doris's conversion to belief in Kringle isn't shown; however, the result of her conversion is. When Doris signs Susan's letter to Kringle, designed to cheer him up, she adds that she too believes in Kringle. The agnostic Susan and the atheist Doris are converted to belief, which seemingly makes Kringle as happy as when the hearing goes in his favor.

SUPERNATURAL INTERVENTIONS

In *The Bishop's Wife* (1947), Bishop Henry Brougham (David Niven) is so obsessed with fundraising to build a new cathedral, he needs supernatural intervention. Like George Bailey in *It's a Wonderful Life*, Henry Brougham hopes he can find happiness in individual fulfillment and career achievement but ends up frustrated with unrealized dreams.

That's because he turns away from the deeper spiritual purpose of his religious vocation and neglects his wife Julia (Loretta Young) and daughter Debbie (Karloyn Grimes). In Henry's home office, a large painting of the envisioned cathedral hangs above the fireplace. A much smaller photograph of Julia is on a table—a visual display of how his ambition supersedes his family relationships. Julia pleads for him to recognize how much he's changed from the free-spirited man who once pastored a struggling neighborhood church. Her plea reflects the postwar anxiety about vanishing community not only in small towns but in city neighborhoods. In an epiphany that leads to a prayer, Henry realizes he's overwhelmed and must make time for Julia. The angel Dudley (Cary Grant) who responds to Henry's prayer says he came because Henry prayed for assistance and guidance, not for a cathedral.

Dudley shows Henry what's important instead: taking an interest in the details of other people's lives, helping those less fortunate, and deepening his connection with people. He's cheerful and optimistic, the antithesis of Henry's cynicism and emotional remoteness. Dudley also demonstrates the right way of living by helping the needy and acting youthful. Although Dudley focuses on important activities he must accomplish, he finds a spiritual pleasure in leisure. He takes a walk before lunch, takes Julia ice skating, and insists she buy a hat she admires in a store window. He shows how the world is too serious and people lose the spirited, idealistic, and youthful parts of their natures. Even when Dudley directs a choir, the hymn they sing is a joyful one that says "your lord is born this happy day" and that he came to "disperse the shades of doom and sadness."

Dudley also uses biblical references. He tells Debbie a story about how Psalm 23 was written. Dudley asks the skeptical Henry, "Do you believe I am what I say I am?" recalling Jesus asking his disciples, "But who do you say that I am?"[181] He gives the taxi driver Sylvester a blessing, saying, "His children and his children's children will rise up and call him blessed," recalling a line from Proverbs that "her children rise up and call her happy."[182] He says at one point, "We are interested in the lowliest sparrow," which recalls "Are not two sparrows sold for a penny? Yet not one of them will fall to the ground apart from your Father."[183] And this all culminates in the ending sermon he writes to remind people that Christmas is associated with the birth of Christ.

Tenth Avenue Angel (1948) is another film with divine intervention, though much less overt than in *A Bishop's Wife*. It centers on the plucky nine-year-old Flavia (Margaret O'Brien), who patrols the New York streets on one roller skate. In addition to being a Depression-era slice of life, it's a coming-of-age film, conveying the disillusionment and loss of innocence central to that genre.[184] Flavia's loss of innocence happens during the beginning of a transition from childhood into early adolescence that starts about halfway through the film. "It's too bad; it had to happen sometime," one adult chillingly says when Flavia begins the conversion out of innocence into disenchantment. Flavia's situation escalates into a spiritual crisis during an argument with her fragile and pregnant mother Helen (Phyllis Thaxter), who asks her if she believes in a Christmas Eve miracle. When Flavia says she can't, it's one of the most heartbreaking moments in the Christmas movie genre. Innocence, belief, and faith vanish from Flavia. She reminds her mother there is no in-between. Either something is true or it isn't. The idea of wanting to believe but being unable to make the leap into belief is the center of Flavia's conversion out of childhood. She can no longer blindly trust. It will take a transcendental experience to move her from skepticism to belief.

RETURNING WAR VETERANS

The first of three films about postwar disillusioned war veterans was originally supposed to be directed by Frank Capra. He read the story for *It Happened on 5th Avenue* and planned to make it his first postwar film after returning from World War II.[185] But he later found the story "The Greatest Gift," to which he bought the rights and renamed "It's a Wonderful Life." It's unfortunate he couldn't make both into films. In 1947, *It Happened on 5th Avenue* was released, but without major stars and the production value the script deserved. Nonetheless, it contains some of the most piercing social commentary in any First Wave Christmas film. A group of homeless war veterans squat in the Manhattan mansion of industry tycoon Michael J. O'Connor (Charles Ruggles) while he's away at his Virginia home for the winter. The movie contrasts the ambition and greed O'Connor represents with the communal family-minded veterans. O'Connor's transformation resolves two postwar anxieties: making a place for veterans and showing how business should not supersede family.

In *Holiday Affair* (1949), war widow Connie (Janet Leigh) must choose between two romantic partners representing differing postwar ideologies. As in *Holiday Inn* and *Christmas in Connecticut*, a woman selecting a marriage partner is really a choice about what belief system to follow. One comes from Carl (Wendell Corey), a lawyer who offers her a comfortable life. Another is from veteran Steve (Robert Mitchum), who drifts from job to job and is saving to move to California to build sailboats. Connie is amused and intrigued by him but views his dreams as unrealistic and his lifestyle far from the security she wants. Carl represents the materialism and faux security of the postwar economic boom. However, Steve tells Connie economic security is not a refuge from life's tribulations. Love is a leap of faith, not an act of safety, he says.

Steve seeks fulfillment away from commerce and convention. He views the postwar economic boom as a trap where one can too quickly lose one's identity. The world-weary ex-soldier is an idealization of the individualist who rejects social norms and economic pressure. Connie's movement toward Steve is a move not only into uncertainty, but away from civilization. She moves into a wilderness where Steve is connected to nature and to moving objects like boats and planes. Connie chooses the man with an independent and unconventional spirit. However, even a rugged individualist like Steve recognizes that the taming nature of marriage is necessary.

In the Christmas noir *Mr. Soft Touch* (1949), Glenn Ford stars as Joe Miracle, a veteran returning home to a postwar nightmare. His business partner has been killed and gangsters have commandeered his business. After he takes his own money from his business, both the gangsters and police pursue him. This follows the film noir convention not only of institutions failing, but of violence not upholding or establishing justice.

Instead, it exists as a malevolent force thriving in the absence of justice.[186] Joe finds what he believes is a safe hiding place at an urban settlement house where social worker Jenny Jones (Evelyn Keyes) works. While staying in the home, he slowly changes by helping with Christmas activities and discretely donating money and goods to the organization. His redemption comes through Jones, whose example of selfless work leads him to overcome his postwar nihilism. Although the settlement house is not an effective solution to the many ills the film presents, Jones's role is venerated because she takes a stand. She attempts to sustain morality in the midst of a corrupt society.

MATERIALISM AND MODERNITY THREATEN THE CHRISTMAS MOVIE

By the early 1950s, postwar anxiety about business was diminishing. So the first half of the 1950s featured Christmas films radically different than 1940s Christmas films. An example is *The Great Rupert* (1950), which favorably portrays characters who invest in the economy and spend while negatively depicting those who save money. It subverts the anti-materialist theme in 1940s Christmas films.

In the second half of the 1950s, it took nostalgia about the war years to produce a successful Christmas movie. *White Christmas* (1954) is not a sequel to *Holiday Inn*. But it features a character played by Bing Crosby, a bachelor entertainer who resists getting into a serious relationship. Crosby's character Bob Wallace and his show business partner Phil Davis (Danny Kaye) are a popular entertainment team a decade after their service in World War II. During what is supposed to be Christmas-related downtime, they unexpectedly find their former army leader General Waverly (Dean Jagger), the owner of a Vermont inn. He's struggling financially and starting to believe his best days are behind him. Wallace and Davis bring their entertainment show to the inn to attract business. They also devise a surprise reunion at the lodge with the general's ex-army troop members on Christmas Eve to show the good-hearted general he isn't forgotten. Like George Bailey in *It's a Wonderful Life*, he's overlooked. And, like Bailey, he is shown his true importance by a group of grateful people whose lives he has touched. It's an homage to an idealization of the American character and a tribute to all veterans who feel dislocated in the postwar society.

Anxiety and concern about being displaced in a postwar economy doesn't concern just the general. Bob and Phil's style of entertainment also is in danger of becoming obsolete.[187] The production number "Choreography" parodies modern dance and warns styles are changing in the entertainment sphere.[188] The duo perhaps identify with the general's plight because they too live with the fear they will be supplanted. To have one's career taken away is to lose a critical part of one's identity. The way to overcome this is to expand one's identity by pairing off into marriage as a refuge, which is another arena where purpose can be established. So the film also contains a romantic plotline to move the male characters from their work and army male-dominated worlds into the domestic female-dominated sphere.[189]

Even with the community unified and romantic relationships established there is a pervasive sense of nostalgia in the film that produces a longing for an unattainable past and a dissatisfaction with the present. When the soldiers are in the war they are nostalgic for home. When they are in the lodge they are nostalgic about their war experience. But this is deeply connected to the pervasive sense of nostalgia associated with Christmas, as indicated in the melancholy entrenched in the film's title song. There is also a feeling of downheartedness in *White Christmas* that the generation and all it represents are on the verge of becoming obsolete.

THE FIRST WAVE ENDS WITH A BLACK COMEDY

The overlooked *We're No Angels* (1955) along with the Laurel and Hardy romp *Big Business* are the forerunners of the black/dark comedies in Third Wave Christmas films. *We're No Angels* shows how criminals are less capable of redemption, that important Christmas movie theme. Instead of a substantial Scroogelike conversion, they are only partially redeemable. That's because they possess a criminal code of morality and justice and a devotion to a criminal subculture that supersedes societal laws or spiritual principles. The characters also employ a sometimes jolting use of black comedy—a combination of gallows humor, shock humor, and comedy about taboo subjects originating in skeptical cynicism.[190]

In *We're No Angels*, most of the black comedy centers around a dangerous snake the prisoners Joseph (Humphrey Bogart), Albert (Aldo Ray), and Jules (Peter Ustinov) keep in a box and which enacts a kind of vigilante justice. This happens after they escape from prison on Devil's Island and devise a plan to rob a family on Christmas Eve and use the money to sail to Paris. But they see the comforts of family life, the family's genuine kindness, and their struggle to maintain their business. Despite Joseph's worry that the three criminals are "getting soft," they help the family. But the criminals find the world outside the prison as exhibiting less morality than the moral code the criminals follow. The true villains in the film are not the criminals, but the business-focused Andre and Paul. They value money above human relationships, an ideology even the criminals disdain.

AN ENDING AND A FALSE START

After peaking during the post–World War II years with movies such as *It's a Wonderful Life*, *Miracle on 34th Street*, and *The Bishop's Wife*, the Christmas movie genre grew less popular by the mid-1950s. The most successful Christmas movie of the 1950s is *White Christmas*, which in many ways is a farewell to the First Wave with its references to the war years.

First Wave Christmas films emphasize small-town values, community, and anti-materialism. However, as the 1950s progressed, perspectives changed. Natalie Wood's wish in *Miracle on 34th Street* to move from a New York apartment to a home with a backyard is representative of a generation pursuing a suburban lifestyle. Between 1950 and 1970 the suburban population more than doubled, from 36 million to 74 million.[191] The average industrial wage for white men had doubled since pre-Depression days, allowing many working-class people to see themselves as middle class.[192] Five years after the war was over, the amount spent on household furnishings rose 240 percent.[193]

First Wave Christmas films emphasize community over career and materialism, as well as extolling traditional values of humility and thriftiness. But 1950s suburbia displayed a more materialistic lifestyle, with larger homes stuffed with material comforts. The suburban lifestyle also became in some ways a political statement about the rewards and benefits of capitalism. In the McCarthy era, the anti-materialism and depiction of greedy business leaders of the First Wave became less popular. Even the movie *It's a Wonderful Life* raised the ire of the FBI. In a memo uncovered years later, the agency stated that the portrayal of Potter maligned the upper class as mean and greedy, a "common trick used by Communists."[194]

However, as the 1960s began, business in a Christmas film was once again critiqued. One film released at the dawn of the decade could have generated another wave of Christmas movies. Instead, it stands as a fascinating anomaly in the Christmas movie genre lodged between the First and Second Waves.

Billy Wilder's *The Apartment* (1960) contains a component central to the First Wave Christmas film. It rejects the morality associated with both urban living and big business, which have an intrusive and corrupting influence. The movie particularly criticizes the hedonism of married corporate leaders who cannot fully embrace their roles as domesticated married men. The executives live a life of infidelity by pursuing women for sex while falsely promising they will divorce their wives.

Within this cauldron of pleasure seeking is C. C. Baxter (Jack Lemmon), who works as an accountant on the nineteenth floor of the insurance company Consolidated Life, a symbolic name that indicates how American lives have become consolidated.[195] Like Bob Cratchit from *A Christmas Carol*, he's a marginalized worker. But it's a far different work environment than the cramped cold office of Ebenezer Scrooge's counting house. The massive office building interior, the crowded elevators, and the carefully timed employee schedules show he's a small cog in an enor-

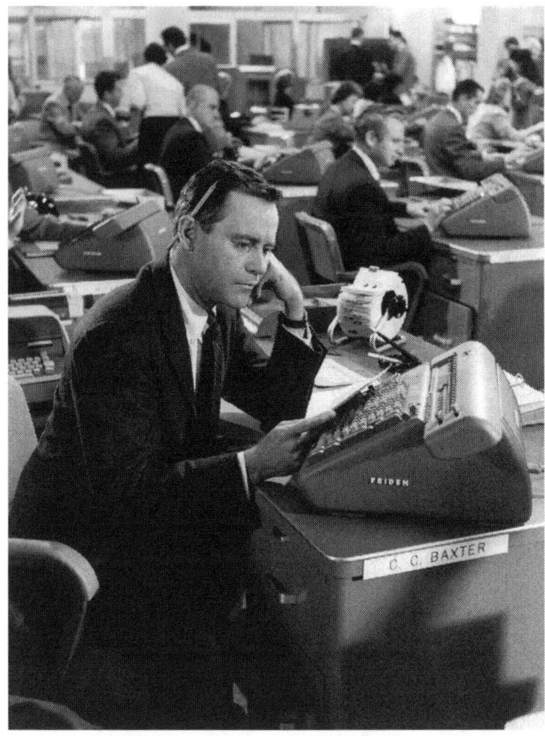

C. C. Baxter (Jack Lemmon) is a modern version of Dickens's Bob Cratchit as a corporate drone in *The Apartment* (1960). The loneliness of the holiday amid urban living is conveyed in the film's tumultuous twin-peaked journey from Christmas Eve to New Year's Eve. Photo courtesy the Everett Collection.

mous corporate machine. As a bachelor living in New York, he doesn't have the family Cratchit had to shape an identity outside of work. He's rewarded with an office not because of the merit of his work but because he lends out his apartment to executives for trysts. This further binds him to the company, where even his home becomes an annex for the corporation.[196] Baxter pays dearly for his cowardice and calculation, for as he lets his superiors into his apartment, he allows the working world into his private life, which has become practically nonexistent.[197]

Baxter takes an interest in elevator operator Fran Kubelik (Shirley MacLaine), who, unknown to him, is having an affair with personnel director Jeff Sheldrake (Fred MacMurray) in Baxter's apartment. Kubelik is a far different character from the strong women of the 1940s First Wave Christmas films. Kubelik is a waiflike self-deprecating woman who is directionless and easily manipulated. When she sees her cracked makeup mirror she says, "I like it that way, it makes me look the way I feel." Fran is a lost soul, not a defiant one.

The Christmas season underscores how the characters are lost in an urban wilderness that offers no real connections. Sheldrake insists on a Christmas tree being put up in Baxter's apartment to add atmosphere for a Christmas Eve rendezvous with Kubelik. So the symbolism of Christmas is only used to add ambiance for a lovers' tryst. There is a raucous office Christmas party that features a woman throwing her pearls in a fake strip tease to the delight of the cheering men. A dejected and jaded C. C. spends Christmas Eve in a bar pursued by a married woman who describes Christmas Eve as "a night like this, it kind of spooks you to walk into an empty apartment."

Both Baxter and Kubelik undergo painful revelations on Christmas Eve. This leads to Baxter's neighbor Dreyfuss (Jack Kruschen) admonishing Baxter for his lifestyle and telling him to grow up and be a "mensch," which he explains means being a human being.[198] This is the sole ethical aspiration presented to Baxter. And it changes him. The way to integrity and a healthy identity is emancipation from a corporate-molded identity, even if the future is uncertain.[199] But giving up material security for freedom and integrity requires courage in an urban culture where material need is so vital.[200]

The Apartment is loaded with possibilities for taking the Christmas movie genre in a more developed direction. Reclaiming individual humanity by leaving behind social institutions became a recurring theme of 1960s culture, exemplified by the novel *Catch-22* and the movie *The Graduate*.[201] But one film wasn't enough to instill these themes into a Christmas film. Instead, the Christmas movie genre was so associated with the World War II years it could have easily ended—yet the genre would live on. But it didn't reboot on the movie screen.

8

Rankin-Bass and The Second Wave

In 1964, many Americans who came of age in the World War II era were young parents spending their evenings home with children. These children came to be known as baby boomers, the largest generation of children in U.S. history. This meant a massive audience awaited family-based entertainment at home. So the Second Wave started with a character that resonated with that demographic in a medium with attentive parents and children: television.

Rudolph the Red-Nosed Reindeer held a connection to the parents of young children in the 1960s. Rudolph wasn't one of the eight reindeer named in Clement Moore's 1823 poem "'Twas the Night Before Christmas." Not until 1939 did the story of Rudolph first appear in an illustrated children's book given away at Montgomery Ward, a department store chain. A misfit deer ostracized for his distinguishing characteristic, which later makes him a hero as Santa's chief reindeer, became a pop culture sensation. In 1964, parents who experienced the initial Rudolph phenomenon were likely nostalgic about Rudolph and encouraged their children to watch a show dedicated to a familiar character.

Rudolph the Red-Nosed Reindeer would become the highest-rated and most watched television show in history.[202] *Rudolph*'s massive success led to the show's creative team Arthur Rankin and Jules Bass largely defining the Second Wave with TV specials that often used a three-dimensional stop-motion presentation. Each model of a character moved slightly between filmed frames to give the illusion of movement. This created a distinctive look that separated it from cel animation.

The Rankin-Bass Christmas specials, along with the cel-animated TV shows *A Charlie Brown Christmas* (1965) and *How the Grinch Stole Christmas* (1966), became the voice of a countercultural movement that questioned materialism, viewed institutions and authority figures as too inflexible, and called for reshaping community to be more inclusive. The Cold War era of the 1950s with its submission to business ideology was incompatible with Christmas movies, which condemned materialism, hyperindividualism, workaholism, and greed. However, as the 1960s counterculture gained momentum, there was a growing suspicion of business, a desire to redefine community as more tolerant and expansive, and an elevation of transcendental experiences. The Rankin-Bass specials feature young or innocent characters embodying those inclinations.

"Kids love to see someone of their own stripe, someone of their own age, someone of their own inferiority achieve things; it makes them feel good," Arthur Rankin said in a 2005 interview. "I think that's probably the reason these films last so long, because, in all our films, that happens. The bad guy becomes the good guy at the end; he's reformed and the underdog fulfills his quest."[203]

Many Rankin-Bass specials employ that twofold narrative device. First, they make their central characters underdogs or misfits who are children, animals, or young adults. These underdogs suffer under obstinate and domineering establishment figures who marginalize the underdogs or force them to leave the community. These underdogs represent the everyman, the "other" in American society, the youth movement, and the voice of spiritual values counteracting material values. Second in the Rankin-Bass formula, many authority figures or villains undergo a conversion experience resulting in acceptance or recognition of the underdog characters. The shows use those two themes to express the conflict during the 1960s and 1970s between baby boomers and establishment figures. And the rise and fall of Rankin and Bass is timed to the rise and fall of the counterculture.

WHO DECIDES THE TEST OF WHAT IS REALLY BEST? RUDOLPH AND A STOP-MOTION REVOLUTION

The year *Rudolph the Red-Nosed Reindeer* was first shown was the beginning of the counterculture penetrating popular culture. In February 1964, The Beatles made a landmark appearance on *The Ed Sullivan Show*, and in December the misfit heroes Rudolph and the elf Hermey in their own way became symbols of the same youth movement. They defied the rigidity and conformity carried over from the Cold War era. Like Rudolph and Hermey, many baby boomers wanted to be accepted for who they were. The boomers grew up in a time of unprecedented economic prosperity, which gave them liberty to pursue their individuality and find a place in society on their own terms. This was a privilege their parents didn't enjoy. The parents' formative years were during the Great Depression and World War II when there was more of an emphasis on economic and physical survival, not the need for self-actualization.

Rankin and Bass's show transformed the Santa mythology dominant in Christmas popular culture. They alter him to be an establishment figure who needs to change. Although Santa possesses godlike powers that enable him to deliver toys to children around the world in one night, he still needs help navigating bad weather on Christmas Eve.[204] This makes Santa irritable and anxious.

This radically changes Santa from the way he's usually portrayed in pop culture, from an easy-going gregarious figure to a workaholic, often frustrated autocrat. In Rankin-Bass's *Rudolph*, he is neither the jovial figure influenced by Thomas Nast's illustrations in the early nineteenth century nor the spiritualized sagely figure shaped by Frank L. Baum's *The Life and Adventures of Santa Claus*, which carries through to movies such as *Miracle on 34th Street.* In *Rudolph*, Santa is a distressed, preoccupied, and somewhat selfish establishment figure. It's difficult to imagine the subversive variations on the Santa Claus persona in Third Wave movies such as *Bad Santa* and *Fred Claus* without Rankin-Bass's reworking of Santa's personality that shattered about a century and a half of pop culture Santa portrayals. *Rudolph* expresses how to overcome unreasonable authority embodied not just in Santa but the majority of elves and reindeer, who are callous and intolerant.

Rankin-Bass's *Rudolph the Red-Nosed Reindeer* (1964) was revolutionary for its portrayal of Santa Claus as a despot and the misfit Rudolph as an outsider hero. The TV show ushered in the Second Wave of Christmas shows with spiritual and religious themes that appealed to the 1960s counterculture. Photo courtesy Rankin-Bass/Everett Collection.

Rankin and Bass's North Pole is not an idyllic community away from modern manufacturing and the troubles of civilization as the North Pole was previously portrayed in Christmas popular culture. Instead, Santa's workshop is an oppressive industrial workplace. A whistle blows when workers can take an allotted break. Each elf has an individual task similar to an assembly line. Even outside the workshop, characters contend to gain approval from a Santa so focused on his work he cannot recognize the needs or emotions of others. To be different physically from others (as Rudolph is) or to want something other than the regimen of factory work (as Hermey does) marks one with the label of "nonconformity," as the snowman narrator describes Rudolph's predicament. The elves dress in matching outfits and look the same except for the misfit Hermey. Those who disagree with the norms or who are different are ostracized, marginalized, or bullied. Surviving life in the remote and cold Christmastown requires obedience to tyrannical male rule.

Rudolph and Hermey are misfits because they don't fit into Christmastown's delineations of masculinity. They are too sensitive, too different, and too "soft" as defined by Christmastown's male-dominated power structure. Other establishment hypermasculine figures assist Santa in his need for conformity. The unnamed overseer called the Head Elf, a supervisor with the demeanor of a military drill sergeant, demands order and subordination. The other tyrannical enforcer of Santa's stern commands is Coach Comet, who trains the young bucks. Although Rudolph flies higher than the other reindeer, he's immediately shunned and marginalized when his disguised red nose is revealed. The conformist culture in Christmastown values not just skills. One must also conform in appearance.

Is Rudolph's physical difference a symbol of racism? The civil rights movement was at one of its peaks during the time the show was conceived and released. So that's one possible interpretation. But part of the power of Rudolph's most distinguishing physical trait is that his nose is nonspecific in what it represents. There is no backstory to why Rudolph has a red nose. What matters is that he's perceived as unusual and is therefore treated differently. Because of this, viewers identify with Rudolph through whatever makes them feel different. That could be race, gender, ethnicity, social class, or, in the era of the counterculture movement when *Rudolph* was made, being young or having a different ideology, appearance, or lifestyle.

One also pays the price for rejecting work that benefits the establishment's goals. Hermey is stuck in a proletariat-style trap of redundant tasks. He is alienated from his work, a deadly form of detachment that disempowers him. There is no encouragement or validation after he announces he wants to be a dentist instead of working in Santa's workshop. Hermey speaks for generations of working-class employees ensnarled in incompatible and degrading work. But rather than rebelling against the system as unjust, his approach is elevating himself to a more appropriate and prestigious job. He wants to join the professional class by being a dentist. Hermey shows no desire to alter the oppressive conditions of the workshop. He's looking for escape and self-fulfillment, not a worker's revolution. Hermey also looks different than the other elves. He has blonde hair that shows from under his elf cap, which also makes him a long-haired symbol of the counterculture. Despite his oppression, he feels empowered enough to leave repressive working conditions.

"Why don't I fit in?" is the question both Hermey and Rudolph ask. *Rudolph* shows the importance of feeling part of a community and the spiritual distress and isolation that comes when one feels like an outsider. But Hermey and Rudolph are outsiders who support each other. They leave Christmastown without a destination. When a community becomes oppressive, one must search for a new community even if it's uncertain where it may be.

On Rudolph and Hermey's journey into the wilderness, they find a companion in the good-natured and boisterous prospector Yukon Cornelius. He lives outside of civilization on a quest for what he thinks will make him wealthy. He possesses the physical traits of a hypermasculine character with his booming voice, flannel shirt, and moustache. Rudolph and Hermey, who are harassed in the civilization of Christmastown by hypermasculine characters, initially hide from him. But they soon find he's an ally. Because he's outside of society and its oppressive categorizations, Yukon possesses a friendliness, a sense of tolerance, and a healthy sense of humor the authority figures in Christmastown lack. So he befriends and helps the underdogs Rudolph and Hermey.

During their trek into the wilderness, the three friends find the Island of Misfit Toys, a place for "homeless toys" that don't conform to expectations of what a toy is supposed to be and therefore are not suitable to be given to children. The island shows that it's not just Rudolph and Hermey who are misfits. It's a worldwide epidemic. King Moonracer travels every day around the world to gather misfit toys and bring them there. They have each other and are not in isolation. But this doesn't make the toys happy. Why is the island more like an orphanage than an alternative community? Why do the characters exist in such a state of despair? Perhaps because, in *Rudolph*, individuals are defined by their market identity. The toys are unhappy because they can't fulfill their market function. They are the establishment's castaways who want to integrate into society but are isolated and despondent, in contrast to Rudolph and Hermey, who leave oppression to go on a quest.

Rudolph and Hermey's absence changes the stern male figures in Christmastown after they return. The Head Elf tells Hermey he can open a dentist's office. Rudolph's father says he's sorry for the way he treated Rudolph. Even the terrifying Abominable Snowman, who "hates everything to do with Christmas," goes through a Scroogelike transformation to redemption. But how much of a happy ending is it? After Rudolph returns, the first characters he encounters are his peers, who still bully him. Even if Santa's elevation of Rudolph to head reindeer ends the bullying, did it stop for the right reasons? Nonetheless, the resolution to the clash between the youthful underdogs and the older establishment is that the establishment becomes more humane.

At the beginning of the counterculture's foray into pop culture in 1964, there is a hopeful resolution that the system can correct its prejudices. The ruling structure can reform. *Rudolph* is an optimistic presentation of how a capitalist society ultimately values individual talents (represented by Hermey wanting to be a dentist instead of making toys) and physical features no matter how unusual (represented by Rudolph's red nose). There is a place for everyone, even misfit toys. For the baby boomer generation, it validated that one could follow one's own calling. The bullying Rudolph undergoes and his isolation in the wilderness are just a temporary phase. That period enhances self-reliance before others finally see what the outsider can offer to improve society.

Rudolph's enduring popularity reveals that the American experience can often be one of an unrecognized outsider. Viewers project their own outsider status onto Rudolph. But, in keeping with the mythology of upward mobility in America, what is a liability becomes in the end an asset. *Rudolph* gives encouragement and reassurance that the larger one's pain, the greater the victory. *Rudolph* assured baby boomers that their period of being independent, misunderstood, and isolated would end. The elders eventually accommodate them. *Rudolph* depicts a generational clash, with Rudolph and Hermey on one side and Santa and his hypermasculine establishment leaders on the other side. But the show promises a truce: the establishment reforms to meet the needs of the younger generation. Six years later another Rankin-Bass TV special showed that optimism had vanished.

DON'T BE THE RULE, BE THE EXCEPTION: A YOUTH REBELLION

By 1970, Rankin-Bass's *Santa Claus Is Coming to Town* presents a much different view on the establishment. Rulers can't reform as they could in *Rudolph*. So the subjugated outsiders form a new community away from the center of tyranny of Sombertown at the North Pole. As *Rudolph* is a marker for the beginning of the counterculture's rise, *Santa Claus Is Coming to Town* shows the counterculture at the height of its power in a full-fledged rebellion against authority, making a well-defined separation from the adult establishment.

When *Santa* was made, the counterculture turned toward creating their own alternative communities as they grew frustrated with the establishment's rigidity. This created a generational clash that divided America into two camps of anti-establishment and pro-establishment forces. This increasing exasperation with the establishment and a growing movement of creating alternative communities merged together in *Santa Claus Is Coming to Town.*

If *Rudolph* made Santa an autocrat, *Santa Claus Is Coming to Town* radically changed the image of Santa to a young rebel. For most of the show, Santa is a long-haired young man, not the roly-poly older man depicted in pop culture for about 150 years. Santa (voiced by Mickey Rooney) leads a rebellious youth movement. He creates his own countercultural community comprised of young people, children, and animals. He defies authority by going on daring nighttime raids to deliver Christmas presents despite the Burgermeister's ban on toys. "You are obviously a nonconformist and a rebel," the Burgermeister tells Santa. The narrator mailman S. D. Kluger (voiced by Fred Astaire) compares Santa to Robin Hood, describes Santa's friends as "a group of outcasts," and says many view Santa as an "outlaw" and "public enemy number one." Adhering to a theme in most Rankin and Bass Christmas TV specials, the underdog hero is outside of the organized power structure while the villain holds institutional power.

Another standard formula in most Rankin-Bass specials is the conversion of a villain or flawed person. However, the Burgermeister never undergoes a conversion. Here, institutional reform isn't possible. From the beginning of the story, the Burgermeister, the totalitarian ruler of Sombertown, is inhumane. A soldier finds an abandoned baby with an attached note pleading with the Burgermeister to care for the newborn, who "will be exceptional if only given the love he needs." The Burgermeister rejects the baby (Santa) and orders him sent to an orphanage.

The Burgermeister is incapable of compassion, reform, or relenting from his oppressive rules. He exhibits traits of a Nazi type of leader (who burns toys instead of books), a communist dictator (who won't allow products into his grim state-run society), and the pharaoh in the Book of Exodus (like the Egyptian leader, his heart only hardens when demands are made upon him to yield his despotic ways).

If the Burgermeister is the Pharoah figure, Santa is a Moses figure. He's an abandoned baby who grows up to liberate an oppressed people (the residents of Sombertown) and those held under the subjugation of the Winter Warlock. Some come with him to build their version of an alternative community away from Sombertown. He even delivers toys to the children of those who don't leave. As a Moses figure, Santa either leads the oppressed to a Promised Land or liberates their spirits by giving toys to those who stay behind in Sombertown. Santa is familiar with creating alternative communities because he grew up in one. After the Burgermeister rejects caring for the baby Claus, characters on the fringes of Sombertown take him to a family of elves named Kringle, who are part of an alternative community, to raise Santa and teach him how to make toys.

When Santa becomes a young man, he takes the toys across the Whispering Winds to Sombertown, a city depicted in a dreary monochrome that makes Santa's red suit and colorful toys stand out. The toys are transcendent objects that not only represent generosity and craftsmanship but are also instruments of pleasure and fun and are an expression of love. There is no association of gifts with commercialism as in *A Charlie Brown Christmas*. Instead, gifts are expressions of love and spirituality.

The children in Sombertown are immediately receptive to the toys, but in the adults, the toys awaken an innocence and kindness they had lost. This is illustrated by three people Santa tries to convert with his toys.

The first is Sombertown's schoolteacher, Jessica, who initially scolds Santa for giving toys to children and wearing his outlandish colorful Santa suit. She reminds him toys are illegal. But after Santa gives her a doll she always wanted, she says the ban on toys is silly. Jessica's conversion experience occurs over time and finally reaches the end of its transforming effect after she becomes disillusioned with the power structure of Sombertown. Jessica is a pivotal character, who changes from being part of the Sombertown establishment to joining Santa's band of rebels and eventually becoming his wife. The final stage of her conversion experience occurs after Santa and his friends are arrested and she asks the Burgermeister to release them. She is a reformist who typifies the dominant ideology in *Rudolph*. But after talking with the Burgermeister, Jessica realizes reform isn't possible. She says, "My eyes are beginning to open for the very first time to what life is really all about." She undergoes a spiritual awakening and marries Kris Kringle on Christmas Eve in an outdoor ceremony. "Since no town would welcome them, they stood before the Lord in the silent winter woods; a grove of pine trees was their cathedral. . . . No church ever looked nicer," says Kluger, emphasizing that God and spirituality are also contained outside of civilization and power structures.

The second authority figure Santa attempts to convert is the Burgermeister. After Santa gives him a yo-yo, he briefly changes from his malicious persona and recalls when he used to do tricks with a yo-yo. However, the Burgermeister only momentarily changes and isn't capable of having his conversion experience endure.

The third figure Santa converts with a toy is the Winter Warlock. After Santa escapes from Sombertown, he passes back through the woods where the Warlock lives. After being captured, he gives the Winter Warlock a toy train. The Warlock says no one gives him any presents. Then, like the Abominable Snowman in *Rudolph*, the Winter Warlock goes through a Scroogelike transformation with "a chance to be reborn," as he says.

The narratives of both *Rudolph* and *Santa Claus Is Coming to Town* show that the system eventually changes for the better. In *Santa*, it doesn't take place until after the death of the Burgermeister. For Rankin and Bass, the system, no matter how cruel, is never overthrown. This indicates an ideology that reform within the system is possible even if it requires more than a generation to occur. Or it suggests that evil cannot be directly confronted because it's just too powerful. Instead of battling it, one must live underground and form communities with like-minded individuals until conditions improve. While Rudolph and Hermey rejoin a community that changes to accept them, *Santa Claus Is Coming to Town* shows that isn't possible. Instead, one creates a new community with other oppressed individuals. But as there was a significant change in the six years from *Rudolph* to *Santa Claus Is Coming to Town,* there would be another momentous change four years later.

BELIEVE IN SANTA CLAUS LIKE YOU BELIEVE IN LOVE

The Year without a Santa Claus was released in 1974 when the counterculture was collapsing. Former radicals, dissidents, and protesters were giving up their activism to settle into conventional roles in society. At the same time, faith in institutions was disintegrating after Watergate, the resignation of President Richard Nixon, and an unsatisfactory end to the unpopular Vietnam War. *The Year without a Santa Claus* reflects a cultural inertia that developed from the counterculture's loss of their idealism as well as a broad pessimism about cultural institutions. There is a worn-out and defeatist Santa Claus and an apathetic public uninterested in Christmas. This fatigue reflects the weariness the counterculture felt about attempting to enact change. If the counterculture was hopeful for reform in 1964's *Rudolph*, and rebellious and separatist in 1970's *Santa Claus Is Coming to Town*, by 1974 there is exhaustion and lethargy. In many ways *The Year without a Santa Claus* represents the mid-life crisis of the countercultural movement.

Santa isn't the establishment figure he is in *Rudolph* or the rebel of *Santa Claus Is Coming to Town*. He is a tired and dejected older man who feels unappreciated and uninspired. Although he feels the aches and pain of age, he also faces a serious spiritual crisis. "Nobody cares about Christmas anymore; it wouldn't surprise me none if nobody believes in you anymore," a visiting doctor tells Santa. The problem is not an authority figure like the Burgermeister in *Santa Claus Is Coming to Town*. It is society itself. There are too many indifferent, cynical, and unbelieving people. There are no clear-cut villains as in most Rankin-Bass specials. Instead there is a collective sense of apathy and disbelief that must be eradicated. If Santa is sometimes a deitylike figure in the Christmas movie genre, *The Year without a Santa Claus* shows him as a supernatural figure who exhibits humanlike traits of depression, resignation, and a longing to feel valued.

Released in the Watergate era, Rankin-Bass's *The Year without a Santa Claus* (1974) shows an exhausted Santa who feels unappreciated. He must take a spiritual journey to overcome his disillusionment and restore his faith and belief in humanity. Photo courtesy Rankin-Bass/Everett Collection.

After Santa announces he won't be delivering gifts, there's initially a feminist response to solve the problem. Mrs. Claus dresses in Santa's suit and sings, "Anyone can be a Santa, why not a lady like me?" But with her back turned to them, the elves Jingle and Jangle still recognize her. She concludes the world isn't ready for a woman to take such an important position. So she'll work behind the scenes and instruct others to ignite Santa's passion about Christmas again. Mrs. Claus sends Jingle and Jangle and the reindeer Vixen to the world below to find examples of

Christmas spirit. She believes that once Santa sees an expression of belief, he will deliver toys again. But when Santa hears what happened, he goes undercover to find them in a harsh and rule-driven world.

As in many Rankin-Bass TV specials, authority figures are antagonistic, unreasonable, and inflexible. When Jingle, Jangle, and Vixen land in Southtown, USA, they immediately encounter a policeman who writes tickets for, among other things, "wearing funny-looking suits on a Sunday." Along with the stern authority, they also find apathy, disbelief in Christmas, and a skeptical political system where the mayor of Southtown wants to see a miracle of "snow in Dixie." Lack of belief in Santa—in the Christmas movie genre often a symbol of disbelief in the spiritual—is rampant in Southtown. However, a turning point comes when Santa incognito sits at a table with the disbelieving child Ignatius and his parents. "I believe in Santa Claus like I believe in love," Santa sings. "There's no question in my mind that he exists, just like love, I know he's there . . . wipe that question from your mind, yes, he does exist."

Santa says if one believes in love, one possesses spiritual belief. While Santa does this to reassure himself as well as Ignatius's family, women work behind the scenes to lift the world out of the inertia and misery created by male dysfunction. Mrs. Claus must convince the Miser brothers to comply with Southtown's mayor's request that it snow in Southtown. The mayor is a deep skeptic who will only believe in the spiritual if a miracle occurs. But the brothers are two show business–like childish entities, the Snow Miser and the Heat Miser, ruling the north and south, respectively. Perhaps reflecting the communist era separation between the east and the west, they cannot get along (they even refer to the telephone as "the hotline," the term used for the phone line between the United States and the Soviet Union to call each other in an emergency). Reflecting the cynicism about politics during the year of Watergate, the bickering brothers cannot transcend their competitive dysfunction and cannot compromise. With all of this male ego, it's up to Mrs. Claus to go "right to the top" to their mother, Mother Nature, a mild-mannered lady who appears to be the ruling force in the world. She simply orders her children to compromise. A woman is in charge in the heavens even if women are not as empowered on earth—as Mrs. Claus's failed attempt to substitute for Santa Claus shows.

By the show's conclusion, the sense of community so important in the Christmas movie genre enlarges to a worldwide one. Children from a diverse group of races, ethnicities, and nationalities collaborate to give gifts to Santa. Santa's definition of spirituality as love widens spiritual belief. Because of this hope, Santa ends his cynicism and resignation. This reflects the era's growing universal spirituality and the spiritual-but-not-religious movement. Seeing this worldwide expression of belief and generosity, Santa is rejuvenated and agrees to go through with Christmas. Children in the film embody hope in the future, perhaps a reflection of the baby boomers' hope that the next generation will enact positive change—an aging counterculture passing the torch to a new generation.

The Year without a Santa Claus is an alteration from the standard Rankin-Bass formula of succeeding underdogs and reforming villains. There is no central villain. Although the Miser Brothers are ego-driven and neurotic, they obey Mother Nature and do not confront others unless their territory is invaded. Neither is the mayor of Southtown, who wants to see snow on Christmas, a true villain. Instead, the villain is an idea. It is the disease of disbelief and cynicism. Rankin and Bass also abandon their customary underdog character and replace it with Santa, a person of power who still has the need to feel reassured and appreciated, and to know that his work contains a clear sense of purpose.

Rudolph the Red-Nosed Reindeer, *Santa Claus Is Coming to Town*, and *The Year without a Santa Claus* form a trilogy chronicling the hope, the rebellion, and ultimately the threat of resignation and despair in the decade from 1964 to 1974. The figure of Santa Claus articulates the reforming establishment in *Rudolph*, the courageous rebellion in *Santa Claus Is Coming to Town*, and the aging figure who needs reassurance about the purpose of his work and hope for the future in *The Year without a Santa Claus*.

9

Rankin and Bass
The Auteurs of the Second Wave

Only *A Charlie Brown Christmas* and *How the Grinch Stole Christmas* matched the popularity of the Rankin and Bass Christmas TV specials. But those were one-off Christmas projects by their creators. Because they released so much material, Rankin and Bass put their personal stamp not only on the three popular shows chronicling the counterculture (*Rudolph*, *Santa Claus Is Coming to Town*, and *The Year without a Santa Claus*) but on their other significant TV shows.

I'LL BE BACK AGAIN SOME DAY: THE RESURRECTION OF FROSTY

Frosty the Snowman (1969) is positioned thematically between the more secular *Rudolph the Red-Nosed Reindeer*, *Santa Claus Is Coming to Town*, and *The Year without a Santa Claus* and the Christian and Bible-based *The Little Drummer Boy* and *Nestor, The Long-Eared Christmas Donkey*. Frosty is both secular hero and religious martyr. He embodies the qualities of a Christ figure who sacrifices himself, dies, and is bodily resurrected. He's also a secular figure of liberation who defies authority.

Frosty is a Christ figure that comes from a humble background, is perceived as a threat by authorities, and makes sacrifices for others. He's also pure of heart, a loyal and concerned friend, and resurrects to return to life. His first words after coming to life are "Happy Birthday!", a possible reference to Jesus being born on Christmas. He's made of Christmas Eve snow, a "special kind of snow," the narrator (voiced by Jimmy Durante) says, that has magic qualities, usually a metaphor in the Christmas film genre for the supernatural or the spiritual. This spiritual matter contrasts with the charlatan nonspiritual magician Professor Hinkle, who wants to generate magic, but can't. Frosty realizes his time is limited if he doesn't get to the cold of the North Pole, a heavenlike realm removed from society where the Christ figure must return. The title song confirms the impermanence of his messianic mission by indicating he will "have some fun before I melt away." Consistent with a Christ figure, Frosty promises he "will be back again someday." Frosty exhibits the Christlike trait of self-sacrifice by putting Karen's life before his own when he carries her into a greenhouse to keep her warm even though it's dangerous to him. This leads to him in a sense dying for others. The ambitious Hinkle is a satanic figure who ultimately causes the death of Frosty. Like Mary Magdalene, Karen weeps for him after his death at the equivalent of an empty tomb, which is the greenhouse. Frosty is reduced to the mere matter of melted water. But death is not the end, the deitylike Santa says. He revives Frosty by using a gust of Christmas wind, a symbol of spirit that can conquer bodily death. Frosty fulfills his promise to return in a resurrection, showing that the spirit-filled substance of the snow is eternal. Unlike other villains in other Rankin and Bass TV shows, Hinkle does not reform. Santa can only neutralize him by threatening not to give him Christmas presents if he won't repent. But the satanic figure doesn't fundamentally change and continues to apparently cause trouble in a world without a Christ figure, who only will return on Christmas.

Frosty also is a secular anti-establishment figure misunderstood and berated by authorities, including the school teacher, the sham magician Hinkle, the policeman who stops Frosty leading a Christmas parade, and the ticket salesman at the train station oblivious to the miracle of a live snowman and instead concerned with receiving money for a train ride. Hinkle is the most heinous authority figure because he obsessively harasses Frosty. He realizes the value of the magic hat that he discarded and wants it returned from Frosty so he can be "a millionaire magician." He wants to reduce a supernatural occurrence to a commercial enterprise. For the children, however, who represent the voice of the counterculture, the transcendental experience of life created and their friendship with Frosty is more important than money. Hinkle locks the door so Frosty will melt. He will destroy life to gain the object of his obsession, which he thinks will bring him money.

THE LITTLE DRUMMER BOY AND REVELATION IN THE DESERT

Although set in the ancient world, *The Little Drummer Boy* (1968) shows similar concerns expressed in modern Christmas movies. That includes commercial exploitation, the idolization of money, and business forces that endanger community and family. However, there's an intense brutality in *The Little Drummer Boy*, with merciless Roman soldiers, murderous marauders, and dangerous thieves. But there also is the redeeming figure of a newborn messiah who draws the disenfranchised to himself, senses the purity of love, and heals and corrects acts of violence. Mostly set in the barren and hostile desert at the time of the birth of Jesus, *The Little Drummer Boy* shows a world stripped to its most basic elements of both savage cruelty and redemptive unselfish love.

The central figure is Aaron, an orphan shepherd boy who roams the desert wilderness with his three animal friends. The devious entrepreneur Ben Haramed, like Professor Hinkle in *Frosty the Snowman*, views others only for financial benefit. He spots Aaron playing a drum as the animals dance and sees the commercial potential. He tries to coax Aaron with promises of making money if he performs for people. But Aaron feels no desire to make other people happy. "I hate people, all people," Aaron says. "And you think I love people?" Haramed answers him. "What a beautiful world it would be without people."

The ancient world in *Little Drummer Boy* (1968) is brutal and makes Aaron misanthropic, with only animals for friends. However, the Christ child reviving his dying lamb restores his faith. Photo courtesy Rankin-Bass/Everett Collection.

The two are in some ways kindred spirits because of their mutual disdain for humanity. But they arrive at their hatred in different ways. Aaron once lived a joyful existence with his loving parents on a farm until desert bandits attacked his family and forced him to flee. Because Aaron has seen the worst of humanity, he's given up on people. But his affections and sense of community must go somewhere, so he becomes attached to his animals. This shows there is hope when there is still a capacity to love, connect, and build community in some way.

The villain in the *The Little Drummer Boy* TV specials (a sequel was released in 1976) is less Ben Haramed in the original and Brutus in the sequel than the dominance of money in both. In *The Little Drummer Boy*, Haramed's disdain for people comes from his lust for money. He admits an evil force controls him to ruthlessly pursue money. "Gold and silver on my mind, mischief in my soul," he sings in a declaration of his obsession, adding, "I want to live like a rich man lives, with life in my control." However, the mania for money controls Haramed more than he controls the world.

To Haramed, everything is a commodity. But Aaron values friendship above money. He refuses the gold he's entitled to and follows the star to Bethlehem. After a Roman chariot runs over his lamb he plays the drum for Mary and Joseph, the shepherds, and the animals in the stable. This act of kindness restores Aaron's faith in humanity again. He realizes the hate he is carrying is wrong. The redemptive power of love heals him and enables him to believe in kindness again. Aaron becomes the embodiment of what the narrator Greer Garson says when she quotes from the Bible: "Blessed are the pure in heart, for they will see God."[205]

WE'LL HELP OUR MAKER MAKE OUR DREAMS COME TRUE

In *'Twas The Night Before Christmas* Santa is an aloof entity who angers quickly and requires belief in him as a prerequisite to distribute Christmas gifts. When disbelief contaminates the community, only a physical monument of faith makes Santa relent and deliver presents.

The figure trying to appease the deitylike Santa is clockmaker Joshua Trundle (voiced by Joel Grey). This is necessary because a letter is published in the local newspaper stating that "Santa Claus is a fraudulent myth rooted in unconscious fantasies and emerging as a deceitful lie," which claimed to be written by the entire town of Junctionville. Albert, the son of Trundle's mouse assistant Father Mouse, admits he wrote it. Father Mouse scolds him, telling him, "You don't know as much as you think, because you only think with your head" and "you have a lot of trouble believing in things you can't hear or touch." This is the clash between atheism and faith. Albert is Rankin and Bass's most blatant atheist. He's a materialist who, even when introduced to the clockmaker by his father, is only interested in how the motors and gears work, not about the faith that motivates Joshua. However, the atheist does convert to belief. "It's not enough to be sorry, when you've done something wrong; you have to correct the thing you did," Father Mouse says. Father Mouse tells Joshua that Albert is responsible for the clock debacle but that he's "repented" and "trying to make amends," which follows the Rankin-Bass theme of reforming villains.

Perhaps the portrayal of a distant and retributive Santa Claus is why the show is underrated. Rankin-Bass featured a despotic Santa in *Rudolph*, but his anger is aimed at the workers in Christmastown, not at children. Santa was both countercultural rebel and Moses figure in *Santa Claus Is Coming to Town*, and a wise supernatural entity who neutralizes a dangerous villain in *Frosty the Snowman*. But in *'Twas the Night Before Christmas*, without explanation Santa rejects the wishes of children for gifts. The only representative of Santa that says anything is the mouse operator, who divulges that Santa is angry about a letter. Otherwise, there is only silence. If Santa fits the prototype in the Christmas movie genre as a supernatural figure, this show's Santa possesses characteristics of an Old Testament god who is distant, is vengeful, abandons people, and punishes a community. This Old Testament idea of collective sin and collective faith is an important concept in *'Twas the Night Before Christmas.*

The solution is building a collaborative relationship with a Santa/God figure. As Joshua sings in a key song, miracles are a collective effort between God and humans. In the Old Testament, altars and sacrifices are made to honor God. Here, Joshua uses his clock-making skill to express his faith and build a two-way relationship with Santa. *'Twas the Night Before Christmas* also employs the Old Testament concept of reparations for sins. After Albert says he damaged the symbol of faith, which is the clock tower, he makes up for it by repairing the clock. In *The Year without a Santa Claus*, the residents of Southtown suffer from apathy and disbelief. They need a miracle of snow falling to believe in the supernatural.

In *'Twas the Night Before Christmas*, the townspeople create their own miracle in collaboration with Santa.

THE FEMINIST UPRISING PART 2

For about a decade, Rankin-Bass largely defined Christmas popular culture in the Second Wave. However, a shift occurred during the second half of the 1970s. Although the team remained popular enough to make more TV specials, the shows premiering after 1974 didn't join their previous efforts as perennial favorites. A repeat audience failed to generate for four new TV specials that were as strong or nearly as strong as the shows that aired before 1975: *The First Christmas, Nestor, The Long-Eared Christmas Donkey*, *Jack Frost*, and *Pinocchio's Christmas*. These largely forgotten four shows spanning from 1975 to 1980 mark a more mature shift in tone and remain some of the best works of Rankin-Bass.

The First Christmas (1975) continues the feminist perspective from the year before in *The Year without a Santa Claus*, which shows women in power, even if from behind the scenes. Similar to Mrs. Claus in *The Year without a Santa Claus*, Sister Teresa (voiced by Angela Lansbury) operates as a wise and moral force even if on the surface it looks like a male figure is in charge—the priest Father Thomas (voiced by Cyril Ritchard).

This conflict first emerges after Father Thomas says that Lucas, the blind shepherd boy whom Sister Theresa took in, must go to an orphanage. The aloof Father Thomas, although not physically blind like Lucas, is morally blind. He plays the role, as in many Rankin and Bass shows, of the villain who must reform. Like so many authority figures he must overcome an ethical defect caused by his institutional position of power. He is too rule-driven, too self-absorbed, and unable to recognize the needs of others, particularly the marginalized such as Lucas. Father Thomas also exhibits a classic trait of a flawed Rankin and Bass character, which is that he doesn't like to have fun. When the nuns and children start setting up decorations for Christmas, he tells them "not to rush the season" and orders the Christmas decorations to be put away. He is stingy with his ability to celebrate, to empathize, or to love. Sister Teresa and the nuns respond by obeying his requests on the surface. But like the women in *The Year without a Santa Claus*, even if they are lower in status than the authoritative male figure, they work behind the scenes to do what they feel is correct.

Lucas as Rankin and Bass's standard underdog character is a figure of faith who never complains about his blindness. He doesn't care about his own misfortune; his concern is about his sheep. He is the opposite of Father Thomas, who cares first about himself. Because Lucas is focused on his sheep and unconcerned about either receiving or giving material objects, he is pure of heart. But as with other characters in Rankin and Bass shows who possess a virtuous spiritual state, he is misunderstood and ostracized. Lucas is shunned and bullied by the other children as they make plans to put on a nativity play. But Lucas is a peaceful and consistent believer, giver, and caretaker. He exhibits a quiet and calm spirituality that shows Rankin and Bass deepening in their spiritual perspective.

NESTOR THE SUFFERING HERO

Another orphan is the subject of *Nestor, The Long-Eared Christmas Donkey*. The show reprises the theme from *Rudolph the Red-Nosed Reindeer* about how a misfit with unusual and unconventional physical features is at first bullied and then admired for his differences. But the show has a much darker tone and shares more in common with Disney's *Dumbo*, where Dumbo, like Nestor, is shunned and disparaged because of his large ears. Both Nestor and Dumbo experience disconnection from their only support system, their mothers. Dumbo's mother is declared mad and separated from Dumbo, and Nestor's mother dies protecting him from the cold. However, Nestor, like Dumbo, ultimately attains acceptance and acclaim because of what his ears can do.

But there's severe anguish and misery for Nestor before that change. In Rankin and Bass's shows, only Aaron from *The Little Drummer Boy* comes close to experiencing what Nestor withstands. There's terror, exploitation, and mastery over Nestor and the other animals, and the bullying Nestor receives because of his ears is widespread and vicious. Yet *Nestor* expresses the themes of the Christmas movie genre carried to their most realized in any of the Rankin-Bass specials: the importance of community, the dismissal of the worldly priorities of materialism, and the ultimate importance of transcendental experiences.

Initially, Nestor lives in a stable under the domination of Olaf, a donkey breeder to whom all living creatures are a commodity. Business and government are a constant threat to community and the family structure. They can be torn apart any time for money. But after Nestor's mother dies protecting Nestor from a snowstorm, Nestor goes out in the wilderness alone. "As savagery often does, it left beauty in its wake," the narrator (voiced by Roger Miller) says. "The good Lord sometimes works in strange ways."

The story of *Nestor* unfolds with a threefold theme the narrator reveals with that statement. First, savagery is what the world generally operates on; second, supernatural events conspire that sometimes don't make sense; and, finally, there is justice when events are ultimately reversed to emancipate the underdog.

Unlike Rudolph, Nestor doesn't have a friend like Hermey. After his mother's death, he walks through a desolate forest on the verge of despair. But a friendly cherub Tilly (voiced by Brenda Vaccaro) says she will guide him. When asked what he should do, she recites something prophetic: that his ears "will guide you on a path that's straight and true" and that "you will save another as your mother once saved you." Nestor sees purpose in this statement to continue. "If that's why mama did what she did, I guess I should follow you," Nestor says. His words reinforce the show's theology that a divine plan is at work even in the most tragic events. His mother's death now takes on significance and is part of a divine design. By Nestor's carrying on to save someone else, his mother's death is given meaning. And it is something God wants, which Tilly reveals when she tells Nestor, "He wants you to" as a celestial light comes down.

Later the Virgin Mary and Joseph select Nestor from all the donkeys in a stable to take them to Bethlehem. Mary and Joseph look at something internal, at quality of character. The rest of the world sees only superficial features and marketability. The stable's dealer first tries to take advantage of Joseph and Mary, then after a celestial light appears around Mary, "Take him, a gift, he's yours," he says. But he soon snaps out of his worldly perspective. "What made me do that?" he wonders. Once again God has a plan, and even a greedy dealer can temporarily change to play a role in the divine plan. After guiding the holy couple to Bethlehem, Nestor is called a hero and welcomed back to his former barn by the animals that once harassed him.

Community is restored despite the enormous pain and loss along the way. But can it make up for the loss of his mother, the loneliness of wandering, and the bullying he suffered for years? Should Nestor return to Olaf, who is responsible for his mother's death? A new beginning might have been a better ending for this character who endured so much. Why does Nestor undergo such severe suffering? Do the individuals who suffer the most receive the most favor from God? Are they most capable of being pure of heart? Both *Nestor, The Long-Eared Christmas Donkey* and *The Little Drummer Boy* suggest that self-sacrifice and suffering are pathways to spiritual progress. *Nestor* is arguably Rankin and Bass's finest show because it plunges the deepest into questions of the nature of suffering, God's providence, and the significance of self-sacrifice.

JACK FROST: AN INCARNATION AND A LOVE STORY

Jack Frost shows a Christmas unlike any other Rankin and Bass show. On Christmas Day there are no presents to give, a tyrannical ruler kidnaps a beautiful young woman, and the hero of the story spends Christmas inside a jail cell. It's one of Rankin and Bass's most fascinating and daring TV specials.

Jack Frost addresses important themes in the Christmas movie genre: the tension between individuality and commitment to community, how obsession with money and power corrupts, and how transcendental experiences reshape lives. It also includes an incarnation that makes the central character a Christ figure. He exhibits the quality of self-sacrifice but also suffers under the burden of a deeply flawed human society. *Jack Frost* also contains one of the few romantic stories in a Rankin and Bass Christmas special, which is an interesting, complex, and unconventional love triangle.

The show is set during the era of King Arthur in January Junction, a peasant rural village ruled by the Cossack Kubla Kraus, who possesses all of the town's horses and money, and who dictates where the peasants can live. Like the Burgermeister in *Santa Claus Is Coming to Town*, he's possessed by an unyielding evil and is incapable of redemption. Jack Frost is a spirit invisible to humans who creates a wintery frost in January Junction and falls in love with the human peasant Elisa. So he wants to become human. "The happiness of me is not what it's cracked up to be / It's lonely being one of a kind," he sings, a song that may have influenced the song "Jack's Lament" in Tim Burton's *The Nightmare Before Christmas*. Father Winter grants Jack his wish, but Elisa doesn't fall in love with Jack.

In the Rankin and Bass specials, only *Santa Claus Is Coming to Town*, with the marriage of Jessica and Santa, and *Frosty's Winterland*, which features children making a wife for Frosty, contain romantic love in their plot lines. But *Jack Frost* puts romance at the center of its story. Even though Jack doesn't attain the object of his affections, the show exhibits how the love embodied in Jack's act of self-sacrifice in creating a snowstorm is stronger than the romantic love he feels for Elisa.

It may initially be puzzling why Elisa and the man she prefers, the Golden Knight, are not more likeable. But their shallowness is the point. Elisa is charming but giddy, naïve, and capricious, while the Golden Knight is sly, aloof, and somewhat manipulative in his quest for Elisa. As physically attractive as Elisa and the Golden Knight are, they don't feel as deeply as Jack Frost does. Elisa is delighted and grateful for Jack Frost's winter magic. But as a human without his powers, he isn't as appealing to her. She only sees an ideal and clichéd version of romance embodied in the handsome but superficial Golden Knight. She is incapable of transferring her affections to someone who doesn't fit her romantic ideal. Elisa is not spiritually developed enough to see beyond her illusion of romance with the Golden Knight, who embodies both high status and physical attractiveness. Frost is capable of a different type of love. He forfeits his own desires for the happiness of someone else.

Because he ordinarily dwells in the spiritual realm and not the physical realm, he operates differently. His sacrifices are, as Father Winter predicted, incompatible with human society. Through his incarnation, Jack Frost learns the perils of being human. When in spirit form, he sees humanity as containing wonderful things, but when experiencing it firsthand, he sees suffering. And as an incarnation of flesh from spirit, his resolution to seeing suffering is to become a Christ figure by sacrificing his humanity to save

***Frosty the Snowman* (1969) is both a messianic figure and secular liberator. The ending resurrection scene is one of Rankin-Bass's most direct Christ figure references.** Photo courtesy Rankin-Bass/Everett Collection.

others. In all the Rankin and Bass TV specials, Jack Frost is the most blatant Christ figure.

THE END OF AN ERA: PINOCCHIO'S CHRISTMAS

For many years there have been two Pinocchios in popular culture.[206] The first is the character from Carlo Collodi's picaresque 1883 novel *The Adventures of Pinocchio*, where the troublesome wooden puppet goes through a series of dark and disturbing events leading to him eventually transforming into a boy. The second Pinocchio is from the 1939 Disney film, which softens the character's dark side, decreases the violence, and expands the cricket character to act as Pinocchio's conscience.

Rankin and Bass create another version of Pinocchio. This Pinocchio combines their two trademark characters of underdog and reforming villain within one character. Pinocchio is partly an underdog but also somewhat of a villain who must reform. Pinocchio is a distinctive character in Rankin and Bass because he is so morally ambiguous.

Usually the Rankin and Bass Christmas TV specials separate major characters into three categories: (1) good characters who embody cheerfulness, generosity, and a focus on others, (2) characters who are loners and who need to have the good brought out of them, and (3) evil characters who are usually capable of reform. Rankin and Bass's Pinocchio doesn't fall into any of these categories. Pinocchio undergoes tests, adventures, and trials that he often fails. He has an underlying sense of what is correct. However, he's easily led astray by characters who tempt him with money or pleasure. Pinocchio's story contains a spiritual dilemma: he wants to do the right thing but struggles to do it. It's an internal battle rather than a battle against an external evil figure, as in many Rankin and Bass shows. Pinocchio is incapable of navigating these decisions on his own. So he has three spiritual mentors representing three different approaches to spiritual discipline.

The first is his creator Geppetto, who accepts Pinocchio unconditionally. "I don't care what you've done, I forgive you, my son," he says while looking through the streets for him. But he doesn't set guidelines for

Pinocchio. If he were more of a disciplinarian, perhaps Pinocchio would not be so susceptible to trouble. The second spiritual mentor is Dr. Cricket, who is as direct and impatient as Geppetto is patient and unconditional. Pinocchio says, "All he did was preach and give advice all day." It's an approach that isn't effective with Pinocchio. While Geppetto is too lenient, the cricket is too impatient and blunt in telling Pinocchio what to do. The third mentor, who strikes the right balance between Geppetto and Cricket, is Lady Azora. Instead of ignoring the problem and always yielding to Pinocchio as Geppetto does or evangelizing as the cricket does, Lady Azora assesses the situation and gently gives him advice. "You really are not a bad boy, just foolish perhaps," is how she sums him up.

The fox joins the Burgermeister from *Santa Claus Is Coming to Town* and Kubla Kraus from *Jack Frost* as one of the few villains in a Rankin-Bass Christmas TV special who does not reform. And of all of the characters in Rankin-Bass Christmas specials, he is the one most associated with evil figures. When he first appears with the cat he says, "We fell from heaven," alluding to Satan as a fallen and rebellious angel. He tries to convince Pinocchio that what he says is "the gospel truth" as he draws a cross in the snow. But he is a deceiver pretending to be Pinocchio's friend. And when turning Pinocchio over to a coach driver who will sell him, the fox receives a bag of gold from the driver, an allusion to Judas betraying Jesus.

Being good is a struggle from the beginning for Pinocchio; his first action when coming to life is kicking Geppetto. As much as Pinocchio progresses, the end of this special illustrates that his resolve to behave is only temporary. "You will try to be a good boy but it will not be easy; you will be led astray, but that is life," Lady Azora ominously says. The peaceful, communal Christmas meal is a respite in Pinocchio's spiritual battle. As Rankin-Bass developed, they didn't present the happy conclusions, such as in *Rudolph*, with trouble behind the protagonist. The hard road ahead for Pinocchio is a fitting end to the last worthwhile Rankin-Bass TV special, which can be read as the counterculture recognizing there are struggles and temptations ahead as they age.

THE LEGACY OF RANKIN & BASS

It's impossible to think of Tim Burton's *The Nightmare Before Christmas* or any Pixar movie being made without the Rankin-Bass influence. And perhaps there would never have been the phenomenon of Japanese anime. Key Rankin-Bass animators went on to join Studio Ghibli, the influential anime company that made movies such as *Spirited Away.*

The best of their shows endure as spiritual fables. What Rankin called underdogs who fulfill a quest are figures on a spiritual journey suffering for a higher cause. Some give up their existence for others, such as Frosty and Jack Frost. Others undergo severe oppression before being vindicated, such as Aaron in *The Little Drummer Boy* and Nestor in *Nestor, the Long-Eared Christmas Donkey.* Sometimes, as in *Rudolph,* there is a hero's journey that ultimately benefits the community. Other times it requires staying where a character is and holding onto faith, as Joshua did in *'Twas the Night Before Christmas* and Lucas in *The First Christmas.* Sometimes it means building one's own community outside of an oppressive one, as in *Santa Claus Is Coming to Town.* In *Pinocchio's Christmas,* it means resisting temptation to do the wrong actions.

The villains of these stories usually transform themselves into better people. In *Rudolph,* Santa and the Christmastown community admit their inflexibility and reform. Characters like the Winter Warlock in *Santa Claus Is Coming to Town* and Jack Frost in *Frosty's Winter Wonderland* change because other characters perform simple acts of kindness to them. Other characters become wiser because others are patient with them, as in *The First Christmas.* Still others, such as Alfred in *'Twas the Night Before Christmas,* are redeemed through making reparations for bad behavior. The redeemed villains show there is always an opening for spiritual transformation.

The Rankin-Bass shows also display a diversity of religious and spiritual influences and ideologies. Elements of Old Testament theology make up *Santa Claus Is Coming to Town,* with its Moses-like protagonist, and *'Twas the Night Before Christmas,* with a Santa that needs to be appeased through displays of devotion. Rankin-Bass made overtly Christian-themed films using the nativity story in *The Little Drummer Boy* and *Nestor, The Long-Eared Christmas Donkey*. They portray a religious community in *The First Christmas*. Their works displayed a diverse set of religious and spiritual beliefs before Third Wave Christmas films redefined the Christmas movie genre as portraying a secular family holiday.

10

The Third Wave
Embracing Materialism and Accepting Dysfunctional Families

Rankin-Bass's *Pinocchio's Christmas* ended the Second Wave in 1980 at the beginning of the decade of the yuppie (young urban professionals). A new generation of well-groomed business warriors and sympathizers proliferated popular culture, including the unabashedly pro-business Alex P. Keaton (Michael J. Fox) on the TV sitcom *Family Ties* and the ruthless Wall Street tycoon Gordon Gekko (Michael Douglas) in the movie *Wall Street*. Pro-corporate policies and a stock market surge led to an emphasis on individualism and materialism. This made the social commentary of *Rudolph*, the anti-commercialism of *A Charlie Brown Christmas*, and the community-oriented World War II–era movies somewhat obsolete.

With social responsibilities deemphasized, the culture also grew more insular. In 1987, British Prime Minister Margaret Thatcher notoriously said, "There's no such thing as society, there are individual men and women and there are families."[207] Reflecting this ideology, the Christmas movie genre narrowed the definition of community to the nuclear family. In the First Wave Christmas film *White Christmas*, a World War II army unit reunites on Christmas Eve to honor their former military leader. In the Third Wave era, being away from one's nuclear family would be unthinkable. The goal in Third Wave Christmas movies is often to barricade oneself with family to negotiate family dynamics and eradicate family dysfunction. The family becomes the primary source for both socialization and morality.[208] Actor Idris Elba of *This Christmas* (2007) summed up that film's intention, which could be the same for most Third Wave films: "This film isn't so much about the religion of Christmas, but it's about that time and what happens is that you see your family."[209] This is prominently exhibited in three influential movies (*A Christmas Story*, *National Lampoon's Christmas Vacation*, and *Home Alone*) that changed Christmas in American popular culture and established the tone of Third Wave movies.

BUYING A PERSONA IN *A CHRISTMAS STORY*

A Christmas Story (1983) is set during the World War II era somewhere in the years 1939 to 1943.[210] But the war years setting is more for ironic nostalgia than era authenticity or employing the themes and tone of First Wave Christmas films. With its homespun voice-over by author Jean Shepherd, who wrote the short stories the film is based on, *A Christmas Story* is an entertaining series of incidents featuring Ralphie (Peter Billingsley), a nine-year-old boy in Indiana who endures humiliation, conjures up wistful and humorous daydreams, and sheds a few tears on the way to finally possessing his coveted Christmas present: a BB gun. It's a coming-of-age story with masculine rites of passage from childhood to early adolescence centered on Ralphie's overriding obsession for a particular BB gun for Christmas.

Never before or since in the Christmas movie genre has there been so much emphasis on a material object. Although set in the 1940s, the extreme attention on the BB gun demonstrates a 1980s ideology of embracing materialism and the idea that brands are not just functional products but transformers of personality.[211] Materialism defines character instead of being an obstacle to character as it was during the First and Second Waves of Christmas films.

The transcendental qualities of the BB gun are illuminated during the opening credits. A crowd stands outside a department store window that looks like an altar of holy objects. Ralphie sees what he calls "the holy grail of Christmas gifts"—a Red Ryder 200-shot range model air rifle. Ralphie's goal is obtaining the BB gun for Christmas. He believes the BB gun contains the power to transform his self-image and masculinize himself. This enables Ralphie to overcome female characters who want to emasculate him. His teacher is a humorless, stern, and moralistic Puritanic figure. Ralphie's mother's warnings about the gun's safety are the "classic mother BB gun block," according to Ralphie's adult narration. Aunt Clara, who the adult Ralphie narrator says holds a delusion that Ralphie is "perpetually four years old and also a girl," gives Ralphie a pink

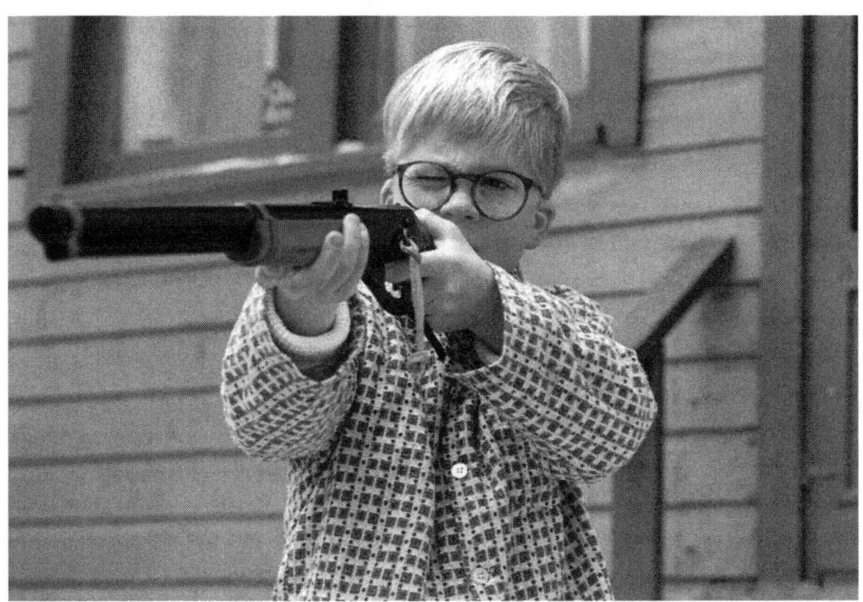

Never in the history of Christmas films has one present been so sought after and revered. *A Christmas Story* (1983) mixes the coming-of-age genre with Christmas films in Ralphie's quest to get his coveted BB gun for Christmas. Photo courtesy MGM/Everett Collection.

bunny suit for Christmas, which he reluctantly and briefly wears. Ralphie's mother, his teacher, and a department store Santa Claus all warn him he shouldn't get the BB gun because, in the movie's catchphrase, "you'll shoot your eye out, kid." But he has fantasies of shooting robbers and defending his family (an inspiration for *Home Alone*?) with a rifle.

The film was influential for showing that the nuclear family is one's sole trustworthy community, despite all of the family's dysfunction. Ralphie's family members have their shortcomings: an impatient hotheaded father with an unhealthy fetish for a risqué lamp, a somewhat meek, overprotective mother, and a younger brother who won't eat his food and locks himself in a cabinet because he's so afraid of his father. Ralphie's father underscores a masculinity with an edge of frustration. His family appears afraid of standing up to him or confronting him. He also exhibits a fetishism and repressed sexuality represented by his fixation on a lamp of a woman's leg, which the narrator describes as "electric sex gleaming in the window." He seems as obsessed with it as Ralphie is with the BB gun.

Despite the family's problems, the rituals of Christmas bring them together. They sing Christmas songs together in the car, revel in an orgy of Christmas presents on Christmas morning, and even amuse themselves when eating a makeshift Christmas meal together in a Chinese restaurant. Life inside the house may sometimes be dysfunctional, but life outside the immediate family is threatening—a theme that would become the norm in Third Wave Christmas films. Ralphie is bullied on his way to school and at school, his father is tormented by unrestrained dogs that belong to the "hillbilly neighbors," and a Christmas tree salesman is a shifty person who tries to cheat the family into buying a substandard Christmas tree. It's far from the idyllic view of small-town life shown in First Wave Christmas movies of the World War II era.

The outside world is an absurdist terrain. The movie at times verges on black comedy as Ralphie navigates his way through a largely hostile environment filled with characters that either threaten him physically or damage his self-identity. Jean Shepherd biographer Eugene B. Bergmann wrote that

Shepherd had a negative view of life and disliked nostalgia, and that "Shepherd's philosophy tended to be that most things in life were going to end in disaster."[212] As a result, the movie employs what the film's director Bob Clark called "an odd combination of reality and spoof and satire."[213]

Even the usually revered images of Santa and his elves become antagonistic figures. In the department store, Ralphie makes his way to a Santa Claus who sits atop a mountain of simulated snow, attended by grumpy elves who escort children to the exasperated Santa's lap. Clark, who also directed the horror movie *Black Christmas*, partially shot this scene with a handheld camera. The movie's most expressionistic and menacing camerawork is Ralphie's view of Santa Claus. As if they are in a horror movie, most of the children scream when they are on Santa's lap and are swiftly sent down a chute into a pillow of fake snow. This is a subversion of the benevolent view of Santa Claus shown in films such as *Miracle on 34th Street.*

The movie avoids both spirituality and religion; Ralphie describes his father as nonreligious: "Some men are Baptists, others Catholics; my father was an Oldsmobile man." The movie also doesn't show Ralphie exhibiting any moral growth associated with the spiritual transformations previously central to the Christmas movie genre. Ralphie is not morally changed by events in the film.

Although the movie was a modest success when released in movie theaters, it became a hit on TV and home video. The movie became so popular that in some polls it replaces *It's a Wonderful Life* as America's favorite Christmas film. Its popularity contributed to a backlash against the themes of community and spiritual transformation in previous Christmas films. A writer in *Time* called *It's a Wonderful Life* "oppressive" and celebrated how *A Christmas Story* overturned the emphasis on the "social good" integral in *It's a Wonderful Life.*[214] "It's the individual Christmas that matters, Bedford Falls can take a hike," he wrote.[215] And in the Third Wave, that "individual Christmas" became linked not to a solitary Christmas but to one's relationship with their nuclear family. For much of *A Christmas Story*, consumerism replaces spirituality.[216] But the movie's ultimate message is that family connection—not consumerism or religion—provides the central meaning of Christmas.[217]

THE ENTITLEMENT AND ASSERTION OF THE SUBURBAN FATHER IN *CHRISTMAS VACATION*

Many critics disdained *National Lampoon's Christmas Vacation* (1989) after its release. The *New York Times* called it "a disjointed collection of running gags."[218] A Canadian review summed it up as "ho-ho-ho ho-rrible."[219] "Rest assured, you won't be seeing *Christmas Vacation* on TV each time you turn the set on 43 years from now as is the case for Frank Capra's *It's a Wonderful Life*," wrote Bruce Rolfsen.[220] But they were wrong. *Christmas Vacation* became the most influential Third Wave Christmas film.

Critically maligned at the time of its release, *National Lampoon's Christmas Vacation* (1989) went on to be the Third Wave's most influential Christmas film. It solidified navigating family dysfunction as the primary goal of Christmas. Photo courtesy Warner Brothers/Everett Collection.

It's significant for shifting the setting for the Christmas film to suburbia. Instead of the First Wave contrast of modest small-town values with corrupt city values, *Christmas Vacation* negatively portrays characters from both small towns and urban yuppie culture. It shows suburbia with all its material comforts as the appropriate setting for celebrating Christmas.

Although *A Christmas Story* depicts a somewhat dysfunctional family, it integrates drama and pathos, and also utilizes conventions from the coming-of-age genre. *National Lampoon's Christmas Vacation* creates a major change in the genre by using minimal drama; the characters display almost no sincere or deep emotion. *Christmas Vacation* makes its characters an often offensive assortment of caricatures and stereotypes. Unlike *A Christmas Story*, where the characters at times show a range of emotions beneath their idiosyncrasies, *Christmas Vacation* features unrealistic and offbeat characters.

Controlling father Clark Griswold (Chevy Chase) tries to create the ideal Christmas, while his family is worn down from Clark's antics. At one point his wife Ellen (Beverly D'Angelo) says a prayer and then says, "Forgive my husband; he knows not what he does."[221] Ellen framing this in a religious context (Jesus's words on the cross) provides some comic relief that she is suffering because of Clark's behavior. In a revealing analysis, Ellen tells Clark he overdoes everything, whether it's Christmas or any other holiday or celebration. Clark Griswold is a prototype of 1980s excess. He is incapable of a humble or modest Christmas celebration. It must contain an enormous Christmas tree, garish lights, and a hefty Christmas bonus. He defines himself by what he can buy, display, or provide for his family. As *A Christmas Story* is centered on Ralphie's desire for masculine self-definition away from female control, and *Home Alone* is driven by Kevin's movement to exert his masculinity through violence, *Christmas Vacation* is propelled by Clark Griswold's drive for domination.

The movie employs a comic component also employed in *A Christmas Story*—setting up the expectation of a Christmas ritual and then showing its dysfunctional reality. This occurs in Ralphie's horror-movie-like visit to a department-store Santa, Ralphie's expectations about how enthused people will be about his desire for a BB gun, and the family's sabotaged Christmas dinner. In *Christmas Vacation*, this cycle occurs during rituals such as cutting down a Christmas tree, relatives arriving at the Griswold home, and a Christmas dinner gone awry.

Clark marches his family through the snowy woods for his ideal Christmas tree. There's a celestial light framing the massive Christmas tree he wants (how far this Christmas tree has come from the lesson about Christmas trees in *A Charlie Brown Christmas*). After returning home, Clark initiates his next obsession, which is to set up a huge display of Christmas lights on his house (how different it is from Charlie Brown exclaiming "my own dog has gone commercial" when Snoopy lights up his dog house). When the lights finally come on in a blast of white light, Handel's "Hallelujah" chorus is played in what is almost a parody of a spiritual revelation.

The dysfunction and challenges in Clark's family aren't just with his passive and exhausted immediate family. Clark and Ellen's parents, as well as Clark's aunt and uncle, are burdens. Clark tells the anxious Ellen "they're family; they're not strangers off the street," indicating his commitment is to his family, but not to anyone he doesn't know. He also says the purpose of Christmas is "seeing through the petty problems of family life," further showing that Christmas is defined by eradicating family dysfunction.

The other components of Clark's family contain the film's most offensive stereotype. Clark's cousin Eddie and his wife and children arrive in a trailer Clark calls a "tenement on wheels," reflecting a worldview of the poor as dysfunctional, uneducated, and responsible for their own impoverished status. Eddie embodies the hillbilly stereotype. He doesn't work, possesses crude manners, and lives in a backwoods home where, as Eddie's daughter says, you "have to put your coat on to go to the bathroom." Clark puts up with Eddie's boorish habits and clothing as well as his destitution. In perhaps his most magnanimous moment, Clark arranges to buy Eddie's children Christmas presents, which he declares not to be charity because Eddie is family. But the shiftless Eddie already has a list ready, showing he anticipated Clark paying for the gifts.

Christmas Vacation changed much about the Christmas movie genre, including how men are often portrayed in Christmas films. Chevy Chase's character introduces a new male personality into the genre, which in recent years has been called a "man boy" or a "man child." One contemporaneous review called Griswold "a boy trapped in a man's body."[222] Chase's Clark Griswold falls into the category of married "man child" films where a man assumes adult responsibilities by having a professional job, raising a family, and having a home. Although he takes on those roles, much of his personality remains lodged in adolescence. Despite Clark's adult responsibilities, he cannot master self-control, which is an important trait of maturity.[223] Part of remaining somewhat in adolescence is living in a near perpetual state of irony. Even in more serious moments, a distance is maintained from sincere emotion. When Clark is trapped in the attic and plays old family films, it is watching himself as a child on Christmas when he feels the most emotion. The "man child" identifies most with himself as a child.

While *A Christmas Story* is somewhat of an anomaly in the Christmas movie genre, with its quirky humor and period setting, *Christmas Vacation* mainstreams a new secular materialistic and insular Christmas. *Christmas Vacation* changed the modern Christmas in movies from spiritual and moral dramas to comedies featuring dysfunctional families.

One reason for the growing popularity over the years of these two movies is because *A Christmas Story* and *Christmas Vacation* utilize irony, an exaggerated comic approach increasingly used in American film comedies.[224] By the 1990s, irony in film and television showed the distance between the expectation and the reality of American life. It expressed the deepening cynicism about institutions, rituals, and societal structures. Stand-up comic Marc Maron in Gina Kim's article "You Thought Irony Was Dead? What a Joke" said the appeal of irony was its distance from sincerity: "People don't like honesty," he said. "They find it boring or too draining for them to engage with. If something's put across in a smug or condescending way, it's got some safety built into it—you can take it in, laugh at it, and it assumes you're in on the joke."[225]

And what could be more of a cultural phenomenon than Christmas to use as an ironic vehicle? *A Christmas Story* and *Christmas Vacation* started the shift toward irony in the Christmas movie genre through the cycle of anticipation and disappointment the protagonists in both films experience about the Christmas season.

SUBMISSION TO THE DYSFUNCTIONAL FAMILY IN *HOME ALONE*

A Christmas Story was a modest financial success when it was released in movie theaters in 1983. And despite mostly negative reviews, *National Lampoon's Christmas Vacation* performed well at the box office partly because it was the third in a successful franchise of *Vacation* movies. But neither movie became a Christmas pop culture staple until shown frequently on television and widely seen on home video. It took years for these two films to become at first cult favorites and then perennial holiday standards.

It was a movie starring a child in the unlikely role of a mini-action movie hero that solidified the Third Wave Christmas film. The enormous success of *Home Alone* (1990) made Christmas films financially viable. After *Home Alone*, studios bankrolled big budget Christmas movies with A-list stars. *Home Alone* became not only the highest grossing film of the year but the third largest grossing film ever at the time, with only *Star Wars* and *E.T.* selling more tickets. It still remains the highest-grossing Christmas film.[226] The movie became a box office smash without extensive special effects, a big name star, or a romantic storyline. Most of its screen time was occupied by an eight-year-old character. However, *Home Alone* developed into a phenomenon because it addresses cultural anxiety over families becoming dysfunctional because of extreme individualism. *Home Alone* illustrates the clash between the materialism and comforts of its suburban setting and underlying family dysfunction.[227]

Like *A Christmas Story*, *Home Alone* is a variation on the male coming-of-age film. And like Ralphie in *A Christmas Story*, an overmothered boy, Kevin McCallister (Macaulay Culkin), is masculinized over the course of the film after his family accidentally leaves him behind when they leave for Christmas in Paris. That's accomplished through overcoming external threats to the family as well as internal strife within the family.

The external threat is surmounted by Kevin using violence to outwit and battle thieves who invade his family's home. He defends the home against an ethnic underclass played by Joe Pesci, who often plays Italian-American gangsters, and Daniel Stern, who in the sequel to *Home Alone* says "Happy Chanukah" while stealing charity money in a crass stereotype of a Jewish criminal.[228] The film ends with the male protagonist as a misunderstood and unrecognized savior who protects the suburban home from the criminal underclass. Another external threat includes institutions outside the family that do not function properly to protect Kevin. When Kevin's mother calls from France to ask police to check on their home, the police and crisis intervention workers are uncaring, unconcerned, and uninvolved. A policeman who goes to Kevin's door leaves too quickly without exploring further. In this dark worldview of apathetic institutions, it's up to the young Kevin to protect the family's home.

The internal threat in *Home Alone* is the dysfunction generated by an overactive, frenetic upper-middle-class lifestyle. Family members are too busy, too careless, and sometimes too cruel to become a solid family structure. The dysfunction and extreme individualism of the McCallister family is apparent in the frantic opening to *Home Alone*. The family, anxiously preparing for a Christmas trip to France, quickly pass by each other and are so self-absorbed they don't notice a thief posing as a policeman standing in their home. If they seem united in anything, it's their disdain or indifference toward Kevin. Apparently this is because his mother, the only family member he appears to have any emotional connection to, plays too dominant a role. Like Ralphie in *A Christmas Story*, Kevin is emasculated by feminine overprotection. As a result, his older siblings harass him.

Kevin's most vicious nemesis is his brother Buzz (Devin Ratray), a scheming bully. Because Kevin's father Peter (John Heard) is distant and largely indifferent, the troublemaker Buzz accumulates power and influence in the household. Kevin appears correct when he declares he's been "dumped on" and asks, "Why do I always get treated like scum?" The viewer sees that underneath the plush suburban home is meanness, dysfunction, and inequality.[229]

This oppression culminates in a disturbing conversation between Kevin and his mother, Kate (Catherine O'Hara), as she takes him to his place of banishment, which is sleeping in the attic. Kevin tries to apologize but his mother says, "It's too late." She does not possess the spiritual value of forgiving. Instead, she enacts punishment. This pushes Kevin into a downhill spiral where he declares that "everyone in this family hates me." His mother replies, "Maybe you should ask Santa for a new family." This propels Kevin into a tirade that he doesn't want to see his family again. The next morning he believes this has actually happened: the power goes out and the alarm clock doesn't go off. During the melee of scrambling to get to the airport, the family is too busy, self-occupied, and segregated to realize Kevin is missing.

While sequestered in his home, Kevin advances through several stages of development that lead to his masculinization. First there is the jubilation of independence. When Kevin realizes his family is gone he feels liberated. He runs through the house saying, "I'm free." Second comes a stage of self-indulgence where he gobbles down ice cream and watches a gangster movie. Kevin deteriorates into gluttony, sloth, and a desire for isolation. But the third stage, fear, becomes his biggest developmental challenge. Even before his family leaves, he's afraid of sleeping alone in the attic. But when he's alone, the fear accelerates. He's afraid of the basement, and he imagines the furnace talking to him. He also becomes scared during a violent scene in a movie and calls for his mother. His fear forces him to hide under his parent's bed after the thieves try to get in the back door and to not answer the front door when a policeman knocks on it.

He reaches his first turning point toward overcoming his fear when he comes out from hiding under the bed. He rouses himself by saying, "I can't be a wimp, I'm the man of the house." Kevin walks outside of his home shouting, "I'm not afraid anymore." Then he sees his neighbor Marley. Kevin is initially afraid of Marley because Buzz had told a story that Marley is a murderous criminal. Kevin screams and runs back to his parent's bedroom. He must overcome his fear of Marley before he can adequately shed his fear.

Kevin does this during a scene within a church, which, in a rarity for a Third Wave film, represents a spiritual sanctuary. Earlier in the film the church was established as a place of protection and safety when Kevin hides from the thieves by wearing a shepherd's cloak in the nativity scene in front of the church. And the thieves chasing Kevin refuse to go in the church. In what is probably the movie's key scene, Kevin goes into the church on Christmas Eve, where Marley is watching a rehearsal for a service. Kevin's fear of Marley dissipates because he apparently feels safe in the church. Marley says he's there to watch his granddaughter sing. He can't see her directly because he and his son became estranged after an argument. Through the conversation it emerges that Marley is a doppelganger to Kevin. Marley also is ostracized from his family. They both are fearful and guilty.

Aside from lashing out at his mother, which in some ways is arguably defending himself, there doesn't appear to be anything Kevin needs to feel guilty about. Yet the specifics of the injustice in his family don't matter. What counts is his allegiance to his family. *Home Alone* demands loyalty to the family structure, no matter how unjust and dysfunctional. Marley tells Kevin, regarding family, that "deep down you always love them, but you can forget that you love them and you can hurt them and they can hurt you."

A large section of *Home Alone* is Kevin manning up by defending the family home against two burglars. Protecting his home recalls vigilante movies, as well as Hollywood Westerns where a settler's home is defended against uncivilized forces.[230] The film's climax is an innovative affluent suburban child protecting the family home from dimwitted lower-class criminals, who receive brutal punishment. The threat in *Home Alone* is very different from threats in previous Christmas films. It's not the effect of materialism, greed, or workaholism. Instead, the threat is criminals from the ethnic lower class.

By defending his home Kevin also breaks free of his overmothering and moves toward being a self-sufficient masculine figure. Like Ralphie in *A Christmas Story*, he's been marginalized by his overprotective mother sheltering him too much. This follows what the film's writer John Hughes said in an interview was at the center of the film: "I felt that the concept, the idea of a kid taking care of himself, was the most important thing."[231] There are opportunities throughout the movie for Kevin to ask for help. But he feels he must take a stand against the criminals on his own through violence that is a combination of comic, if unrealistic, punishment.[232]

After masculinizing himself by defending his home, Kevin must still repair his relationship with his mother to restore peace. Kate's anxiety and guilt exposes a threat to the family—the fear of a mother unable to manage the demands of a busy household. Kevin must help her overcome that by overlooking dysfunction out of loyalty to the family rather than correcting the family dysfunction. This temporary truce between Kevin and his mother does not mean the household has fundamentally changed. The ending line is Buzz yelling, "What did you do to my room?" showing Kevin still faces oppression.

11

Christmas and the Family under Siege

In the early 1980s American divorce rates were at an all-time high.[233] Students graduating with bachelor's degrees tripled from 1960 to 1980.[234] That meant more family members left home for higher education and jobs. In 1960, 73 percent of American children under age eighteen lived with two married parents in their first marriage. That dropped to 61 percent in 1980 and by 2013 to fewer than half.[235] Also by 2013, more than half of parents said it was difficult for them to balance work and family.[236] Third Wave films temporarily resolve these pressures by using Christmas to bring together family members to repair physical and emotional separation.

In the First Wave, being home at Christmas was important to reestablish a sense of community after the war and to reconnect with pro-family small-town ideals. However, the American yearning for home goes back further. Since the Industrial Revolution, home has offered an oasis away from a sometimes dehumanizing workplace.[237] Home is also crucial in the American immigrant experience to provide comfort in an unfamiliar culture. Leaving family for economic independence generates anxiety.[238] Third Wave films attempt to alleviate that tension through family members reconnecting at Christmas. That often means temporarily overcoming family dysfunction produced by the independent lives of family members.

Another trait of the Third Wave is the marginalization of female characters. Traditionally in American literature, home is associated with a nurturing feminine sphere, which provides a refuge from a difficult world.[239] This concept changed in the Third Wave with divorce and the increasing number of working women. As a result, most protagonists in Third Wave films are men feeling apprehension about gender role changes. In Third Wave films, the voices of women are minimized, and Christmas becomes a time for men to express their angst and reassert their identities in the home.

THE ANTI-FAMILY THREATS IN *DIE HARD*

Die Hard (1988) is the most far-reaching Third Wave Christmas film in showing the extent of threats to the American family. It begins with a conflict between a married couple over competing careers and ends as an exposure of how malfunctioning institutions jeopardize the family. It also indicates the subjugation of the American proletariat through its depiction of the film's protagonist John McClane (Bruce Willis), who, despite his competence and insight, is unrecognized, unappreciated, and disdained. The movie links McClane and the movie's sympathetic characters to Christmas and the family while portraying business, law enforcement, and criminals as opposing both Christmas and the family.[240]

Because *Die Hard* was released in a decade deluged with mediocre action films, most critics initially dismissed it. Some writers categorized *Die Hard* as another Reagan-era "hard body" film. Susan Jeffords's 1993 *Hard Bodies: Hollywood Masculinity in the Reagan Era* popularized the term to describe the male body types in films starring Sylvester Stallone, Arnold Schwarzenegger, and Chuck Norris. Jeffords and others also pigeonholed these films as espousing a right-wing political agenda with violent outsider, white male characters confronting bungling bureaucracies.[241] They felt this reflected a disturbing resurgence of militarism, individualism, and vigilantism. Other critics labeled *Die Hard* as sexist, racist, and xenophobic, including a writer who called it a "fantasy of white male dominance."[242]

However, McClane is not part of what he at one point calls the "macho assholes" in law enforcement who lack the vulnerability and attentiveness he and his adopted partner Al Powell possess. As the movie unfolds, McClane regrets his lack of support for his estranged wife, Holly. At the end of the film he accepts her identity as Holly Generro by introducing her with that name to Powell. He's progressed from the beginning of the film when he confronted Holly about using her maiden name. McClane's only other alliances are with two African-American characters who are also vulnerable and marginalized. The film is not racist or sexist. Because blacks and whites can be either good or bad characters, the emphasis is more on class conflict.[243] And in 2013, a *New York Times* evaluation pointed out why *Die Hard* has been elevated so highly in recent years. The flawed, self-deprecating, and angst-ridden McClane endures while the machine-like implausible characters that Stallone, Schwarzenegger, and Norris played haven't aged well.[244]

The film starts with the anti-family demands of corporations that workers who should be home on Christmas Eve are in the workplace. It also shows how dual career marriages can create tension. McClane and his wife Holly (Bonnie Bedelia) are separated because of it.

Soon after their disagreement on Christmas Eve, terrorists fronted by the well-dressed, urbane, and classically educated Hans Gruber raid the office Christmas party. McClane methodically sabotages their plans to unlock a vault that contains $640 million in bearer bonds. The police and FBI arrive but don't want McClane's help, even though he's the only one effective in trying to stop the heist. He forms a bond through radio transmission with Al Powell (Reginald VelJohnson), a police sergeant, who, like McClane, is disregarded by authorities.

Christmas in *Die Hard* is an ideology connected to family that divides characters into two camps: pro-Christmas and anti-Christmas.[245] The pro-

Christmas characters include McClane, who carries a giant teddy bear to give to his children for Christmas and asks Argyle to play Christmas music when they're in the limo together. At a critical moment when he appears to be unsure if he will live or die, he says, "It's up to the man upstairs." He tells Hans he attended Catholic school and when he sees the roof wired to be blown up he says, "Jesus, Mary, mother of God." Another character who makes religious references is Powell, who tells McClane he must know when it's the appropriate time to pray. Powell too is associated with Christmas. He sings "Let It Snow" and has a Christmas ornament in his police car.[246]

Holly is a mixture of pro- and anti-Christmas viewpoints, but is mostly anti-Christmas because she's immersed in her corporate job. However, she fends off advances by her co-worker Ellis by reminding him Christmas is, among other things, about family. And her name is linked to the Christmas season. However, Holly is unable to let go of her business obligations to enjoy the Christmas party, showing how business pulls individuals away from family and community. She tells a co-worker to stop working and enjoy the party because she's beginning to feel like Ebenezer Scrooge. And, consistent with a Scrooge-type character, she's linked to excessive submission to business. Although she's still married, Holly uses her maiden name at the company because she believes it will help her succeed, showing that for her, business identity supersedes family identity.

The workplace contains anti-family values and is anti-Christmas.[247] The Christmas party is a commemoration of financial success with Baroque era music, not Christmas music. Ellis, the stereotype of the 1980s yuppie, snorts cocaine and propositions Holly. A Christmas party tryst occurs between two co-workers. When John arrives, Ellis wants Holly to show John the pricey watch he gave her, suggesting there is some connection between Ellis and Holly through a material object that is a symbol of success. Later in the film when John rescues Holly from Gruber's clutches, loosening this watch indicates she's free of Ellis's influence as well as released from her corporate identity. Earlier when John tells her Ellis has his eye on her, she replies that she's got her eye on his office. Human relationships in the corporate world are dysfunctional because they are disingenuous.

The terrorists are also in the anti-Christmas camp. By attacking a Christmas party, they attack Christmas. They mock and subvert traditional Christmas by creating variations on Christmas stories and Christmas carols.[248] The terrorist and computer hacker Theo recites the beginning of the poem "'Twas The Night Before Christmas" as the terrorists attack authorities trying to enter the building. Hans Gruber says because it's Christmas, it's the time of miracles. This turns out to be the incompetent FBI agent who cut the building's power, which enables the terrorists to enter the vault. When the vault finally does open, Theo says, "Merry Christmas."

There are also connections between the terrorists and the corporate leaders, suggesting they operate by a similar mentality. Ellis tells Gruber "Business is business. You use a gun, I use a fountain pen. What's the difference?" Like the executive Takagi, Hans likes classical music and hums Beethoven. Gruber admires Takagi's suit and says he owns two suits from the same designer. Gruber's goal is to be "on a beach earning 20 percent." He's not a common thief; he's a business-minded one. When John says to Takagi that he didn't know the Japanese celebrated Christmas, Takagi says, "We're flexible. Pearl Harbor didn't work out, so we got you with tape decks." Although jokingly stated, it indicates he thinks of business as a war-like enterprise. When Holly is summoned away to speak to the employees, her co-worker calls employees "the troops."

What makes *Die Hard* consistent with traditional Christmas movie genre narratives is the moral transformation McClane undergoes. The movie depicts not only how McClane fights cultural problems but also how he battles the demons within himself.[249] The action is not just a movement to stop terrorists, it's a journey for McClane into self-examination, confession of shortcomings, and even acknowledgment of a higher power.

As the action intensifies and his physical body becomes bloodier and more battered, McClane's feelings of regret and his inner battle increase. The vulnerability McClane exhibits defies the convention of a protagonist in the action movie genre. Usually the protagonist possesses a hardness of character, boastful humor, a lack of vulnerability, and a formulaic and implausible sense of inevitability that the protagonist will triumph. In an interview Willis said, "I think John McClane is the opposite of a superhero," he said. "He's not invincible; he's a very vulnerable guy. He's capable of being afraid, making mistakes, and feeling pain."[250]

The only one who understands McClane is Powell, an African-American policeman who communicates with McClane, but whose advice is ignored by the power structure of the police and FBI. The working-class white American male and the working class African-American are marginalized in a system that doesn't acknowledge their wisdom or abilities. McClane and Powell are more thoughtful, introspective, and intuitive in juxtaposition to the other male characters, whom Powell describes as textbook and play-by-play. McClane and Powell share gallows humor, not boastful humor. Because of their ability to be self-reflective, they are more perceptive. When Powell says he has a hunch McClane is a cop, the police chief dismisses it. He doesn't value intuition, observation, or anyone in a lower position of power. Powell tells McClane "the guys" and "the boys" appreciate McClane's efforts, which indicates a split between working-class police and the law enforcement power figures.

McClane and Powell also connect through their recognition of family. The two say their children will play together at some future time. When McClane starts to bond with Powell, they share their regrets. They are both living with remorse that isolates them. Powell is living with the guilt of accidentally shooting a thirteen-year-old. McClane has his own confession, when he is the bloodiest after running barefoot through broken glass and when things appear the bleakest for him. McClane painfully picks glass out of his bloody feet, calling to mind the image of a suffering savior in Christian imagery.[251] Facing a possible impending death, he regrets the way he treated his wife: "I should have been more supportive and I just should have been behind her more . . . She's heard me say I love you a thousand times; she never heard me say I'm sorry."

Even after everything he's accomplished, at the end of the film McClane is harassed by law enforcement and the media. McClane is unappreciated by the larger society, but what does matter to him is that his family is restored.[252] Through McClane, the movie offers men a cathartic vehicle to lash out at an oppressive power structured while at the same time learning to become more sensitive to accept female independence.[253]

CHRISTMAS IN ACTION MOVIES

Since the 1934 film *The Thin Man*, action or crime films have utilized Christmas to display an ironic distance between a character's actions and what's associated with the Christmas season, such as spirituality, community, and family. *Lethal Weapon* (1987) is an example of how Christmas is used for irony and characterization but falls short of being a true Christmas action film like

Yes, internet, *Die Hard* (1988) is a Christmas film. John McClane (Bruce Willis) finds redemption and restores his marriage by battling the anti-Christmas terrorists and corporation. Photo courtesy 20th Century Fox/Everett Collection.

Die Hard. Other action-based films such as *Kiss Kiss Bang Bang* (2005), *Three Days of the Condor* (1975), and *Reindeer Games* (2000) also use Christmas imagery as an ironic backdrop without being full-fledged Christmas films. These films do not show Christmas as a transformative force.

Lethal Weapon uses Christmas symbolism ironically at times, such as when Christmas lights are reflected in a mirror where a woman is snorting cocaine and also when a drug deal is made where Christmas trees are sold.[254] Christmas also illustrates the difference between the film's two protagonists. The beginning of the film depicts Roger Murtaugh (Danny Glover) in his warmly lit suburban home with his wife and family. In contrast, Martin Riggs (Mel Gibson) slumps on a sofa alone in his dark, cluttered trailer watching *Bugs Bunny's Christmas Carol* and feeling suicidal because of his wife's death in a car crash.

The emotional states of the two characters are amplified because of the Christmas season. Murtaugh is more connected to his family while Riggs feels despondent in his isolation. Christmas is associated again with family at the end of the film when Riggs is invited into the Murtaugh home, indicating he is part of a community and no longer isolated. However, the movie never allows Riggs to be introspective enough to execute a truly convincing epiphany and utilize Christmas for transformation. Riggs may be in spiritual distress, but he only briefly mentions it. In one quick banter of dialogue Murtaugh says, "God hates me, that's what it is" when he finds out Riggs is his new partner. Riggs says, "Hate him back; it works for me." But the movie never takes this further.

DIVORCE AND MALE ANXIETY

In *Die Hard,* the tension between home life and career creates a crisis for a family that culminates during the Christmas season. But by the end of the film, a family emerges intact. However, some families in Third Wave Christmas films can't resolve parental disagreements. As a result, divorce threatens to sabotage Christmas and the family itself. Many Third Wave Christmas films make divorce the central conflict.

The first major Christmas film to cover this is *All I Want For Christmas* (1991), with the outcome that divorce is incompatible with Christmas and therefore the American family. However, by the 2006 film *Unaccompanied Minors*, children no longer address divorce by attempting to reunite their parents. Their goal is to create a substitute family, not of surrogate parents but of surrogate siblings of other divorced parents. More than a decade later in 2017, in *Daddy's Home 2*, the burden of resolving the dilemma of divorce shifts to divorced fathers. In the era of guilt-ridden parenting because of divided homes and busy work schedules, the children possess power to dictate what the parents do.

A significant Third Wave Christmas film addressing male anxiety about divorce is *The Santa Clause* (1994), where a divorced man transforms into Santa Claus after a rooftop mishap with the real Santa Claus on Christmas Eve. His new role lifts him out of divorce-fueled anger and isolation. He then bonds with his son, develops emotionally to manage divorce, and attains work with purpose. Becoming Santa remasculinizes him against the effects of divorce, which had threatened to make him archaic and incompetent.

In the Third Wave era, divorce affects a man's confidence and makes him angry, insecure, and somewhat immature. This is apparent in the beginning of the film as Scott Calvin (Tim Allen) spends a strained Christmas Eve with his son. There is a palpable emotional distance between Scott and his son. Some of it is because of Scott's dismay and resentment about his ex-wife remarried to a touchy-feely psychologist Neal (Judge Reinhold). He represents a new breed of man who threatens the power of the traditional masculine father figure Scott represents. Neal is a docile New Age version of the villain psychologist in *Miracle on 34th Street*.

However, a supernatural solution occurs after Santa falls off the roof and in an unexplained incident his body disappears, leaving only a Santa suit. Scott puts on the Santa suit and uses the sleigh to deliver presents with his son Charlie by his side. After the Christmas delivery is over, Calvin starts to assume the physical appearance of Santa. Through his new appearance and duties as Santa, Scott possesses heroic qualities his son admires to overcome the threat to his masculinity because of divorce.

Romance may be a contrived end product of *Surviving Christmas* (2004), but the real issue is male neurosis and divorce. When Drew (Ben Affleck) finally confesses what is so disturbing from his childhood Christmas, he reveals that his father left them on Christmas. Because of this he cannot commit or be truthful in a relationship. The arc of the romantic plot in this film is to overcome the fallout from divorce that extends into adulthood. *Four Christmases* (2008) is another movie that on the surface appears to be a Christmas romance, but is really about the effects of divorce that make adult children of divorce incapable of committing in relationships. Initially Brad (Vince Vaughn) and Kate (Reese Witherspoon) vow to stay unmarried and childless. "We're both from families that are divorced," Brad says. "We've seen it play out. We don't need to repeat the pattern." The crisis of masculinity in *Jingle All the Way* (1996) culminates in the threat of divorce because of the father's workaholism and the hazards of a feminized male similar to the Neal character in *The Santa Clause.* The father's search in *Jingle All the Way* for an elusive toy shows the fear fathers feel of disappointing their children.[255] The shopping mission, some of it with ironic use of Christmas music, goes further than most Third Wave films in satirizing consumerism. But it stops short, which makes it an ideologically confused film.[256]

Male anxiety is also shown through the warring male neighbors in *Deck the Halls* (2006), one of the worst Third Wave movies, and in *Jack Frost* (1998), where Jack (Michael Keaton) dies in a car accident and returns as a snowman to mentor his son and repair his regrets about placing too much emphasis on his career. Jack doesn't return to resolve unfinished business with his wife. The message is that the father-son bond is a man's primary role and that men will feel deep regret if they pursue individualistic career goals too voraciously.

Besides divorce, other family dilemmas lead to a crisis in masculinity for Third Wave Christmas protagonists. In *I'll Be Home for Christmas*, Jake (Jonathan Taylor Thomas) must accept his new stepmother after his father remarries following the death of his mother. *Christmas with the Kranks* (2004) covers the effect of empty-nest syndrome on Luther Krank (Tim Allen), who convinces his wife Nora (Jamie Lee Curtis) to skip Christmas because their daughter won't be home. But Luther doesn't fall into a full-blown mid-life crisis. This movie isn't that deep. Luther calculates they spent more than $6,000 on Christmas the year before. For half the money, they can go on a Caribbean cruise starting on Christmas Day. They vow to boycott all Christmas activities. However, the couple receives a torrent of criticism, antagonism, and biting comments from neighbors, co-workers, and even their priest. But after their daughter unexpectedly calls to say she's returning home for Christmas, neighbors who harassed and shunned the Kranks put together a Christmas Eve party to welcome her back. For the Kranks, Christmas is worth celebrating only when the nuclear family can be together.

IF NOT CHRISTMAS, THEN WHEN? CHRISTMAS ROMANCES IN THE THIRD WAVE

Although mending family problems is the prevailing story arc in Third Wave Christmas films, a handful of Christmas films feature romance as the central subject. Romance-based Christmas films show the Christmas season as a period when emotions are elevated. Thus, a single person is acutely aware of the loneliness of not having a romantic partner and therefore more likely to pursue romance.

There's a significant difference between Christmas romances from the World War II era and Third Wave romances. First Wave movies often make the choice of a romantic partner a moral and spiritual decision. Also, a balance occurs between the viewpoints of the male and female protagonists, where they usually both pursue each other during different stages of the relationship. However, Third Wave romances are largely from a male point of view, with an infatuated male pursuing a woman.

This is particularly pronounced in *Love Actually* (2003), featuring a collection of characters and narratives during the Christmas season in England. Most of the storylines involve men aggressively pursuing a partner who is either in a different social class, a temptress, or someone who appears to be unattainable. To achieve the object of their intended conquest, they go to obsessive levels to chase the object of their infatuation. A British prime minister (Hugh Grant) pursues Natalie (Martine McCutcheon), one of his staff members; writer Jamie (Colin Firth) falls for Aurélia (Lúcia Moniz), an exotic Portugese housecleaner; Daniel (Liam Neeson) encourages his son Sam (Thomas Sangster) to pursue the most popular girl in Sam's school. Colin Frissell (Kris Marshall) leaves England for America, where he instantly establishes himself as a babe magnet because of his British accent. Even marriage is not a deterrent for obsession. A groom's best man, Mark (Andrew Lincoln), is secretly in love with his best friend's wife, Juliet (Keira Knightley). A married business executive, Harry (Alan Rickman), is tempted by his secretary, Mia (Heike Makatsch). The message in these plotlines is to man up and chase your woman. As Jamie says to his family gathered for Christmas before he leaves to pursue Aurelia, "A man's gotta do what a man's gotta do." Romance is such a strong pull in *Love Actually* that it supersedes family.

The portrayal of love in *Love Actually* is a product of physical attraction and requires virtually no verbal communication or emotional affinity.[257] Several of the characters have little or no conversation with the women they are pursuing, including Colin Firth, who must learn Portuguese to ask a woman to marry him. Sam hasn't even spoken to the girl in his class who is the object of his obsession. Hugh Grant's character only has a few short conversations with his assistant before she declares his love for him in a card and he goes on a Christmas Eve search for her. Daniel says he'll only date someone after his wife's death if she looks like

Most of the storylines in *Love Actually* (2003) feature men obsessively pursuing women they barely know. That includes the English prime minister (Hugh Grant), who chases after his staff member, Natalie (Martine McCutcheon). Photo courtesy Universal/Everett Collection.

Claudia Schiffer. And that happens. A woman named Carol (played by Claudia Schiffer) becomes Daniel's new love interest. In the famous cue card doorway scene, Mark writes that he'll only get over Juliet by marrying one of four supermodels whose photos he's fastened to a card. Colin goes to America to find women, believing women there are easier targets, because English women are too stuck up. On his first night in America he instantly meets three sexually assertive and attractive women and returns to England with two attractive sisters (played by ex-models Shannon Elizabeth and Denise Richards).

Women who don't fit this fantasy version of a romantic partner and who have other priorities are lonely and discontented. Sarah (Laura Linney) abruptly stops a sexual liaison with a long-sought-after partner because she must take a phone call from her mentally ill brother. She apparently cannot pursue a relationship because of her devotion to her brother. The movie portrays Karen (Emma Thompson) as a cold person whose iciness may have left a void in her marriage.

Perhaps the intense pursuit of an idealized version of beauty in *Love Actually* is based on an ideology inherent in another Christmas romance, *Serendipity* (2001): the "soul mate." That's someone who in the film's definition of spirituality fate brings together with another. In the film, Jonathan Trager (John Cusack) and Sara Thomas (Kate Beckinsale) reach to buy the same pair of gloves in a department store while Christmas shopping. After some banter, they go to a restaurant called Serendipity because Sara says it's her spiritual philosophy. "I don't really believe in accidents; I think fate's behind everything," she says. After a gust of wind blows away Sara's phone number, she refuses to give it to Jonathan again. She insists fate must bring them together. Because of Sara's interpretation of fate, she cannot make a decision, which leads both of them into substandard relationships that keep them apart for years. It's an ideology that appears to leave one both powerless to make decisions and powerless to believe in a higher power that can be attentive to one's needs.

While You Were Sleeping (1995) and *The Holiday* (2006) are atypical for Third Wave films because women play the dominant roles. However, the appeal of a partner in *While You Were Sleeping* is that he also provides a new family to Lucy Moderatz (Sandra Bullock), whose parents have died. In *The Holiday*, two women don't need family to define themselves; they create new identities without it. Using a website where people can temporarily swap houses, Iris Simkins (Kate Winslet), an English journalist who finds out the man she is in love with is engaged to someone else, trades houses for the Christmas season with American Amanda (Cameron Diaz), a movie trailer editor who finds out her live-in boyfriend is cheating on her. Because they are largely removed from family, they create identities for themselves through work and romantic relationships. They appear to have no real friendships or connections. In their family-deprived world, without romantic partners, they are lost. Instead of returning to a supportive family, these solitary figures use their economic status and technology to build a new identity.

The most interesting Christmas romance is *Family Man* (2000), which updates both Scrooge's fateful decision to choose business over marriage and explores a "what if" idea influenced by *It's a Wonderful Life*: What if George Bailey never married his wife and followed his own ambitions instead?

Jack Campbell (Nicholas Cage) is leaving for an internship at a financial company in London. His girlfriend Kate (Tea Leoni) plans to go to law school. They say they'll reunite in a year. But as he's about to board the plane, Kate says she has a bad feeling. She wants to start building a life together right away. But Jack insists they stick to their plan. Like Ebenezer Scrooge choosing business over love when he won't marry his fiancée, Jack gets on the airplane.

Thirteen years later, Jack is an unmarried workaholic executive. While walking home alone on Christmas Eve after helping prevent a robbery, a mysterious man hints to him that maybe Jack doesn't have all he thinks he does. When Jack wakes up the next day, he's married to Kate and they live in suburban New Jersey with two children. The movie never offers a clear explanation of whether this alternative life is a dream or is a supernatural occurrence. But whatever the reason for what later is called a "glimpse" of another life, Jack figures out that in this alternate life he came back the next day on the plane from England. He and Kate have been together ever since. In the scenario, like George Bailey, he sacrificed ambition for a family life.

The movie comes down on the side of suburban family life despite its limitations. Like *It's A Wonderful Life*, the compromises and sacrifices required for a home life and children are more fulfilling than the individualism of career success. And like First Wave Christmas movies, it shows that small family business is superior to big city business. Perhaps the reason the movie didn't succeed at the box office is because it doesn't offer a happy ending. It concludes with the weight of loss because of decisions one makes. As in *A Christmas Carol*, it shows the enormous consequences of choosing worldly ambition over marriage.

12

I'm Dreaming of a Dark Christmas

Black Comedies, Stanley Kubrick, and Christmas Horror

With so much emphasis on family in Third Wave Christmas movies, a backlash against idealized presentations of families at Christmas developed. Some Third Wave Christmas movies explore how emotional or physical separation from family creates neurosis, anger, and depression. Some of these films are black comedies, some horror movies, others the product of visionary directors using Christmas to express social commentary.

BLACK COMEDIES

A few films employ what is called either black comedy or dark comedy to make Christmas a holiday that encompasses either violence or severe neurosis. Black comedy focuses on the macabre, the vulgar, and the grotesque, with disturbing subject matter often consisting of violence, death, or mental instability. Andre Breton coined the phrase in 1940 when he compiled an anthology of writers representing the genre, including Edgar Allen Poe, Baudelaire, and Nietzsche. They wrote in different styles in diverse eras but the common ground is that black comedy is "the mortal enemy of sentimentality."[258]

Third Wave Christmas movies are notable for sentimentality because of the reverence for family. Even Third Wave films that flirt with black comedy such as *A Christmas Story* ultimately rein the story back into sentimentality. But during the 1990s, black comedy movies became mainstream. *Heathers* (1988), *The War of the Roses* (1989), and *Pulp Fiction* (1994) were successful, and the black-comedy-fueled *Fargo* (1996) and *American Beauty* (1999) both won Academy Awards for Best Picture. Black comedies suited a postmodern era where universal and traditional truths in narratives were subverted or scorned.

In 1994, three Christmas-focused black comedies were released. Because the approach was new for the genre, it produced very mixed results. The most disjointed is *Mixed Nuts*, where characters affiliated with a suicide hotline serve as a surrogate family. Rather than spiritual transformation, the film shows the chaos and absurdity of life working against the characters until an ending makeshift nativity-laced birth scene. *Trapped in Paradise* also uses black comedy and an atmosphere of crime-fueled chaos but concludes with bank robber Bill Firpo (Nicholas Cage) deciding to stay in a small town, a throwback to a theme in First Wave films.

Both *Trapped in Paradise* and *Mixed Nuts* use black comedy elements but end with sentimental transformations. There is no such sentimentality in *The Ref* (1994). Instead of a criminal undergoing redemption, the outcast and outspoken criminal not only escapes but becomes the most likeable and truthful character. The movie suggests it is the affluent suburbanites who need redemption, not the criminal. If there's any growth in the characters it's generated by Gus (Dennis Leary), who robs upscale houses on Christmas Eve and holds a squabbling married couple, Caroline (Judy Davis) and Lloyd (Kevin Spacey), hostage.

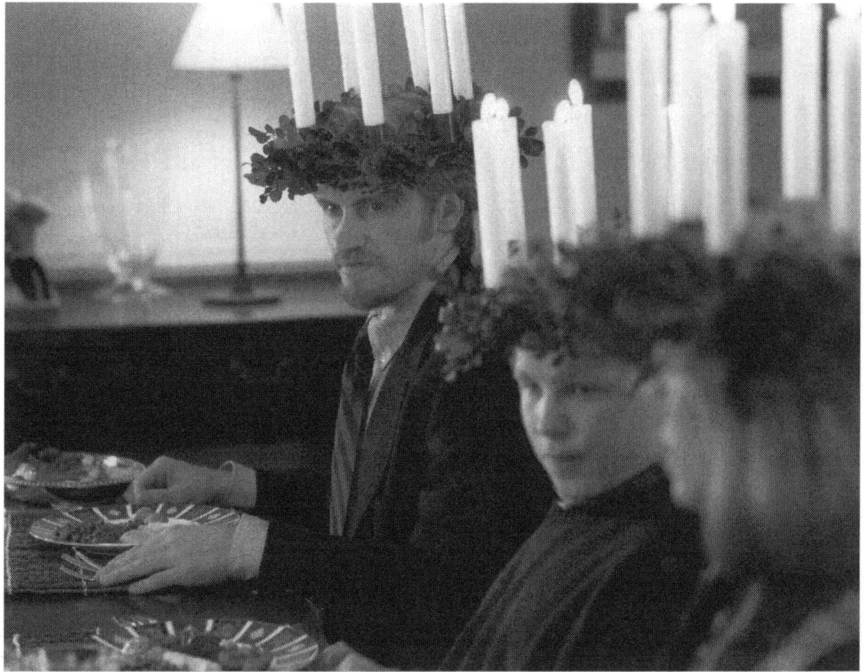

The burglar Gus (Denis Leary) participates in a Christmas celebration in *The Ref* (1994). Gus calls out the suburbanites for their hypocrisy in one of the Christmas genre's best black comedies. Photo courtesy Touchstone/Everett Collection.

This film is much more consistent than *Mixed Nuts* and *Trapped in Paradise* because it unyieldingly aims at an explicit target: upscale suburbia with its affluence, dysfunctional families, and old money roots embodied by Lloyd's tyrannical mother Rose (Glynis Johns). Gus serves as a mediator, faux psychologist, and social class critic. He directs some of his wrath at the upper-middle-class lifestyle, which he views as generating entitlement, insulation, and laziness. Gus voices outrage about how the family members treat each other. "You're supposed to be a family; how can you talk to each other like that?" he asks and later tells Lloyd's mother, "I know loan sharks that are more forgiving than you." Gus acts as a surrogate psychologist to confront the characters about their problems, which ultimately empowers them.

After these movies underperformed at the box office, this subgenre stopped for about a decade. It emerged again in 2005 with *The Ice Harvest*, a film noir–inspired black comedy. The moral and spiritual vacuousness of the characters is more far reaching than in previous Christmas black comedies. They cannot forge positive relationships because they possess an emotional numbness and lack of self-knowledge that produces dishonest and manipulative relationships.

The film's director, Harold Ramis, said the movie is an exploration of existentialism. The central tenants of existentialist ideology, according to Ramis, are that "life is meaningless, that we're all going to die, that we're alone in the universe, and we're responsible for everything we do."[259] This manifests in the film as "people who have lost any sense of meaning in their lives," as Ramis says.[260] The characters don't find purpose in the areas of life where most people find it: work, families, and friendships. So they distract themselves from their inner turmoil with alcohol and a seedy world of strip clubs and pornography.

The characters in *The Ice Harvest* have a dark restlessness that manifests in violence, sex, and drinking. The only thing they think may change their unhappiness is an outlaw dream of freedom.[261] Thus, lawyer Charles Arglist (John Cusack) and pornography dealer Vic Cavanaugh (Billy Bob Thornton) steal $2 million from a mob boss. The movie subverts the Christmas movie genre by having the longing for redemption come through money, not through a spiritual or moral epiphany. The result of this pursuit is violence, which unfolds during the night as the characters plan their getaway on a bleak rainy Christmas Eve.

Earlier in the film, there's a revealing exchange where Charlie and Pete (Oliver Platt) talk about life as chaotic without a sense of justice or fairness:

"Everybody has regrets," Platt says. "Guys our age, what else is there?"

"It is futile to regret," Charlie says. "You do one thing, you do another, I mean, so what? What's the difference? Same result."

Charlie illustrates this with a story about his father and his uncle. They both die prematurely within a day of each other. One led a good life; the other did not. Charlie doesn't see the ultimate outcome as any different. Because he's living in a consumerist culture, it's the end game that matters, not the person one becomes despite the external results. In existentialism, when people make their own meaning from life, they can create something positive out of it. But these characters are so far beyond connection, so numb, and so far on the fringes they appear incapable of finding meaning.

CHRISTMAS HORROR

Starting in the 1970s, a subgenre of Christmas horror movies emerged that associate violence with Christmas. Christmas horror conveys fear by making familiar icons of Christmas frightening. Several of these films are what critic Kim Newman calls "the psycho Santa slasher film."[262] In movies such as *Christmas Evil* (1980) and *Silent Night Deadly Night* (1984), deranged men dressed as Santa Claus go on murder sprees. Other symbols associated with Christmas also became violent threats, such as a snowman in *Jack Frost* (1997) and elves in *Elves* (1989).

Black Christmas (1974) was the first notable movie to inject horror into the Christmas movie genre by, like film noir Christmas films, using Christmas as a backdrop to violence. *Black Christmas* is a slasher film with an unseen male killer terrorizing a group of women in a sorority house. It's significant not only for being the first significant Christmas horror movie but for creating many devices employed in the slasher film genre. These include point-of-view shots from the killer's perspective, primitive methods of killing victims with knives and other objects, a killer motivated by a psychosexual fury, and what film critic Carol Clover labels the "final girl," the distressed but courageous female character who ultimately confronts the killer.[263] Clover points out that on the surface it appears horror films want the audience to identify with the male killer. But she argues the audience identifies with "final girl," not the killer.[264] In *Black Christmas*, the "final girl" is Jess Bradford (Olivia Hussey), a prototype for the "final girl" in films such as *Halloween*, *A Nightmare on Elm Street*, and *Friday the 13th*.

The film contains a feminist perspective absent from most slasher films that would follow. *Black Christmas* depicts a threatening, incompetent, and controlling patriarchy. Because the killer isn't shown and the only sounds he makes over the phone are threats and psychotic ramblings, the killer is a symbol of the dark side of the male id threatening the solidarity of the women who live together. Almost all the male characters are seriously flawed. They provide no salvation to the women in the film.[265] Jess's angry and neurotic boyfriend Peter tries to control her, and the men in law enforcement are largely incompetent or unhelpful. The girls are a surrogate family that decorates the sorority house with a Christmas tree and Christmas lights. The killer invades and violates this feminine domestic sphere. Christmas is used ironically during a scene when Christmas carolers sing as the killer stabs one of the women, Barbara (Margot Kidder), with a unicorn figure. Her screams aren't heard over the singing. The film also uses Christmas imagery by subverting the genre's birth narrative when Jess declares she will have an abortion.

Some 1980s Christmas horror films follow the conventions of the slasher genre of *Black Christmas* but shift the killer to a misguided, damaged, and maladjusted individual who dresses as Santa Claus. These films are based on the novelty of reshaping the benevolent character of Santa Claus into an instrument of terror. The pattern in these films is that a child experiences a trauma related to Santa Claus and then later, as an adult, the disturbed individual adopts the persona of Santa Claus to inflict violence.

In addition to this trope of undergoing a traumatizing Santa experience as a child, *Christmas Evil* (1980) borrows heavily from 1970s antihero films. The protagonist is more a misguided vigilante Santa Claus than a deranged individual. One writer describes the film as "The *Taxi Driver* of Christmas Movies."[266] The film's director, Lewis Jackson, considers the protagonist "an innocent gone wrong."[267]

As a child, Harry Stadling (Brandon Maggart) is disturbed after seeing his mother seduced by his father dressed as Santa Claus. Years later he works in a toy factory and lives a secret fantasy life as Santa Claus. After realizing he's an object of ridicule, he dons the Santa suit to enact his definition of justice, which means toys for children and death for anyone who disparages him. *Christmas Evil* is in some ways a tragedy about an outsider driven to murder after being bullied. In the "psycho Santa" movies, he is the most sympathetic deranged Santa, more consistent with an ambivalent psychological antihero than a maniac killer.

Although it's gained a cult following, the quirky *Christmas Evil* remains in the shadow of the inferior *Silent Night Deadly Night* (1984), another "psycho Santa" film that became notorious even before its release. After lurid TV ads featuring an upcoming movie about an ax-wielding Santa aired, parent organizations formed a campaign against the film. The controversy forced the movie studio to not only yank the ads but cut short

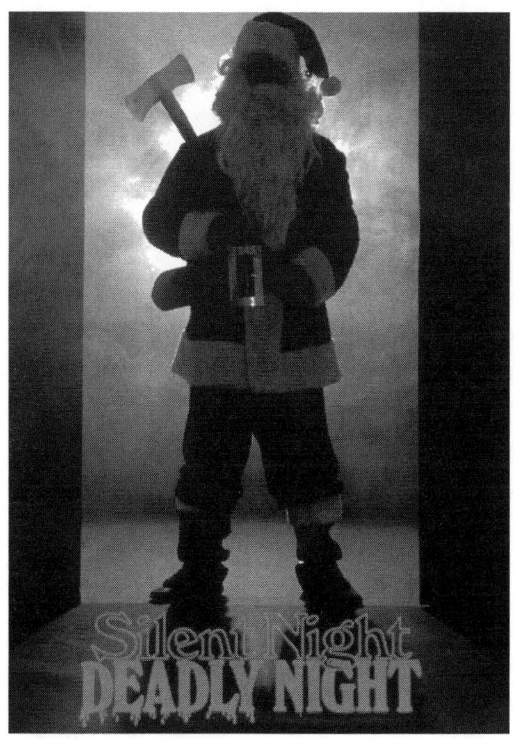

The most notorious "psycho Santa" film is *Silent Night Deadly Night* (1984). After protests over both its advertising campaign and the film, the film was pulled from some movie theaters. Photo courtesy Tristar Pictures/Everett Collection.

the film's run in theaters. Even though the film's run ended prematurely, the notoriety persisted. The movie's marketing machine exploited the idea that audiences were prevented from seeing it. When the movie was rereleased a year later, the movie poster read "They tried to ban it" and "They didn't want you to see it!"

Another reason the film was remembered over the years was the reevaluation of slasher films. Critics largely dismissed most slasher films at the time of their release. But in the 1990s some academics elevated slasher films that were once dismissed as sexist and loaded with gratuitous violence. Some film scholars recategorized slasher films by pointing out what they believed were more complicated themes. They wrote about the "final girl" prototype of a brave young woman confronting the threat of the male killer and how deranged killers are part of a larger statement about violence in American culture.

As a result, the substandard *Silent Night Deadly Night* (which doesn't have the "final girl" trope as *Black Christmas* does) was placed in a canonized group of films from the mid-1970s through the mid-1980s that included *The Texas Chainsaw Massacre*, *Halloween*, and *Friday The 13th*. Because *Silent Night Deadly Night* was released during the same era as those other films, it helped the enduring reputation of the film. Still, it's impossible to separate the film from the media controversy. The film's depiction of a murdering Santa Claus and the backlash against it exposed a cultural dichotomy in Santa Claus between Santa's judgmental nature and his generous characteristics. Usually in American pop culture that dichotomy tipped in favor of the jovial and benevolent figure. The "psycho Santa" film elevated the punishing attributes. It manifested in a damaged adult character who violated and exploited the trust children established in Santa Claus.

While *Christmas Evil* makes the grownup person a misguided and at times somewhat sympathetic vigilante, *Silent Night Deadly Night* turns the protagonist into an unsympathetic frenzied killer. *Silent Night Deadly Night* is a botched attempt at a psychological portrait of a man traumatized by violence. Five-year-old Billy's parents stop to help a man dressed as Santa Claus who appears to need help. However, the man murders Billy's father and rapes and murders his mother. Billy is sent to a Catholic orphanage where there are two differing approaches on how to deal with Billy's trauma. His teacher Sister Margaret (Gilmer McCormick) believes Billy must be dealt with kindly because "it's still inside him, all the terrible violence he saw," as she says to Mother Superior (Lilyan Chauvin). But the Mother Superior is unsympathetic and more interested in punishing Billy for his disobedience. As a young adult, Billy works in a toy store and, after being forced to be a fill-in Santa, Billy in the Santa suit warns the children about Santa's wrath. At the store's Christmas party, he sees a worker trying to rape an employee and kills both the rapist and the victim—one with a string of Christmas lights. He goes on to commit a series of murders.

The film never explains why Billy adopts the persona of the figure he was traumatized by. However, a somewhat coherent theme is that the most dangerous figures are related to religion and the supernatural. The Mother Superior represents the unmerciful, nonempathetic punishment associated with a stern and unforgiving definition of Christianity. The film also defines Santa Claus (who with his supernatural characteristics becomes a figure of faith in some Christmas films) as a punishing figure. These characters represent an unmerciful and punishing interpretation of Christianity. This contrasts with Sister Margaret, who is compassionate toward Billy. But in *Silent Night Deadly Night*, hers is a minority view.

While the psycho slasher Santas adopt their own individual twisted notions of punishment, the idea of a darker side to Christmas manifested in a surge in the popularity of the figure Krampus, a half-goat, half-demon folk figure. In festivities dating back to the 1600s in Austria and Germany, someone dressed as St. Nicholas offers small gifts to good children while Krampus rattles chains and shakes birch switches to intimidate bad children.[268] In folk legends, Krampus collaborates with St. Nicholas to ensure children behave properly.[269] This was a tradition in Europe for many years, but recently in the United States, Krampus festivals, parades, and pub crawls are becoming increasingly prevalent.

However, in Krampus's most popular depiction in a Christmas film, he is severed from St. Nicholas to become an anti–Santa Claus. *Krampus* (2015) extracts the figure of Krampus from its European tradition to adhere to a horror movie convention of constructing a menacing supernatural force. There isn't the "naughty" and "nice" dichotomy of St. Nicholas as a rewarding being and Krampus as a punishing entity. Instead, St. Nicholas is absent and Krampus is an unbridled force inflicting punishment, fear, and even death. Krampus becomes an extension of the psycho slasher Santa.[270] Instead of being St. Nicholas's disciplinarian, Krampus is a deitylike figure who unleashes forces to terrify and punish.

In *Krampus,* punishment is triggered by a lack of belief in Santa Claus, who is often in the Christmas movie genre a metaphor for spiritual belief. The movie depicts a fear of retribution from a vengeful supernatural force that punishes unbelievers. However, in the family-obsessed Third Wave era, what triggers the disbelief is a breakdown of the family. Family dysfunction is why the protagonist loses faith in Santa Claus, which unleashes the violence of Krampus and his frightening underlings. But because of the Third Wave's obsession with family, the movie follows the convention of restoring a dysfunctional family under threat. The invasive supernatural entities give the sparring family members a common enemy.

As in *Gremlins*, evil forces attack the technology the suburbanites are dependent on. But *Krampus* is never daring enough to imply that a supernatural force punishes the suburbanites because of collective wrongs such as materialism or consumerism. Instead, it's triggered by Max's declaration of a lack of faith in Santa Claus and thereby a disbelief in the supernatural. The movie is also surprisingly devoid of Krampus. Most of the attacks on the family come from a legion of minions ranging from the comic to the surreal.

THE AUTEUR'S CHRISTMAS: VISIONARY DIRECTORS MAKE CULTURAL OBSERVATIONS

Two directors (Tim Burton and Stanley Kubrick) made Christmas films in the auteur tradition of a filmmaker exerting distinctive creative control. They both used associations of Christmas with benevolence, community, and family to contrast it with a culture centered on sex, violence, hedonism, conformity, and greed.

Instead of churning out an imitation sequel after the massive success of *Batman* (1989), director Tim Burton used his clout to make a movie set at Christmastime incorporating a combination of horror movie conventions, German expressionism, and dystopian elements.

Batman Returns (1992) opens on Christmas with the wealthy parents of a violent and deformed baby throwing their newborn child inside a baby carriage into a river in a subversion of the birth associated with Christmas.[271] The baby carriage floats down the water until a group of penguins discover the creature and raise it. More than thirty years later, Gotham City is a dystopian city. Schreck (Christopher Walken) is a ravenous businessman building a monopoly. "One can never have too much power; if my life has a meaning, that's the meaning," is his philosophy. *Batman Returns* presents a grim view of society. It's being destroyed from within by an establishment that appears respectable but is deeply corrupt. And it's being attacked from outside by thugs led by the abandoned baby who, now in his thirties, is dubbed the Penguin (Danny DeVito). Another threatening villain is Selina Kyle (Michelle Pfeiffer), who, after being a mousy assistant to Schreck, transforms into the criminal Catwoman.

In dystopian literature, the rebels and outcasts are often heroes who overthrow the establishment. But in *Batman Returns*, the oppressed, marginalized, and rejected characters Penguin and Catwoman instigate violence, sometimes aimed at the innocent. Instead, the film's hero is Bruce Wayne (Michael Keaton), who uses his Batman persona to impart a brand of justice that works within the system, as corrupt as it is. Batman is the dispassionate, detached man of few words. His moral dominance in the film indicates the idealization of the moderate over the chaotic revenge of the underclass and the corruption of the establishment. As much as *Batman Returns* is a visual marvel and contains social commentary akin to a dystopia, Burton can't escape the campiness that ultimately undermines a larger critique of a corrupt culture.

Batman Returns is the second in a trilogy of films Burton created that feature Christmas. Before *Batman Returns* and *The Nightmare Before Christmas* was *Edward Scissorhands* (1990), where a suburban Christmas shows an inability to accept "the other" different from the dominant group. The protagonist is so physically different in appearance, intention, and personality he cannot successfully integrate. This makes him an outcast Christ figure while Christmas serves as the culmination of the community's shunning of him. The suburbia of *Edward Scissorhands* is not a community capable of showing acceptance of "the other." The Christ figure Edward (Johnny Depp) must ultimately ascend back to a celestial home (his castle outside of town) because the community cannot appreciate or understand him.

Stanley Kubrick's *Eyes Wide Shut* (1999) integrates Christmas into the mis-en-scène of the film to embellish the filmmaker's commentary on contemporary American culture. Christmas serves as a backdrop to Kubrick's story that is both psychological, sociological, and spiritual.

On the psychological level, it shows that underneath its façade of upper-middle-class comfort, a marriage contains concealed fantasies and urges. It's a descent into the psyches of the characters, from which they try to emerge more self-aware.[272] The movie is also a sociological odyssey through a culture with a rigid and oppressive class structure ruled by a dominant oligarchy that exploits and oppresses. The patriarchal ruling class subjugates women of the lower classes and delivers retribution to the film's protagonist, who threatens their power.[273] In the end, the odyssey the protagonist Bill Hartford (Tom Cruise) undertakes leads to, not genuine transformation, but a return to a flawed status quo. The film emphasizes Kubrick's belief that "most of humanity is not quite bright enough to know what they want and plan how to get it."[274]

The mis-en-scène of Christmas décor does much more than just establish that a film is set during the Christmas season. Christmas lights and paraphernalia become an extension of character and social class. At a party given by the oligarch Victor Ziegler (Sydney Pollock), the Christmas decorations are ostentatious and merely spectacle. In a sex worker's apartment, a modest Christmas tree indicates her lower economic status. In the apartment that Bill and his wife Alice (Nicole Kidman) share, the decorations give the appearance of a family Christmas. Two important scenes that in some ways parallel each other—the scene of Ziegler around his pool table telling Bill about the party, and the secret society—do not have any Christmas trees. Christmas songs aren't performed at Victor's party. The absence of Christmas in these scenes shows how distant the characters are from the ideals associated with Christmas. Kubrick uses Christmas imagery in a way no other filmmaker has. He creates a dreamscape the characters inhabit that establishes a conflict between the culture they live in and the spirituality of sacrifice and salvation Christmas imagery is associated with.[275]

The Christ figure attribute of self-sacrifice comes in an unlikely situation, during a party Bill goes to featuring the oligarchy engaging in orgies between masked characters. The wayward Bill is threatened, but a masked naked woman says she will sacrifice herself for Bill so he can escape unharmed. The woman, who stands like a crucified Jesus, is transformed from sex worker into a savior.[276] It is this idea of self-sacrifice—associated with Jesus, who sacrifices himself on the cross—that Bill responds to. In his somewhat empty life and his misguided search for some sensation or meaning, this act of self-sacrifice holds meaning for him.

In some ways the film is a commentary on how relationships are based on sexual possibilities.[277] But the movie also de-eroticizes sex through a dispassionate employment of nudity. This reflects what Kubrick's wife said of the film, that "it has nothing to do with sex and everything to do with fear."[278] Sex is either a vehicle of exploitation or the unleashing of dark impulses that take one away from fidelity. In its tour of the underbelly of New York, the movie also depicts the social problems of contemporary times, including AIDS, drug use, hedonism, homophobia, and income inequality.[279]

Despite the nudity and sometimes disturbing events and subject matter, *Eyes Wide Shut* is a deeply moral commentary on how decadent contemporary culture is under its façade of comfort and respectability. It also shows a culture divided into distinct social classes, with Victor representing the wealthy oligarchy, Bill and Alice the upper middle class, and the sex workers an exploited proletariat. Bill realizes during the course of the film that he's dominated by an older male order and threatened by the feminine independence of his wife.[280] Despite the harrowing psychological and sociological journey, the protagonists aren't empathetic. The result is that the viewer can't fully engage with the two main characters.[281] Alice comes across as privileged and aloof and Bill largely has shallow or superficial responses to many events.[282] When Bill finally collapses into tears and confesses to Alice what has happened, it is not really about psychological, moral, or spiritual insight he's attained; it's as if he is a child who underwent a frightening experience.

Unlike *Less Than Zero* or Christmas black comedies, *Eyes Wide Shut* doesn't use Christmas symbolism as blatant irony. In *Eyes Wide Shut*, there is a more subtle moral distance in the culture and the characters from what Christmas represents, including spiritual rejuvenation, antimaterialism, and community. Kubrick's final film is a compelling social commentary on how far contemporary society has come from values typically associated with Christmas.

13

The Minority Report
A Return to Transcendentalism

Third Wave films reshaped Christmas as a secular family holiday. However, a minority of films continued the traditional Christmas movie genre themes of condemning materialism and putting characters through a transformative spiritual awakening.

Some include innocent, childlike, or naïve characters having faith in the transcendental despite a cynical or antagonistic world. In *Ernest Saves Christmas* (1988), the innocent character is Ernest, a happy-go-lucky cab driver who, like John Payne's character in *Miracle on 34th Street*, sacrifices his job for his belief in Santa Claus. *One Magic Christmas* (1985) features the child Abby as a believer in the transcendental and portrays Santa Claus as a godlike figure. When Abby visits Santa at the North Pole, she recognizes a janitor at her school who died but now works in Santa's workshop. It's clear she's gone to the afterlife, where Santa (the God figure) dwells. In *Arthur Christmas* (2011), which details Santa's operation to distribute Christmas gifts, the film expresses anxiety about technology replacing "magic," a metaphor for the spiritual. It's up to the humble, innocent Arthur to correct this.

A supernatural experience occurs in one plotline in *Noel* (2004), where a woman visiting her mother in a hospital on Christmas Eve encounters a mysterious stranger who helps her overcome her doubts about the existence of God. Tyler Perry's comedy *A Madea Christmas* (2013) features a character who in her feisty way is a crusader for the transcendental and for creating community. Madea (Tyler Perry) executes an unorthodox combination of moralism, politically incorrect humor, and sincere but unconventional religiosity to overcome racism, political correctness, and corporate greed—at least in one small southern town.

TRADING PLACES: FINANCIAL OVERLORDS WITH GODLIKE POWERS

Trading Places (1983)—set during the Christmas season with much of the action occurring between the double peak of Christmas Eve and New Year's—is in some ways a reworking of Mark Twain's *The Prince and the Pauper*, about two characters from different social positions exchanging roles. But in this variation, the men have their lives altered by financial overlords with deitylike powers to control lives.

Randolph and Mortimer Duke (brilliantly played by Ralph Bellamy and Don Ameche) disagree about an article in a science magazine regarding whether heredity or environment shapes an individual's destiny. So they devise an experiment to switch the social positions of wealthy commodities broker Louis Winthorpe (Dan Aykroyd) with street beggar/con man Billy Ray Valentine (Eddie Murphy). They conspire to take Valentine off the streets of Philadelphia and put him in Winthorpe's luxury home. They also give him Winthorpe's high-paying job at their financial company. At the same time, they strip Winthorpe of his job, home, money, and social connections to test whether he will turn to a life of crime.

Randolph's idea to take away Winthorpe's good fortune is reminiscent of the Book of Job, where Job's good fortune is taken away after a wager

In *Trading Places*, deitylike financial overlords rearrange the lives of Billy Ray Valentine (Eddie Murphy) and Louis Winthorpe III (Dan Aykroyd). But the duo work together to turn the tables on the bigoted moguls with the Christmas season as a backdrop to social and racial injustice. Photo courtesy Paramount/Everett Collection.

between God and Satan.[283] Mortimer defends Winthorpe, similar to how God says the "blameless and upright" Job is prosperous, dutiful, and "turn[s] away from evil."[284] In the Book of Job, Satan encourages God to "stretch out your hand now, and touch all that he has, and he will curse you to your face."[285] God agrees to see what happens and lets Satan inflict suffering on Job. So Job loses his property, his servants, his children, and his health as Satan imposes painful sores on him. In *Trading Places*, the wealthy financial magnates Randolph and Mortimer possess similar god-like powers to impose suffering. Randolph hopes to see Winthorpe curse his fate as Satan hoped to see Job curse his fate.

The movie forces the audience to consider the moral and spiritual consequences of economic determinism and social stratification. This is set up at the beginning of the film during the opening credits, a masterful series of images that recall the montages of the early Soviet filmmaker Eisenstein, who contrasted shots to create harsh collisions that are jolting and dialectical.[286] Images of symbols and icons of American history—including the Liberty Bell, Independence Hall, and sculptures of American political and war figures as well as powerful institutions such as Philadelphia's ornate City Hall and the Dukes' company—contrast with images of homeless people and unemployment lines.

First Wave Christmas films depict greed in the business world as an enormous obstacle to spiritual and moral growth. Usually this is shown by characters choosing career over relationships or a potential romantic partner who overvalues money and materialism. *Trading Places* presents a deterministic view of the world. The characters don't have the free choice that characters in First Wave movies have to change their spiritual condition. Unlike First Wave films, *Trading Places* depicts economic deprivation not as something to endure, or a noble sacrifice for one's principles, but as a circumstance creating despair, violence, and racism.

Although *Trading Places* criticizes the power structure and the financial system, it approves of material success for the worthy. It redistributes wealth from the bigoted "old boy network" represented by the Dukes to a more inclusive team, which include Winthorpe and Valentine, the two victims of the bet, as well as a sex worker (Jamie Lee Curtis) and Winthorpe's servant (Denholm Elliott). Winthorpe's redemption occurs after he's removed from his elitist network. He's exposed to the lower classes, which has a humanizing effect on him.

GREMLINS: SUBURBIA AS A FALLEN EDEN

In most Third Wave films the family suburban home is revered as the ideal setting for Christmas. In *Gremlins* (1984), it's a place of dysfunction and irresponsibility. *Gremlins* also examines the perils of consumerism, overreliance on technology at the expense of real human connection, and how humans create disorder because of negligence, disobedience, and self-centeredness.

Inventor Randall Peltzer (Hoyt Axton) is an incompetent and manipulative entrepreneur who is ambitious with his business dealings—traditionally an indication of a flawed character in the Christmas movie genre. He visits a store and spots a small furry animal called a mogwai he wants to buy for his son Billy (Zach Galligan) for Christmas. The owner, Mr. Wing (Keye Luke), declines. "With mogwai comes much responsibility; I cannot sell him at any price," he warns. But his grandson sells the creature to Randall. He cautions Randall about three directions he must obey about the mogwai: don't expose him to light, don't get him wet, and never feed him after midnight. Like God's warning to Adam and Eve in the Garden of Eden, the instructions are ignored or fumbled and enormous consequences follow. After water is poured onto the mogwai—renamed Gizmo—he spawns mogwai more devious than himself. After they trick Billy into feeding them after midnight, they turn into podlike forms they call gremlins, which change into rebellious, hedonistic, violent, and uncontrollable creatures.

A climactic scene occurs in the typical center for Christmas commercialism, a department store. The major areas of devastation in the film are consumerist centers including the suburban home and the shopping mall.[287] Later, Wing reprimands the suburbanites. "You do with mogwai what your society has done with all of nature's gifts," he says. "You do not understand; you are not ready." Wing frames the movie with a warning at the beginning and a condemnation at the end.

Wing makes the movie's most substantial statements about the spiritual shortcomings of modern American culture. But *Gremlins* also uses conventions of the horror movie genre to formulate social and spiritual commentary. Horror movies are often about the collective anxieties and fears a culture holds.[288] *Gremlins* conveys specific fears of the 1980s: consumerism, technology, and the dysfunction of suburban living that creates negligence, unhealthy escapism, and lack of community.

To contrast this with the themes of First Wave films, the setting of *Gremlins* reworks the locale of *It's a Wonderful Life.* Billy works in a bank as George did. *It's a Wonderful Life* plays on television in the Peltzer family's kitchen, and the town is called Kingston Falls, similar in name to George Bailey's hometown of Bedford Falls. George Bailey created a fantasy life to travel to foreign lands and go to college to study architecture. But this 1980s variation on George Bailey is Billy, who is reduced to essentially living in his bedroom shut off from his family, watching horror movies, snacking on food, and drawing comic-book influenced illustrations. He exists in a combination of inertia and escapism. Billy's family is dysfunctional; the three family members rarely gather together in the same room. To establish a solid connection outside his family, Billy turns to his pretty co-worker Kate Beringer (Phoebe Cates). But she is immersed in a Christmas-related depression. More than any other character, she embodies the movie's combination of comedy and horror. "While everybody else is opening up their presents, they're opening up their wrists," she says about suicide during the Christmas season.

The movie serves as a cautionary tale, warning that suburbanites cannot handle responsibility. Their self-absorption makes them reckless. The movie also expresses anxiety about an overreliance on technology. The gremlins grasp society's dependence on technology and manipulate it to use against the humans. Gizmo also represents a subversion of the nativity story by making a venerated infant the subject of neglect rather than proper devotion.[289] This neglect leads to the gremlins unleashing violence, which goes against the cultural expectation of childhood innocence.[290] *Gremlins* also removes the security and virtue associated with children's movies, such as home, family, Christmas, and Walt Disney films.[291] However, the movie never becomes a full-fledged horror film. It's a combination of the visions of director Joe Dante, who is more steeped in horror films, and the film's family-film-friendly producer Steven Spielberg.

Because Christmas movies fit into existing genres, in some ways the gremlins adhere to the horror convention of a monster film where society is changed because of the monster and its force.[292] The film is also an example of what Angus McFadzean calls "the suburban fantastic," a series of films in the 1980s including *Poltergeist* and *E.T.* in which preteen and teenage boys living within the suburbs confront a disruptive fantastic influence, such as ghosts, aliens, vampires, and gremlins.[293] This forces the male protagonist to resolve his gender-related issues, settling the conflict between insulated suburbia and the terrors of the adult world.[294] *Gremlins* shows young adults who are not only irresponsible but are past high school age but incapable of becoming independent adults.[295] The gremlins force Billy to change—to fight against them and move from the isolation of his home, where he is directionless and immobilized, into a relationship with Kate. However, the movie is ultimately antithetical to the Third Wave veneration of family because it shows the suburban family home as unresolvedly dysfunctional.

MAGICAL REALISM AND NEOREALISM

Prancer (1989) is a significant film not just for its confirmation of the transcendental but because of its gender concerns, understanding of social class, and combination of realism and magic realism.

Many female protagonists propelled the plots of First Wave Christmas films. Women are often central characters, at a critical point redefining their worldview, trying to live a more authentic life, or making crucial decisions about how to move forward with a romantic relationship. By the Second Wave, only Karen in *Frosty the Snowman* (and perhaps Lucy in *A Charlie Brown Christmas*) had significant roles in the TV Christmas specials dominating that era. In Third Wave Christmas films, women don't usually occupy main roles even in romances, a genre where women often are protagonists. Only in *The Holiday* do two women have the dominant perspectives and make decisions that move the narrative forward.

So it's somewhat of a revelation that an eight-year-old girl, Jessica Riggs (Rebecca Harrell), is the center of a Third Wave Christmas film. She not only believes in the transcendental but asserts a feminine mysticism in a bleak and male-dominated family and community. Jessica is the sole female in the family (her mother has died before the film begins) and is marginalized by both her father and her brother. Her father, John Riggs (Sam Elliot), is exasperated by her questioning, her enthusiasm for Christmas, and what he feels is a dangerous imagination holding her back from responsibility and submission. But ultimately Jessica transforms her relationships with her father and brother while maintaining her core identity. She employs valuable maternal and caring instincts for an animal, which for most of the film isn't valued or appreciated in a male-dominated pragmatic community. She also brings a community together through her faith.

The movie is also rare for a Third Wave Christmas film because it portrays working-class life in a rural community. In Third Wave films aside from *Prancer*, only Eddie Murphy's character in *Trading Places* is a major character from the underclass. Otherwise, Third Wave Christmas films generally show characters in homogeneous suburbia, where no class tensions are evident. In *Prancer*, economic adversity, loss, and isolation exhaust the rural community and emotionally harden the characters, who exist in a remote snow-filled Michigan landscape where they appear exiled.

Prancer uses an effective variation on two film movements. The first is neorealism, developed in postwar Italy, which showed the economic challenges and adversities of the working class, was shot largely on location, and used children as important characters in films—such as *The Bicycle Thief* and *Shoeshine*. The other technique *Prancer* employs is magic realism, which uses dreamlike sequences and injects mythic, mystical, or fantastic elements into a realist setting.[296] In *Prancer*, a mild form of magic realism occurs with a reindeer that Jessica believes is Santa's Prancer.

Magic realism is set into motion when, on the way home from school, Jessica sees workers hanging a display of wooden reindeer on a wire in the center of town. Jessica calls out to the reindeer as Santa would ("now Dasher, now Dancer, now Prancer, now Vixen") and one of the reindeer falls and breaks. Jessica figures out that, according to the order of Santa's reindeer, the fallen reindeer represents Prancer. This triggers the film's magic realism: a reindeer subsequently appears to Jessica during her eerie twilight walk through the snow-covered woods. After her father sees that the deer is wounded and grabs a rifle to shoot it, the deer vanishes, seemingly by magic. Jessica appears to have a psychic connection with the reindeer. She awakens from a dream about a wooden Christmas display of Prancer falling on her to hear the sounds of a real wounded reindeer in the family's barn. The deer is somewhat of a resurrection or incarnation of the wooden reindeer that broke. Although not specifically a Messianic or Jesus figure, the reindeer appears from an unknown place and lands in an out-of-the-way town—even staying in a makeshift stable. And at the end of the film Jessica sees the reindeer ascend into the heavens.

But while this magic realism occurs, neorealism is also used to portray a community where people work hard, struggle economically, and suffer from loss. One of the most effective elements of realism the film uses is the tension between Jessica and her father. John Riggs is worn down with bitterness, disillusionment, and financial distress. Loss, economic struggle, and isolation make him so preoccupied and agitated he overlooks the best of what's in front of him, which is the innocence and faith and the love of his daughter. Jessica's dreaminess, imagination, and unyielding focus on spirituality is her reaction to living under her father's anger and oppressive and insecure economic conditions.

The film's ending suggests that, given the choice between descending to believing in nothingness (believing the reindeer fell off the cliff) and the transcendental (the reindeer ascended into the sky), one must believe in the transcendental. Is Prancer's ascent to join Santa an affirmation of the transcendental? Is it something Jessica imagines? Is Prancer a symbol of her innocence leaving her as she stands on the verge of adolescence? Does it affirm that her mother is in heaven? Does the ending aerial shot suggest that a supernatural force is watching over the town? It's one of the movie's strong points that there are multiple interpretations of this fascinating ending.

A MODERN INCARNATION: *ELF*

Elf (2003) advocates not only a belief in the transcendental but a transformation of personality as a solution to overcoming cynicism, harshness, and self-centeredness produced by urban living and the modern workplace. Buddy (Will Farrell) is a human brought up at the North Pole as an elf, which leaves him in a state of arrested childlike development. However, this gives him a cheerfulness, optimism, and creativity that contrasts with the hardness of the world in New York City after he leaves the sanctuary of the North Pole.

While *Prancer* shows the economic results of living on the fringe in the rural Midwest, *Elf* shows the center of American commerce in New York City. People there, from retail workers to business executives, are anxious, insecure, and deadened by jobs they feel no joy doing. Although the film

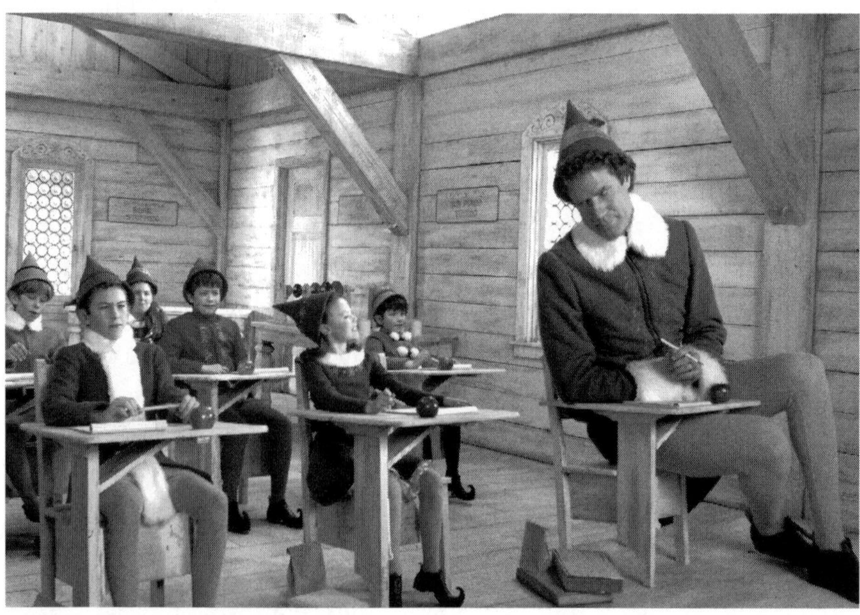

With allusions to Rankin-Bass TV specials, *Elf* (2003) shows an elf who becomes a liberator to humans plagued by deadening work and urban alienation. The key to the film is Will Farrell's non-ironic performance, the antithesis to Chevy Chase's humor in *Christmas Vacation*. Photo courtesy New Line/Everett Collection.

doesn't challenge the economic system, the result of the economic structure is shown by how the workplace deadens the spirit.

Buddy is a love child of a hippie-era liaison. His mother died, and his father is workaholic children's book publishing executive Walter (James Caan), who is on Santa's "naughty list"—seemingly because of his inattention to his family and his lack of business ethics. So Buddy visits his father "down south" where there is doubt in the transcendental, represented by a growing disbelief in Santa Claus.

Buddy finds a sense of mission and purpose to spread Christmas spirit to his father. Like Bill Murray's Francis Cross of *Scrooged*, Buddy's father abandoned his 1960s youthful lifestyle for a ruthless business persona. But Santa tells Buddy it's not too late for his father to reform, which expresses the genre's traditional component of spiritual transformation. Buddy finds New York a hostile place where advertising is deceitful (Buddy believes a business that advertises "the world's best coffee") and where work isn't fun (his co-workers at Gimbel's are insecure, skeptical, and cynical—even smiling is met with suspicion).

Buddy's quest to spread "Christmas cheer" results in him being viewed as insane, or at least, as a doctor explains to Buddy's father, that Buddy is "reverting to a state of childlike dependency." As in *Miracle on 34th Street*, in a cynical world of business, individualism, and survivalism, belief in the transcendental and spirituality can be viewed as a type of mental illness. Buddy becomes a liberator, however, through returning joy to people. He restores a sense of innocence and fun to his co-worker Jovie (Zooey Deschanel). He takes mailroom workers out of their deadening routine by doing a dance while they cheer him on. He builds a bond with his brother. And he leads his father to leave a demanding, greed-filled workplace to enjoy his family and start what is traditionally in Christmas films a noble way of work, a small business.

In some ways, *Elf* is an homage to themes and characters in Rankin-Bass TV specials. Santa's North Pole workshop is, like in *Rudolph the Red-Nosed Reindeer*, a factorylike assembly line. The snowman in *Elf* references the snowman in *Rudolph*, and Buddy goes on a hero's journey on a snow float, as Rudolph did. Like Hermey in *Rudolph*, Buddy realizes he's a misfit who doesn't have a place in Santa's workshop. Buddy is also similar to Santa Claus in *Santa Claus Is Coming to Town* because he's a liberating figure who inspires happiness. And as in *The Year without a Santa Claus*, there's a descent by an innocent character into a world filled with disbelief. Similar to the oppressive law and order of that story's Southtown, USA, Santa in *Elf* faces a menacing team of horse-riding police called Central Park Rangers, who pose a threat. As in the counterculture driven Rankin-Bass specials, authority is dangerous.

The movie also validates belief in the transcendental. Santa's sleigh, which runs partially on Christmas spirit, breaks down in Central Park. It requires "Christmas spirit," a metaphor for spiritual belief, to make it rise again. "Christmas spirit is about believing, not seeing," Santa says. Like *Miracle on 34th Street* the film uses Santa Claus (Ed Asner) as a symbol for spiritual belief.

If Santa is a godlike figure, Buddy is a Christ figure who suffers for his innocence and is an outsider in an antagonistic world. He leaves the North Pole not only to "find out who you really are," as his mentor snowman tells him, but to be a spiritual liberator for his father and other people he comes into contact with. He frees people through convincing them to adopt a childlike perspective. As Papa Elf says in a narration toward the end of the film, "Buddy managed to save Christmas, and his spirit saved a lot of other people too."

Unlike Chevy Chase's ironic performance in *National Lampoon's Christmas Vacation*, Ferrell plays Buddy as a convincing innocent character. He told one journalist that was his intention: "I thought Buddy had to be the most unjaded creature," Ferrell said. "There's not a single cynical part of him. I thought it must be played in complete earnest, without any winking to the audience in any way. Hopefully, the comedy comes from Buddy's unjaded view of things that we take for granted."[297]

THE POLAR EXPRESS: A MYSTICAL ENCOUNTER WITH THE TRINITY

The theme of transcendence in Third Wave Christmas films also comes through in *The Polar Express* (2004), a film where a mystical experience instills a boy with faith. In the adaptation of Chris Van Allsburg's children's book, a life-changing train ride to the North Pole on Christmas Eve becomes a spiritual journey and supernatural encounter that converts the protagonist from doubt to belief.

Van Allsburg said the story is about "a protagonist who is torn between believing in an idea, which he cherished, and not believing in it because it defies reason."[298] As in *Prancer*, the spiritual dilemma of belief and doubt is embodied through a child at the age where rationality threatens to supersede belief in the supernatural. The protagonist's train ride in *The Polar Express* is a spiritual journey for himself and three other children. They are at differing stages of spiritual development and they all receive crucial spiritual guidance on their trip.

The central character (simply called Hero Boy) is a child at the turning point of belief or nonbelief about Santa Claus. He is on the verge of a descent into cynicism and doubt. However, on Christmas Eve the force of a train rattles the walls of his bedroom. He goes outside and sees the Polar Express with a celestial light coming from inside.

"This is your crucial year," the conductor tells him, confirming the boy is at the critical tipping point between belief and disbelief. The conductor tells the boy it's his choice whether he wants to get on the train or not, but he recommends that he do it. The boy hesitates but climbs on board, showing that a spiritual journey is a choice. When the boy first gets on the train, a girl tells him it's a "magic train." Like the magic snow that creates Frosty in the Rankin-Bass TV special *Frosty the Snowman*, magic is a metaphor for the spiritual.

The movie also features three other children with spiritual challenges. There is a "know-it-all" kid who recites statistics about the train and is lost in rationality and hubris. He looks at gifts in a storefront window and says he wants them all. He's at the lower spiritual stage of arrogance, greed, and too much trust in rationalism. The "Hero Girl" thinks of others, shows an interest in the oppressed, and takes charge at crucial times. But perhaps she is a bit too unwilling to act on her leadership instincts. Billy, a boy from "the other side of the tracks," is in a state of despair and says, "Christmas never works out for me." He isolates himself, has low self-esteem, and is in need of community. He doubts because he has experienced hard times, not because of rational disbelief like that of the Hero Boy.

During the journey three mentors instruct the Hero Boy. The first is apparently a ghost of a hobo. This mentor wants the boy to acknowledge his dark side of doubt, which is his spiritual crisis. The hobo exposes the Hero Boy as a Doubting Thomas who fears believing in something without proof. The second mentor is the train conductor. He represents someone who keeps the spiritual journey on task. He's disciplined, mindful of time, and won't let obstacles stop him from his destination. He exerts compassion when necessary, but is determined and conscious of keeping the spiritual journey moving forward. The third mentor is Santa Claus, who is a cross between a guru and a rock star. After the train arrives at the North Pole, a crowd of elves and children chant the song "Santa Claus Is Coming to Town" before Santa appears out of a celestial light. However, a bell comes off the sleigh, the music slows and then stops, and there is silence as the Hero Boy picks up the bell. At first he can't hear its sound, until his faith and belief begin to grow. But then he holds it next to his ear and says, "I believe," which is what Natalie Wood's character, Susan, says in *Miracle on 34th Street* before she sees the visible result of her Christmas wish for proof. After he declares this belief, Santa Claus appears directly to him.

Santa offers spiritual advice to the four children. Santa tells the "know-it-all" kid to learn humility, that Billy must experience community to grow, and the Hero Girl needs to take the next step into leadership. "Now what would you like for Christmas?" Santa asks the Hero Boy. He wants the sleigh bell from Santa's sleigh because he wants some physical object from his encounter to sustain his belief. As someone on the verge of falling into disbelief, the Hero Boy needs visible proof. Santa tells the Hero Boy the bell is merely a "symbol" of spirit, because "the true spirit of Christmas lies in your heart." But the Hero Boy carelessly puts it in his pocket where, he has forgotten, there is a hole. This perhaps signifies something in his character—that he doesn't protect what is valuable or is too reckless. This means he will lose the bell. That will once again place him in the precarious position of not having the discernable proof he requires.

It's also possible to view the movie's three mentors as variations on the three ghosts in *A Christmas Carol*, with the hobo representing the past (although he utilizes fear usually associated with the Ghost of Christmas Yet to Come), the conductor the present (a time-conscious person who introduces the Hero Boy to community like the Ghost of Christmas Present), and Santa Claus the future (someone insuring the boy will continue to believe, which, like Scrooge, will make him a better person). A Scrooge puppet in the train car is a Marley-type character who warns the boy of the distress he could face.

Another spiritual reading of the film is that the three mentors represent the three parts of the Christian trinity. The hobo denotes the Holy Spirit (a spiritual entity who rides on top of the train and offers assistance in life-and-death situations). The conductor is a Jesus figure, who escorts people to the heavenlike North Pole (literally bringing people to the Santa Claus/God figure and thereby offering them salvation by asking them to get on the train). He also punches out spiritual advice on tickets (a variation on creating a Holy Scripture?). Santa represents God, with supernatural qualities and an omniscient insight into people's spiritual conditions.

Before boarding the train for their homes, the four children also receive spiritual advice from the Hero Boy's other mentor, the conductor, who completes punching their tickets. Earlier on the trip he gave them a few letters, but now he completes the words, which are a type of spiritual mantra or advice to implement. The "know-it-all" kid receives "Learn," indicating he must humble himself to realize he doesn't know everything. Billy gets the words "Depend on, rely on, count on," showing he must acquire dependability to overcome his insecure and oppressive conditions. Hero Girl receives "Lead," showing she must seize the opportunity to take charge. And the Hero Boy, described as "the young man with all the questions" (the spiritual seeker), receives the word "Believe."

Although the boy is devastated that he loses Santa's sleigh bell, the next morning under the Christmas tree there is a present with the bell and a note from Santa. When his parents try to ring the bell, they can't hear it, and they tell him it's broken. But the Hero Boy and his sister both hear it. The poignant final line is "though I've grown old, the bell still rings for me as it does for all who truly believe." The bell transfers faith from something abstract to something concrete only heard by believers.[299]

Conclusion
Where Is the Christmas Film Genre Going?

After Christmas romances and family films were churned out in the theaters since the 1990s, Christmas films appeared to run their course after the first decade of the 2000s. That's because Third Wave Christmas films exhausted variations on how to preserve the American family through a suburban Christmas gathering. *Happy Holiday* (2020), about a woman bringing her girlfriend home for Christmas, may appear different on the surface. But its structure is still based on the formula of a suburban family Christmas disturbed by family conflict, a storyline central to Third Wave films.

The Christmas movie genre isn't growing because it didn't evolve out of the Third Wave. And audiences may have grown bored with Christmas films because the Dickens model of spiritual transformation seems to have ended. Additionally in the Third Wave, only two movies prominently featuring African-American characters (*Madea's Christmas* and *Best Man Holiday*), and the white working-class movie *Prancer* feature spirituality and religion significantly in a positive way. Otherwise, representations of religious figures in Christmas movies are generally negative.

In *Four Christmases* (2008), unmarried couple Kate (Reese Witherspoon) and Brad (Vince Vaughn) satirize a nativity story as if it is an obsolete, archaic, and outrageous artifact to the holiday. Churchgoers are too dimwitted to understand the mockery and sarcasm. The Myers family members who return home for Christmas in the dramedy *Almost Christmas* (2016) respond to attending church with apathy or mockery. The minister says the patriarch widower of the family Walter Myers (Danny Glover) is a faithful member but hasn't attended much since his wife died almost a year earlier. The message is that the younger generation views church in stereotypes, and the older generation doesn't see the church as a place of consolation during a crisis. In *Nothing Like The*

Some of the few films with overt religious references in the Third Wave are films featuring African Americans characters, such as *A Madea Christmas* (2013). The film culminates in a clash between secularism and Christianity in the public sphere. Photo courtesy Lionsgate Films/Everett Collection.

Holidays (2008), with the family's parents facing divorce, one of the sons invites a priest to come talk to them. But the priest is so ineffectual that when he says, "Maybe we should say a prayer," the family members in unison immediately silence him. Later, after the family and the neighbors gather to sing Christmas carols, they go to the church for a party and food. The purpose of church is providing a space for community, not for spiritual answers.

For a short time the genre tried to move in a different direction. *The Night Before* (2015), *Office Christmas Party* (2016), and *A Bad Mom's Christmas* (2017) all show a group of millennial friends becoming a surrogate family and celebrating Christmas together rather than with one's nuclear family.

The precursor to these films is the Christmas romance *The Holiday* (2006), which shows directionless thirty-something professionals without family connections. Another influence is *A Very Harold and Kumar Christmas* (2011), which integrates elements of teen sex comedies and stoner movies. The roots of this may go back further to the 1999 indie film *Go*, which features a Christmas Eve night of partying from different points of view, as well as the 2002 comedy *Friday After Next*. The dramedy *Best Man Holiday* (2014) is another millennial-centered film where thirty-something uberprofessionals gather together for Christmas and try to shed their college-era identities to confront their growing pains into adulthood.

These films suggest that millennials want to create their own Christmas rituals outside of the traditional family gathering. The family-focused Third Wave tried broadening its definition of family to include a surrogate family of tight-knit friends, particularly in *The Night Before*, *Office Christmas Party*, and *A Bad Mom's Christmas*.

The Night Before assures young men they can rely on the male friends from their youth as they transition into adult responsibilities. They feel unprepared for adulthood because they cling to their college-age identities. Starting a family and settling down isn't a trap that prohibits individual ambition and self-expression as it did for George Bailey in *It's a*

Wonderful Life. There are no dreams deferred when there are no dreams in the first place. Instead, settling down means leaving behind a lifestyle associated with being young. Their developmental crisis occurs when transitioning from a college-age identity to becoming a young adult. A Christmas Eve night of drinking and taking drugs leads them to reveal their insecurities, including commitment phobia and career anxieties.

The movie subverts the Christmas movie genre's former convention of characters having transcendental experiences or epiphanies. Instead of this occurring through moral growth, a shortcoming conquered, or a spiritual awakening, it happens during a night of partying, with drugs as transcendental tools. When Isaac (Seth Rogen) opens the box of drugs his wife gives him, a bright light emanates as if they are sacred objects. At one point Isaac says, "Those drugs you gave me, they put me on a spirit quest, like in an Oliver Stone movie or *Young Guns*." A drug dealer they later encounter says he's a believer in Jesus, dispenses wisdom like a guru, and acquires angel wings and ascends into the skies. The Nutcracker Ball they attend is located through a white-filled tunnel as if they are entering a celestial space.

In *Office Christmas Party* (2016), the partying co-workers at a hi-tech company form a surrogate family of sorts. At the center of the movie is a sibling rivalry between Clay Vanstone (T. J. Miller) and Carol Vanstone (Jennifer Aniston). They represent two approaches to business. Carol is bottom-line driven, whereas Clay is more laid back and employee-focused.

As in *The Night Before*, the solution to problems is a party. But unlike in *The Night Before*, it isn't partying to loosen up enough to reveal insecurities. The party is motivated by inviting an important executive to try to land a business deal. The characters in *Office Christmas Party* are completely defined through their job identities, with the workplace an extension of a college dorm.

Unlike the three men in *The Night Before* transitioning from single young adulthood to committed relationships and parenting, in *A Bad Mom's Christmas*, Amy (Mila Kunis), Kiki (Kristen Bell), and Carla

(Kathryn Hahn) already have cleared the hurdle into parenthood. Their goal is to return to college-era style partying as an outlet when adult pressures intensify. The anchor of the three women's lives is not their families but their bond with each other. The three women are surrogate sisters in the same highly idealized presentation of female friendship found in the TV show *Sex and the City*. The movie instills a fantasy that women weighed down by adult responsibilities can still retain a close-knit bond with a few friends with whom they don't have conflicts. To escape their responsibilities, they occasionally leave their families to party together.

Why all the partying in these films? It's an escape from adult responsibilities and allows the characters to reach what they feel is a truer identity: their adolescent or college-era selves. It's a connection to their younger and more hedonistic and carefree lifestyle before the onslaught of adult responsibilities.

After a failed attempt to reboot the genre through this trio of Christmas party films, it looked as if the genre might again switch to television, as it did in the Second Wave. Audiences embraced the predictable romances and family made-for-TV movies on The Hallmark Channel and other TV networks in a way that they didn't respond to Christmas rom coms and family Christmas films in theaters.

Just when it appeared the genre was disintegrating, in 2019 *Last Christmas* was released. It did well at the box office and convincingly (even if at times clumsily) took the genre back to its roots. Like Dickens's *A Christmas Carol* and some key First Wave films, it utilizes the theme of redemption by supernatural intervention. A flawed character transforms through a movement from individualism, career ambition, and hedonism to community and selflessness.

In *Last Christmas*, the character based on the Dickens model of a reformed Scrooge character is a twenty-six-year-old immigrant to England from the former Yugoslavia. Kate (Emelia Clarke), between auditions for plays, lives a transient lifestyle drifting from bar to beds in hit-and-run affairs. Her life changes after she meets a mysterious man, Tom (Henry

Goulding), who appears to be more mentor than romantic partner. But that doesn't mean there isn't some romance. There's an homage to the famous scene in *The Bishop's Wife* when the angel Dudley (Cary Grant) takes the neglected wife Julia (Loretta Young) ice skating.

Nearly two decades after *Elf* and *The Polar Express*, a Christmas film once again embodied the central traditional theme of the genre. Even with its flaws, *Last Christmas* (2019) showed a character undergoing a spiritual transformation. Photo courtesy Universal/Everett Collection.

The movie starts as a romantic comedy but then shifts to a redemption story. Tom nudges Kate into a change of character. He volunteers at a homeless shelter, and soon she's volunteering there too. She drops trying out for stage parts and instead puts her time into raising money for the homeless. She makes amends with friends and family and appears to find meaning in her life.

Kate is not the workaholic of so many Christmas films. What sets her apart is a kind of lostness. Her only real motivation is a good time and the need to perhaps be famous by acting. This suits the current cultural climate of a younger generation that feels somewhat directionless with limited opportunities. This is a shift from the success-oriented workaholic characters in Third Wave films from *Scrooged* to *Jingle All the Way*. Kate's movement is from aimlessness to purpose rather than from workaholism to making more time for family, which is a Third Wave trope.

However, *Last Christmas* is unclear in its portrayal of the supernatural represented by Tom. It's unclear by the end of the film if he is an angel, a ghost, or a projection of Kate's fantasies. Unlike the clear explanation of the supernatural in First Wave films, it's an ambiguous intervention. Marley in *A Christmas Carol* explains who he is and what will come to Scrooge, in *It's a Wonderful Life* there is an opening exposition from the cosmos about the mission of the angel Clarence, and in *A Bishop's Wife* the angel Dudley explains the parameters of who he is and why he has come to earth as an angel. There are no such explanations in *Last Christmas.* Even with this ambiguity, *Last Christmas* is a fascinating return to the supernatural in the Third Wave era when the transcendental is mostly ignored. It's the first meaningful or enduring Christmas film since *Elf* in 2003 and *The Polar Express* in 2004.

Despite some flaws, *Last Christmas* is a mini-triumph that may resuscitate the Christmas movie genre by returning it to its roots of redemption and spiritual transformation. Will its box office success mean a true revival of the genre? Time will tell.

Acknowledgments

First and foremost, thank you to my wife, Kim, for all of her support, patience, and critical insights. May we stay forever young by watching these movies and TV shows every year. Thanks to Lou Vetri for encouragement and spiritual wisdom. Thank you to Don Bertram for his friendship and spirtual mentoring. Many thanks to all the libraries I used—too numerous to mention. But a particular thanks to Miriam Stone and Val Schaeffer for diligently and cheerfully fulfilling so many interlibrary loan requests. I thank Rick Goldschmidt for his kindness and for preserving the memory of the Rankin-Bass canon. Thanks also to Michele Hadlow and the Everett Collection for the use of the photographs. Thanks to Rachel Hackenberg, Adam Bresnahan, and Kris Firth for their editing and guidance and to Pilgrim Press for believing in this project. And, of course, thanks to all the auteurs of the Christmas genre: the creators, producers, writers, directors, and actors that made such an impact on me and so many other people over the years, including Frank Capra, Ernst Lubitsch, Preston Sturges, Billy Wilder, Jimmy Stewart, Barbara Stanwyck, Deanna Durbin, Margaret O'Brien, Bing Crosby, Cary Grant, Arthur Rankin and Jules Bass, Charles M. Schultz, Dr. Seuss, Tim Burton, and Stanley Kubrick.

Appendix

Christmas and Christmas-Related Movies

Ratings:
★★★★—A Christmas classic and must-see film
★★★—A very good movie worth seeing
★★—A mediocre film with some good moments
★—Avoid

All I Want for Christmas (1991) ★★
In this early Third Wave film, with children asking Santa to work his magic so their parents won't divorce, Lauren Bacall plays the grandmother and gives the film some gravitas, but not enough.

All Mine to Give (1957) ★★★
The oldest brother of an orphaned family must find new homes for his siblings in time for Christmas. Devastating. A bona fide tearjerker.

Almost Christmas (2016) ★★
An African-American family returns to the home of their father (Danny Glover) for the first Christmas since his wife died in this standard "home-for-the-holiday" plotline of squabbling siblings sorting out their problems.

The Apartment (1960) ★★★★
This brilliant Billy Wilder film stars Jack Lemmon as an office drone at an insurance company who loans out his apartment to executives for

trysts. It is seminal for its depiction of the loneliness surrounding the holidays for single urbanites and its bleak view of the modern corporation.

Arthur Christmas (2011) ★★

This animated film showing Santa's military-style Christmas Eve delivery operation until one present is left behind is significant for its depiction of Santa as a kind of royalty succession starting with St. Nicholas.

Bachelor Mother (1939) ★★★

Ginger Rogers plays a department store worker coming to the aid of a baby left on the doorsteps of an orphanage in this most realized Depression-era Christmas-themed film.

A Bad Mom's Christmas (2017) ★

The rushed Christmas-based sequel to the 2015 surprise hit *Bad Moms* features unlikeable millennial mothers defending their homes against their invasive and irresponsible baby boomer mothers.

Bad Santa (2003) ★★★

A foul-mouthed criminal playing a department store Santa (Billy Bob Thornton) ultimately undergoes a Scroogelike redemption. Thornton's performance as a self-loathing alcoholic adds complexity to what could have been a one-dimensional character.

Bad Santa 2 (2016) ★

This is an unnecessary sequel, with Thornton's nasty Santa returning to arrange a heist with his estranged mother. Avoid.

Batman Returns (1992) ★★

Tim Burton's dystopian portrayal of Christmas in Gotham City is visually spectacular but undermined by overacting. Burton's Yuletide vision worked better in his two other Christmas films, *The Nightmare Before Christmas* and *Edward Scissorhands*.

The Best Man Holiday (2013) ★★

The first part of the film is a Christmas gathering of affluent college friends, the second part a downer with a serious illness undermining their reunion.

Beyond Tomorrow (1940) ★★
Three businessmen bring together a couple for Christmas Eve dinner. The men later die in a plane crash and return as ghosts to oversee the couple.

Big Business (1929) ★★★★
Laurel and Hardy play Christmas tree salesmen who meet their match in a grumpy suburbanite. This is comedy at its finest and the screen's first black Christmas comedy.

A Bill of Divorcement (1932) ★★
This dated depiction of mental illness is now most notable for being Katherine Hepburn's debut film. Her father, played by John Barrymore, returns home on Christmas Eve after fifteen years in an asylum to threaten his wife's plans to remarry.

The Bishop's Wife (1947) ★★★★
David Niven plays a New York Episcopal bishop so fixated on plans to build a cathedral that he neglects his wife. Cary Grant plays an angel who shows him the true value of his life.

Black Christmas (1974) ★★★
Olivia Hussey convincingly plays what may be the horror genre's first version of the "final girl," the courageous last girl standing who confronts a psychopathic killer. This groundbreaking slasher film had more influence on the horror genre than the Christmas movie genre.

Black Nativity (2013) ★★
This musical contemporary adaptation of the nativity story is hit and miss, mostly miss. Jennifer Hudson is the standout as a struggling single mother.

Blast of Silence (1961) ★★
A low-budget neo noir about a hit man in New York City during the Christmas season, this film features an overbearing voiceover. Stick with 1940s Christmas noir.

Bundle of Joy (1956) ★
This remake of *Bachelor Mother* as a musical is a misfire but is notable for the onscreen pairing of Debbie Reynolds and Eddie Fisher.

A Charlie Brown Christmas (TV) (1965) ★★★★
The animated adaptation of comic strip "Peanuts" characters deservingly remains a Christmas pop culture staple. The modern materialistic Christmas makes a community dysfunctional until a religious component is introduced.

The Cheaters (1945) ★★★
A screwball comedy-influenced film with a madcap spoiled family duping an heiress so they will inherit her fortune, this one deserves more recognition.

Christmas Eve (1947) ★★
This gangster comedy starring George Raft and Randolph Scott is a rare post–World War II era dud.

Christmas Evil (1980) ★★
One of several "psycho Santa" films, this one at least has a healthy sense of humor.

Christmas Holiday (1944) ★★★
Gene Kelly and Deanna Durbin both play against type as a doomed married couple after Kelly's hidden criminal life is exposed. The effective atmosphere of New Orleans and a Hitchcock-style overbearing mother make it a compelling Christmas film noir.

Christmas in Connecticut (1945) ★★★★
Barbara Stanwyck shines in this classic Christmas comedy. Her masquerade as a food columnist is threatened when her publisher wants to spend Christmas with her at a country home in Connecticut.

A Christmas Carol (1938) ★★
This Reginald Owen version has its moments but mostly misses the mark. It's shockingly devoid of Depression-era realism, which could have effectively updated Dickens's story.

A Christmas Carol (1951) ★★★★
Alastair Sim stars in what many *Carol* fans feel is the definitive film Scrooge. An outstanding performance is enhanced by an extensive backstory for Scrooge's character.

A Christmas Carol (1971) (TV) ★★
Twenty years after starring as Scrooge on film, Alastair Sim provides the voice of Scrooge in a Gothic animated version of the story.

A Christmas Carol (1984) (TV) ★★★★
George C. Scott joins Alastair Sim as one of the best Scrooges ever. This version depicts Scrooge as a gruff out-of-touch businessman, which reflects the economic and cultural shifts of the 1980s.

A Christmas Carol (1997) ★★
This forgettable animated *Carol* with Tim Curry voicing Scrooge is the most generic and undistinctive of the major animated versions of *A Christmas Carol.*

A Christmas Carol (TV) (1999) ★★★
Like the George C. Scott version of Scrooge, Patrick Stewart is a detached and callous businessman in this competent and compelling adaptation.

A Christmas Carol (2001) ★★
Simon Callow plays Scrooge in yet another animated film version, notable for its alteration to the story, which has Scrooge reuniting with his lost love Belle (voiced by Kate Winslet).

A Christmas Carol: The Musical (2004) ★★
Kelsey Grammer is a stagey Scrooge; forgettable songs drag this down.

A Christmas Carol (2009) ★
Dickens meets the horror genre and *Alice in Wonderland* in this bloated, dizzying version starring Jim Carrey as Scrooge. Dickens's story is buried in a spectacle of distracting special effects.

A Christmas Story (1983) ★★★
Ralphie (Peter Billingsley) wants a BB gun for Christmas but adults warn him, in the movie's catchphrase, "you'll shoot your eye out, kid." This is essentially a comical coming-of-age film set during the Christmas season.

Christmas with the Kranks (2004) ★★
An affluent suburban couple (Tim Allen and Jamie Lee Curtis) see no reason to celebrate Christmas if their daughter isn't coming home, but the neighbors try to shame them into celebrating Christmas. It fails as a satire and as a drama.

The Cricket on the Hearth (TV) 1967 ★
Rankin and Bass's Christmas special follow-up to their revolutionary *Rudolph the Red-Nosed Reindeer* is a complete misfire. Based on a Dickens story.

Daddy's Home Two (2017) ★
Divorced dads, played by Will Ferrell and Mark Wahlberg, are best buds, but that's threatened when their fathers, played by Mel Gibson and John Lithgow, show up for Christmas. Painfully unfunny.

Deck The Halls (2006) ★
This *Christmas Vacation*–inspired Christmas tree light contest ignites a feud between two neighbors (Matthew Broderick and Danny Devito). One of the worst Third Wave comedies.

Desk Set (1957) ★★★
A sizable chunk of this office comedy is set during a Christmas party. Spencer Tracy and Katherine Hepburn are always a delight to watch.

Die Hard (1988) ★★★★
John McClane (Bruce Willis) fights terrorists in a skyscraper on Christmas Eve and finds some redemption along the way. Over the years *Die Hard* has achieved iconic status because of Willis's believable performance as a New York cop battling not only terrorists but an incompetent bureaucracy.

Die Hard 2 (1990) ★★
The rushed inferior sequel has McClane fending off terrorists at a Washington, D.C., airport. The only other *Die Hard* sequel to date set during Christmas.

Edward Scissorhands (1990) ★★★
A well-meaning housewife (Dianne Wiest) takes in a man with scissor blades for hands (Johnny Depp). At first he's regarded as a creative novelty, but suburbia turns against him.

Elf (2003) ★★★★
Orphan child Buddy (Will Ferrell) is raised at the North Pole but goes to New York to find his father, who is a ruthless businessman. In some ways an homage to Rankin and Bass, this film largely succeeds because of Ferrell, who plays the role with a lack of irony.

Ernest Saves Christmas (1988) ★★
An aging Santa is looking for a successor, and Ernest (Jim Varney) helps him find one. The new Santa turns down a role in a horror movie to deliver presents just in time.

Eyes Wide Shut (1999) ★★★★
Stanley Kubrick's final film is a mesmerizing and penetrating study of the moral flaws in contemporary society. Tom Cruise and Nicole Kidman play a married couple who take journeys through the New York underworld during the Christmas season.

The Family Man (2000) ★★★
In many ways this is a variation on *It's a Wonderful Life*: What if George Bailey left town instead of staying? Nicholas Cage plays a successful executive who gets a glimpse of the life he would have had if he had married his college girlfriend (Tea Leoni).

The Family Stone (2005) ★★
A white, liberal suburban family comes together for Christmas and endures tension from a conservative (Sarah Jessica Parker) girlfriend of one son. It never becomes the social satire that would make it interesting.

The First Christmas (TV) 1975 ★★★
This touching Rankin and Bass story of a boy who loses his sight and is taken in by a group of nuns led by Angela Lansbury is underrated.

Four Christmases (2008) ★
Vince Vaughn and Reese Witherspoon can't make a Christmas getaway and are forced to spend their time with their four families, all dysfunctional and unappealing. One of the genre's most star-heavy failures.

Fred Claus (2007) ★
Santa's brother Fred (Vince Vaughn) goes to the North Pole to help Santa (Paul Giamatti) prepare for Christmas. In the Third Wave where it's the norm for families to be dysfunctional, even the Claus family has issues.

Friday After Next (2002) ★
In this unfunny stoner comedy, on Christmas Eve a man in a Santa suit breaks into the apartment of Craig (Ice Cube) and Day Day (Mike Epps) and takes, among other things, the rent money.

Frosty the Snowman (TV) (1969) ★★★★
This animated story develops an important friendship between the child Karen and the snowman the children create that comes to life. Like Rankin and Bass's *Santa Claus Is Coming to Town*, there's a generational clash and the godlike Santa intervenes to save Frosty from disintegrating.

Frosty's Winter Wonderland (TV) 1976 ★
In the disappointing sequel, children create a mate for the lonely Frosty.

Ghosts of Girlfriends Past (2009) ★
Ghosts confront a womanizing bachelor (Matthew McConaughey), so he realizes his romantic blunders. *A Christmas Carol* inspired romantic comedy that goes nowhere.

The Great Rupert (aka *The Christmas Wish)* (1950) ★★★
Louie Amendola (Jimmy Durante) is the happy-go-lucky leader of a vaudeville family act who talks his way into living in an apartment vacated by a friend. Soon a squirrel in the rafters brings down money to the family.

Gift of the Magi (1952) ★★★
This final section of the anthology movie *Full House* stars Jeanne Crain and Farley Granger as a struggling couple who unwittingly buy each other gifts they can't use. O. Henry's classic story fits nicely into the First Wave themes of antimaterialism.

Go (1999) ★★
This cult indie film only alludes to the events occurring a night near Christmas from differing points of view. It was the first in the stoner Christmas films where a drug experience is a faux spiritual transformation.

Good Cheer (1926) ★★
The *Our Gang* short isn't sophisticated but contains an interesting plotline, with the real Santa Claus appearing in spiritlike form to guide the children against criminals dressed as Santa.

Gremlins (1984) ★★★
This effective satire of suburban culture and consumerism strikes the right balance between horror and comedy and even imparts a lesson to irresponsible suburbanites.

The Grinch (2018) ★
This politically correct, nonthreatening Grinch is even more defanged than the Ron Howard 2000 film. Bah humbug to this sanitized Grinch.

Hail Mary (1985) ★★
The nativity story updated to the modern day is all art film, not exploitative. Mary is a student who likes to play basketball and Joseph a taxi driver.

Happiest Season (2020) ★★
The *Home for the Holidays* narrative is updated with an LGBT storyline. Abby (Kristen Stewart) seems like a real person while everyone else appears to be in a mediocre TV movie.

Hell's Heroes (1929) ★★★
The first talkie version of the silent film *Three Godfathers* is gritty and gripping. It features harrowing desert scenes where the criminals come across a dying woman and promise to take care of her newborn child.

The Holiday (2006) ★★
Kate Winslet and Cameron Diaz swap houses for Christmas and find love. Ho-hum rom com.

Holiday Affair (1949) ★★★
Janet Leigh is a war widow who can't move on with her life. She thinks she will find security in marrying the "safe" Carl (Wendell Corey) but finds herself attracted instead to a rugged war veteran (Robert Mitchum).

Holiday Inn (1942) ★★★★
A formative film in the Christmas movie genre, this film is about road-weary entertainer Jim Hardy (Bing Crosby) creating his own inn where he'll only work on holidays. Establishes the First Wave theme of romantic partner as a moral decision.

The Holly and the Ivy (1952) ★★★
Lackluster recent films featuring dysfunctional families returning home for the holidays to work out problems can take a lesson from this fasci-

nating film. Ralph Richardson is a minister who is the head of a family facing a myriad of problems in postwar England.

Home Alone (1990) ★★
After the busy McCallister family forgets Kevin (Macaulay Culkin) in a mad dash to the airport to leave for Paris, Kevin mans up by defending the upscale suburban home from burglars. Its surprise success solidified family-oriented Christmas comedy as a money maker.

Home Alone 2: Lost in New York (1992) ★★
The sequel is proof that the McCallister family remained lodged in dysfunction after their reunion at the end of the first film. Once again Kevin is separated from his harried parents; this time he ends up in New York and his family in Florida.

How the Grinch Stole Christmas (TV) (1966) ★★★★
A misanthropic Grinch undergoes a Scroogelike conversion experience after he sees he can't make Christmas go away by taking away Christmas presents. Brilliant adaptation of Dr. Seuss children's book with memorable narration by Boris Karloff.

How the Grinch Stole Christmas (2000) ★
The Dr. Seuss story has an ineffective backstory and a script that takes all of the bite out of the Grinch. Jim Carrey hams it up in an oversized suit for an hour and a half. Not fun.

The Ice Harvest (2005) ★★★
This existentialist crime drama with John Cusack uses Christmas as a backdrop for a piercing social commentary on the dispossessed American male in middle America. More noir than black comedy. Fascinating.

I'll Be Home for Christmas (1998) ★
College student Jake (Jonathan Taylor Thomas) must find a way to get across the country to see his family and patch things up with his hometown girlfriend. One of the all-time worst Christmas films.

I'll Be Seeing You (1944) ★★★★
Ginger Rogers is out of jail for Christmas after being imprisoned for killing her boss as she fended off an attack, and Joseph Cotten is on leave from treatment as a soldier suffering from "shell shock." This mature romance represents the First Wave's emphasis on healing and bringing society together again after the devastation of war.

In Bruges (2008) ★★★
An intriguing crime story, *In Bruges* features the Belgian town at Christmastime serving as a backdrop for two hit men (Colin Farrell and Brendan Gleeson) hiding out after a job gone wrong.

Iron Man 3 (2013) ★★
As with many of Shane Black's films, it's set during the Christmas season. But this time it's also a convoluted adaptation of *A Christmas Carol.*

It Happened on 5th Avenue (1947) ★★★
A vagabond squats in the Manhattan mansion of the second wealthiest man in America. Soon he's taking in some homeless war veterans.

It's a Wonderful Life (1946) ★★★★
Not only the pinnacle of Christmas films but one of the great moments in American popular culture. Over the years this movie has become a near religious text about the story of a small-town American everyman George Bailey (Jimmy Stewart) who appears to be forgotten and at the mercy of a greedy banker.

Jack Frost (1997) ★
This is an absurd horror film about a murderer on his way to his execution becoming doused with toxic chemicals and turning into a killer snowman.

Jack Frost (1998) ★
In this bizarre story, a musician father (Michael Keaton) dies in a car crash and returns to mentor his son as a snowman.

Jack Frost (TV) (1979) ★★★
Truly underrated, this Rankin and Bass story is about the figure of Jack Frost, who wants to come to earth to learn how mortals live.

Jingle All the Way (1996) ★★
Buried in this film is a critique of consumer culture and workaholism, with Arnold Schwarzenegger ditching his family and trying to find a popular Christmas toy for his son. But the filmmakers don't explore this enough.

Just Friends (2005) ★
Overweight teen (Ryan Reynolds) returns to his hometown as a slim hot-shot music producer trying to woo his old crush. Wrong in, oh, so many ways.

Kiss Kiss Bang Bang (2005) ★★
This self-conscious neo noir starring Robert Downey Jr. is too artificial and overtly clever. As is common for writer/director Shane Black, the movie uses the Christmas season as a backdrop.

Krampus (2015) ★★
A Christmas horror film that severs Krampus from the more benevolent St. Nicholas who traditionally accompanied him on his "mini-judgment" of children. Krampus has godlike powers and enacts vengeance on a suburban boy who loses his Christmas spirit.

Lady in the Lake (1946) ★★
A gimmicky noir film, this is shot from the point of view of the protagonist, who is another screen version of Raymond Chandler's Phillip Marlowe—this one played by Robert Montgomery. Christmas is an ironic backdrop to the crime drama, not a vehicle for redemption.

Lady on a Train (1945) ★★★
Deanna Durbin's best adult role balances her talents for both drama and comedy in this thrilling noir. Stunning scene of Durbin singing "Silent Night" to her father over the telephone.

Last Christmas (2019) ★★★
After the many Christmas movie disappointments over the previous fifteen years, this comes closest to a modern Christmas classic. The life of a London Christmas store worker (Emilia Clarke) is transformed from selfishness to purpose after she meets a mysterious stranger (Henry Goulding).

The Lemon Drop Kid (1951) ★★
Bob Hope plays a shady criminal who botches a racetrack bet and has until Christmas to give a gangster the money. The Christmas song "Silver Bells" debuted in this film.

The Leprechaun's Christmas Gold (TV) (1981) ★
This low point in the career of Rankin and Bass appears to be a St. Patrick's Day story half-baked into a Christmas TV special.

Less Than Zero (1987) ★
A handsome preppie (Andrew McCarthy) returns home to visit his hometown friends. Like the Christmas crime films, Christmas imagery serves as an ironic backdrop—in this case it's a string of drug-filled parties.

Lethal Weapon (1987) ★★
The first of several Shane Black Christmas-related films, *Lethal Weapon* mainly uses Christmas as a barometer of characterization with the family-connected Murtaugh (Danny Glover) contrasted with the tormented widower Riggs (Mel Gibson).

The Life and Adventures of Santa Claus (TV) 1985 ★★
This Tolkien-influenced adaptation of Frank Baum's 1902 novel falls mostly flat. Rankin and Bass did much better with the Baum-inspired *Santa Claus Is Coming to Town.*

The Little Drummer Boy (TV) (1968) ★★★★
This compelling film tells the dark story of Aaron, a boy whose life is shattered when his parents' village is ransacked and they are killed. After much hardship he finds kindness in the newborn Jesus.

The Little Drummer Boy Book 2 (TV) (1976) ★★★
The best of Rankin and Bass's sequels picks up right where *The Little Drummer Boy* left off. To help spread news of the Messiah's arrival, Aaron helps rescue bells from the clutches of Roman soldiers.

The Long Kiss Good Night (1996) ★★
Samantha Caine (Geena Davis) suffers from amnesia and is living as a suburban mother where she plays Mrs. Claus in a Santa parade. But when she starts to unravel her violent past, she's led away from her domestic life. Interesting premise, inadequate execution.

Love Actually (2003) ★★★
A rom com with multiple plotlines, this movie features everyone from Britain's prime minister to a stand-in double for movie nude scenes. Although the movie claims to be about all types of love, it's heavy on male obsession for unattainable or sexy women.

Love Finds Andy Hardy (1938) ★★
One of the few Depression-era Christmas films features a teenage Mickey Rooney, whose problem is too many girls to take to a Christmas Eve dance. Underutilization of Christmas is typical for the 1930s Christmas-themed film.

Love, the Coopers (2015) ★★
Another "home for the holidays" movie shows the family's parents (John Goodman and Diane Keaton) considering divorce. Following this subgenre's pattern, there are bickering siblings and a health crisis.

A Madea Christmas (2013) ★★
Feisty Madea (Tyler Perry) fights against racism, bullying, and a company's attempt to remove Christ from public displays of Christmas. A grab bag of what appears to be mainly improvised jokes.

The Man Who Came to Dinner (1942) ★★
A belligerent author visits an Ohio town and injures himself on the steps of a small businessman's home. Confined to a wheelchair during the

Christmas season, he insults and generally terrorizes the homeowners. Not as fun as it should be.

The Man Who Invented Christmas (2017) ★★
This disappointing mini-biopic about how Dickens wrote *A Christmas Carol* is more of a concocted psychological profile than a reliable or compelling historical account.

March of the Wooden Soldiers (1934) ★★
The appearance of Santa Claus in this Laurel and Hardy fairy tale satire somehow got this film connected to the Christmas movie genre. The standout Laurel and Hardy Christmas film is *Big Business.*

Meet Me in St. Louis (1944) ★★★★
A career-focused father threatens to uproot his household to New York. One of the most iconic moments in any Christmas film is here: Judy Garland singing "Have Yourself a Merry Little Christmas" to Margaret O'Brien.

Mickey's Christmas Carol (1983) ★★★
Clocking in at less than half an hour and thankfully free of musical numbers, it's a concise and effective version of *A Christmas Carol.* Naturally, Scrooge McDuck plays Scrooge.

Miracle on Main Street (1939) ★★
As in the Depression-era *Bachelor Mother*, an abandoned baby serves as a figure of redemption. A burlesque dancer decides to raise the infant and salvation follows.

Miracle on 34th Street (1947) ★★★★
Aside from *A Christmas Carol* and *It's A Wonderful Life*, this is the most enduring Christmas story and cinema's most penetrating example of making Santa Claus a symbol of spirituality and faith, which clashes with a modern skeptical society.

Miracle on 34th Street (1994) ★
This lifeless remake of the 1947 classic embraces the materialism critiqued in the original film and veers off course.

Mixed Nuts (1994) ★
A star-studded flop, Nora Ephron's follow-up to *Sleepless in Seattle* is a failed black comedy starring Steve Martin, Madeline Kahn, and Juliette Lewis among a group of suicide hotline workers and their troubled callers.

Mr. Magoo's Christmas Carol (1962) (TV) ★★★
The near-sighted curmudgeon plays Scrooge in a Broadway production with memorable songs by songwriters Jule Styne and Bob Merrill. The animated format forever changed how *A Christmas Carol* was portrayed in popular culture.

Mr. Soft Touch (1949) ★★★★
This stellar Christmas noir stars Glenn Ford as a jaded World War II veteran who returns home to find his business taken over by gangsters. He meets a social worker played by Evelyn Keyes, who offers him a chance for redemption.

A Muppet Christmas Carol (1992) ★★★★
Michael Caine may be the most emo Scrooge in screen history. Be sure to watch the uncut DVD version with the devastating "When Love Is Gone," sung during the Scrooge-Belle breakup.

National Lampoon's Christmas Vacation (1989) ★★
Besieged by bad reviews at the time of its release, the comedy featuring Chevy Chase as the comic patriarch of a suburban family has over the years become canonized as essential Christmas pop culture. Every dumb Third Wave Christmas comedy owes something to this film.

Nativity! (2009) ★★★
This winning British comedy features a disillusioned schoolteacher (Martin Freeman) who finds meaning in a musical presentation of the nativity story.

The Nativity Story (2006) ★★★
The only feature movie to date about the birth of Christ stars Keisha Castle-Hughes as the virgin Mary and Oscar Isaac as Joseph. Initially resistant, they find purpose in the impending birth of the holy child.

Nestor, The Long-Eared Christmas Donkey (TV) (1977) ★★★★
The most heart-wrenching Rankin and Bass story, *Nestor* features a donkey with big ears who is ostracized and led on a long and lonely journey before the virgin Mary selects him for a special mission. Harrowing.

The Night Before (2015) ★★
Part stoner movie, part bromance, this movie takes place on Christmas Eve as three friends party for what they say is the last time through Christmas Eve. Amid the bedlam, lots of male insecurity surfaces.

The Nightmare Before Christmas (1993) ★★★
Tim Burton's Gothic-style twist on the stop-motion Christmas TV special has Jack the Pumpkin King terrorizing the residents of Christmas Town before he realizes his errors. The Christmas genre's biggest cult film.

Noel (2004) ★★
In this fragmented and disjointed ensemble Christmas film with several storylines taking place on Christmas Eve, the standout plotline is Susan Sarandon caring for her ailing mother. She meets a mysterious man (Robin Williams) who gives her insight into her life.

Nothing Like the Holidays (2008) ★★
This Latin variation of the "home for the holidays" subgenre of Christmas movies contains the usual sibling conflicts, parental crisis, and an outsider threatening the family's principles.

The Nutcracker and the Four Realms (2018) ★
There's not much Tchaikovsky music in this Disney imagining of the Christmas fantasy story. Dull.

Office Christmas Party (2016) ★
It's not bold enough to be a satire of corporate culture, not intelligent enough to be a screwball comedy, and not raucous enough to be a party comedy.

One Magic Christmas (1985) ★★
This variation on *It's A Wonderful Life* has an angel (Harry Dean Stanton) arranging events so a working mother (Mary Steenburgen) realizes the value of her life.

Pinocchio's Christmas (TV) 1980 ★★★
To earn money for Christmas presents, Pinocchio joins a puppet show and is duped by villainous characters. The last meaningful Rankin and Bass TV special.

The Polar Express (2004) ★★★★
As in *Miracle on 34th Street,* Santa represents spirituality and faith itself. A boy teetering on the edge of disbelief takes a train north to meet the Big Man himself.

Prancer (1989) ★★★★
Employing both neorealism and magical realism, this understated gem handles a crisis of faith of a rural Michigan girl trying to maintain her faith amid life's hardships. Sam Elliot plays her cantankerous father, who feels unable to make his daughter happy.

The Preacher's Wife (1996) ★★
Denzel Washington does his best to fill Cary Grant's shoes in this remake of *The Bishop's Wife*. Severe script deviations and a lackluster performance by Whitney Houston as the neglected wife sink this one.

The Ref (1994) ★★★
Captivating and effective, this Christmas black comedy features Dennis Leary as a burglar of upscale homes who meets his match in a dysfunctional family and a squabbling married couple. It shows the underside of suburbia that's both penetrating and comical.

Reindeer Games (2000) ★
This Christmas crime film stars Ben Affleck as an ex-con duped by Charlize Theron. It really doesn't work as a crime film and doesn't work as a black comedy.

Remember The Night (1940) ★★★★
In one of the all-time great Christmas films, Barbara Stanwyck is a jewelry thief bailed out for Christmas who returns to Indiana for Christmas with her prosecuting attorney (Fred McMurray).

Rent (2005) ★★★
The story of a group of struggling downtown New York friends in the 1980s doesn't pack the punch of the stage musical. But it features key members of the original cast, which makes it a credible, if flawed, film adaptation.

Rudolph the Red-Nosed Reindeer (TV) (1964) ★★★★
The Second Wave began with this story of a misfit reindeer who goes on a hero's journey and returns home to assist Santa on a fog-filled Christmas Eve. This groundbreaking story launched the career of Rankin and Bass, who became the auteurs of the Second Wave.

Santa and the Ice Cream Bunny (1972) ★
In this notoriously bad Christmas film, Santa's sleigh gets stuck in the sands of a Florida beach. Before the Ice Cream Bunny comes to the rescue, there's a film-within-a-film of the fairy tale *Thumbelina.*

Santa Baby! (TV) 2001 ★
After sixteen years, Rankin and Bass release their first TV Christmas special about a songwriter looking for inspiration. The magic is gone.

Santa Claus (1925) ★★★
This fascinating half-hour silent film depicts Santa in the polar wilderness. Two children ask Santa what he does when it's not Christmas time and, in a flashback, he shows them his life in the frozen land he calls home.

Santa Claus (1959) ★
Bizarre, trippy, and surreal, this film shows Lucifer trying to stop Santa from delivering presents, but Merlin the magician comes to Santa's aid.

Santa Claus: The Movie (1985) ★
Perhaps the biggest box office Christmas flop of all time as well as one of the worst Christmas films, in this dud Dudley Moore plays an elf in a movie that's half Santa origin story and half corporate management strategy.

The Santa Clause (1994) ★★★
Divorced dad (Tim Allen) can't get on the good side of his son, who seems to prefer his mother's touchy feely psychologist boyfriend (Judge Reinhold). But after Santa is accidentally killed on Scott's roof, Scott takes over for Santa, and father and son start to bond.

The Santa Clause 2 (2002) ★★
Lightning doesn't strike twice. The sequel to the massively successful *The Santa Clause* is only sporadically funny.

The Santa Clause 3: The Escape Clause (2006) ★
The franchise is out of steam in this cash grab second sequel with Martin Short as Santa's nemesis Jack Frost.

Santa Claus Conquers the Martians (1964) ★
Low budget sets, appalling acting, and all the attributes of B movies come to the Christmas film. It's not a case of a movie so bad it's good. It's just bad.

Santa Claus Is Coming to Town (TV) (1970) ★★★★
In this film that borrows heavily from Frank Baum's novel *The Life and Adventures of Santa Claus*, Mickey Rooney plays a countercultural Santa who rebels against the tyrannical establishment figure the Burgermeister.

Santa with Muscles (1996) ★
If there was a fourth film to be added to the three that are routinely lampooned (the 1959 *Santa Claus, Santa Claus Conquers the Martians,* and *Santa and the Ice Cream Bunny*) this would be it. Ruthless businessman Hogan comes down with a case of amnesia and believes he's Santa Claus.

Saving Christmas (2014) ★
Kirk Cameron advocates to uphold the American Christmas celebration to rescue it from downers who think the holiday isn't religious enough or is too materialistic. Much of the film takes place in a car as a conversation, which makes it more commentary than narrative film.

Scrooge (1935) ★★
This largely forgettable version of *A Christmas Carol* stars Seymour Hicks as Scrooge. The 1951 Alastair Sim version is the go-to British black-and white-adaptation of Dickens's famous novella.

Scrooge (1970) ★★
A too-young-for-this-role Albert Finney overacts in this big budget musical version of *A Christmas Carol.* Much less about moral transformation than a hippie-fueled ideology of just being less uptight, man.

Scrooged (1988) ★★
Baby boomer anxiety about losing their countercultural foundation surfaces in this work-heavy contemporary adaptation of *A Christmas Carol* starring Bill Murray as a television executive. Murray played this type of role far better five years later in *Groundhog Day*.

Serendipity (2001) ★★
John Cusack and Kate Beckinsale run into each other at a New York department store while Christmas shopping and leave it up to fate if they will meet again.

Shop Around the Corner (1940) ★★★★
This classic Ernst Lubitsch story of antagonistic employees (Jimmy Stewart and Margaret Sullavan) at a department store, who are secretly

pen pals, was remade as the musical *In the Good Old Summertime* and the corporate comedy *You've Got Mail.*

Silent Night Deadly Night (1984) ★
This awful "psycho Santa" slasher movie would have deservedly fallen into obscurity if not for the controversy surrounding its release. That stirred enough interest to spawn several sequels worse than the original.

Star in the Night (1945) ★★★
An Oscar-winning short, *Star in the Night* successfully updates the nativity story to the modern era. A pregnant woman and her husband arrive at a desert motel with no lodging available.

The Stingiest Man in Town (TV) (1978) ★
This Rankin and Bass adaptation of *A Christmas Carol* with Walter Matthau as Scrooge is disappointing and dull.

Surviving Christmas (2004) ★
Ben Affleck is a wealthy executive who is so lonely at Christmas he pays the blue-collar family in his childhood home to adopt him for Christmas. One of the worst Third Wave Christmas comedies.

Susan Slept Here (1954) ★★
A teenage delinquent (Debbie Reynolds) is dropped off for Christmas at the home of a has-been film screenwriter (Dick Powell) who is doing research on contemporary youth. A somewhat icky plotline ensues.

Tenth Avenue Angel (1948) ★★★
Margaret O'Brien plays a child in poverty-stricken downtown New York during the Great Depression. She suffers a crisis of faith, which culminates in what appears to be a Christmas Eve miracle. Underappreciated.

The Thin Man (1934) ★★★★
This film featuring a sleuthing martini-soaked married couple (William Powell and Myrna Loy) invented the crime story set during Christmas that is not a full-fledged Christmas film. Christmas imagery is used for ironic effect and to contrast home life with criminal life.

This Christmas (2007) ★★
This African-American home-for-the-holidays dramedy hits all the clichés of the Third Wave Christmas family gathering film: affluence, unrealistic careers, sibling tension, a parental crisis, an outsider threatening the family unit, and a family member who needs to be brought back into the fold.

Three Days of the Condor (1975) ★★
The Watergate-era thriller uses Christmas as a backdrop as a CIA worker (Robert Redford) tries to figure out who he can trust after his co-workers are murdered.

Three Godfathers (1936) ★★★
This adaptation of Peter B. Kyne's book is solid, with Lewis Stone and Walter Brennan especially effective as two of the three cowboys who find redemption in the desert.

Three Godfathers (1948) ★★★★
John Ford's epic adaptation of Peter B. Kyne's often filmed 1913 novel stars John Wayne as one of three thieves finding redemption through a newborn baby. It features visually stunning desert sequences and one of Wayne's best performances.

Tokyo Godfathers (2003) ★★★
The animé version of *Three Godfathers* brings the story to contemporary urban Japan, maintaining the spirit of the original story while making it unique to its time and culture.

Trading Places (1983) ★★★★
In this successful updating of screwball comedy to the 1980s, Eddie Murphy and Dan Akyroyd swap roles as financial executive and homeless criminal after executives (brilliantly played by Ralph Bellamy and Don Ameche) strike a bet to see if it's environment or genetics that makes the man.

Trail of Robin Hood (1950) ★★
The low-budget Western starring Roy Rogers plays out the First Wave dichotomy between greedy business and altruistic business—at least when it comes to selling Christmas trees.

Trapped in Paradise (1994) ★
"Trapped in bull****" is how Jon Lovitz referred to this dismal attempt at a black comedy about three brothers fleeing New York to the small town of Paradise, Pennsylvania. The oddball brothers Lovitz, Dana Carvey, and Nicholas Cage stage a bank robbery but cannot leave town.

'Twas the Night Before Christmas (TV) 1974 ★★★
This Rankin and Bass TV special is underrated. After a letter appears in a newspaper doubting the existence of Santa Claus, a clockmaker tries to show his faith in Santa by building a clock tower.

Unaccompanied Minors (2006) ★★
Grumpy airport employee (Lewis Black) confines a group of parentless tweens to an airport holding room. They escape to talk about their family problems in somewhat of a cross between *The Breakfast Club* and *Home Alone.*

A Very Harold and Kumar Christmas (2011) ★
Not the first stoner Christmas comedy, this is the most overbearing one. Bromance is more fully realized in *The Night Before*, a 2015 stoner Christmas film starring Seth Rogen.

We're No Angels (1955) ★★★
The final film of The First Wave is somewhat of a redemption story laced with black humor. Humphrey Bogart, Aldo Ray, and Peter Ustinov are three escaped convicts from a prison who enter a family business to rob it but end up helping the family.

While You Were Sleeping (1995) ★★
In this dated Christmas rom com, subway token taker Lucy (Sandra Bullock) falls for a dishy executive she sees at the train station. After being

attacked by robbers on Christmas, he lies in a coma while his family mistakenly believes she's his fiancé.

White Christmas (1954) ★★★★
Bing Crosby and Danny Kaye are performers honoring their former army general struggling in a snowless Vermont lodge at Christmas. Fun, entertaining, redemptive. What's not to love?

Why Him? (2016) ★
On the surface a Christmas romance, *Why Him?* is really more of an intergenerational clash between a dot-com exec Laird (James Franco) and an old-school business father Ned (Brian Cranston), father of the college student Laird wants to marry.

The Year without a Santa Claus (TV) (1974) ★★★★
Although this movie is best known for the Snow Miser and Heat Miser characters, Mickey Rooney plays an exhausted Santa who feels unappreciated. The world's not ready for a Mrs. Claus making the deliveries, so Santa heads to Dixie to find some Christmas spirit. Iconic.

GOSPEL-BASED MOVIES WITH NATIVITY STORIES

The Life and Passion of Christ (1903) ★★★
This fascinating forty-four-minute early silent film on the life of Christ contains painstaking hand-painted color tints.

From the Manger to the Cross (1912) ★★★
An hour-plus silent gospel film, this one is notable for being filmed on location in the Middle East, with stunning shots of the holy couple at the Egyptian pyramids during the flight into Egypt.

Ben Hur (1925) ★★★
The first feature-length adaptation of Lew Wallace's *Ben-Hur: Tale of the Christ* includes color footage during the nativity scenes.

Ben Hur (1959) ★★★★
The action-packed big budget remake of the epic silent film includes a legendary chariot race sequence. However, it reduces the nativity to a three-minute scene of shepherds and magi together at the birth of Christ.

The Messiah (1975) ★★★
Roberto Rosellini's class-conscious opening depicts Herod's decadent and violent rulers against the oppressed Jews.

Jesus of Nazareth (TV) (1977) ★★★
There is extensive nonbiblical material in the birth narrative that focuses more on Joseph's backstory than Mary's.

King of Kings (1961) ★★
Sometimes called *I Was A Teenage Jesus* because of heartthrob Jeffrey Hunter's role as Jesus, it's a squeaky clean variation on the birth narrative.

The Gospel According to St. Matthew (1964) ★★★★
Pasolini's masterpiece is overall the best gospel film to date—partly because it most closely follows the gospel. Told from the Joseph-centric Gospel of Matthew, it nonetheless has compelling shots of a young mystical and vulnerable Mary.

The Greatest Story Ever Told (1965) ★
The cumbersome and plodding biblical epic features a stagey and formal birth narrative sequence. As in many gospel films, there's a lot more Herod than holy couple.

Life of Brian (1979) ★★
The star/magi/manger nativity clichés are so standard that, until the end of the nativity segment, this parody is indistinguishable from a straight gospel story.

Son of God (2014) ★★★
The birth narrative is reduced to less than a minute in this somewhat stiff but watchable film.

Notes

CHAPTER ONE: What Is a Christmas Movie?

1. Penne L. Restad, *Christmas in America: A History* (New York: Oxford University Press, 1996), 171.

2. Mark H. Glancy, "Dreaming of Christmas: Hollywood and the Second World War," in *Christmas at the Movies: Images of Christmas in American, British, and European Cinema*, ed. Mark Connelly (London: I.B. Tauris, 2001), 60.

3. Restad, *Christmas in America*, 137.

4. Mark Connelly, ed., *Christmas at the Movies: Images of Christmas in American, British, and European Cinema* (London: I.B. Tauris, 2001), 3.

5. Steven Nissenbaum, *The Battle for Christmas: A Social and Cultural History of Our Most Cherished Holiday* (New York: Vintage Books, 1997), 73.

6. Ibid., 74.

7. Ibid., 81.

8. Restad, *Christmas in America*, 155.

9. Nissenbaum, *Battle for Christmas*, 172–75.

10. Restad, *Christmas in America*, 149.

11. Ibid., 143.

12. Ibid., 52.

13. Russell Belk, "Materialism and the Modern U.S. Christmas," in *Unwrapping Christmas*, ed. Daniel Miller (Oxford: Clarendon Press, 1993), 83.

14. Ibid.

15. Ibid., 82.

16. Ibid.

17. Gerry Bowler, *Santa Claus: A Biography* (Toronto: McClelland & Stewart, 2005), 194.

18. Ibid., 229–30.

19. Glancy, "Dreaming of Christmas," 60.

CHAPTER TWO: The Birth Narrative of Jesus on Film

20. Bruce Francis Babington and Peter William Evans, *Biblical Epics: Sacred Literature in the Hollywood Cinema* (Eugene, OR: Wipf & Stock, 2009), 420.

21. Ibid., 99.

22. George Buttrick, ed., *The Interpreter's Bible,* vol. 7 (Nashville: Abingdon Press, 1951), 256.

23. Barnes W. Tatum, *Jesus at the Movies: A Guide to the First Hundred Years and Beyond* (Salem, OR: Polebridge Press, 2013), 13–14.

24. Raymond E. Brown, *The Birth of the Messiah: A Commentary on the Infancy Narratives in the Gospels of Matthew and Luke* (New York: Doubleday, 1993), 167, 182.

25. Tatum, *Jesus at the Movies,* 10.

26. John 1:14.

27. Lloyd Baugh, *Imaging the Divine* (Lanham, MD: Sheed & Ward, 1997), 78.

28. Rose Pacatte, "The Nativity Story," *St. Anthony Messenger* 114, no. 7 (Dec. 2006): 34.

29. Ty Burr, "'The Nativity Story': A Reverent Retelling," *Boston Globe*, Dec. 1, 2006, D1.

30. Lee Lourdeaux, *Italian and Irish Filmmakers in America: Ford, Capra, Coppola, and Scorsese* (Philadelphia: Temple University Press, 1990), 123.

31. Joseph McBride, "John McBride on *Three Godfathers,*" *Film Comment* 9, no. 4 (Jul./Aug. 1973): 55.

32. Lourdeaux, *Italian and Irish Filmmakers,* 123.

33. Joseph McBride, *Searching for John Ford* (New York: St. Martin's Press, 2001), 442.

34. Peggy Polk, "Pope Condemns Controversial 'Hail Mary' Film," UPI, April 23, 1985.

35. Vincent Canby, "Godard's Hail Mary," *New York Times*, Oct. 7, 1985, C16.

CHAPTER THREE: How *A Christmas Carol* Shaped the Christmas Movie Genre

36. Peter Ackroyd, *Dickens* (New York: Harper Collins, 1990), 410.

37. Charles Dickens, *American Notes and Pictures from Italy* (Oxford: Oxford University Press), 249.

38. Ackroyd, *Dickens,* 408.

39. Paul Davis, *The Lives and Times of Ebeneezer Scrooge* (New Haven, CT: Yale University Press, 1990), 7.

40. Ackroyd, *Dickens,* 409.

41. Davis, *Lives and Times,* 41.

42. James Chapman, "God Bless Us, Every One: Movie Adaptations of *A Christmas Carol,*" in Connelly, *Christmas at the Movies,* 14.

43. Luke 16:19–21.

44. Charles Dickens, *A Christmas Carol and Other Christmas Writings* (New York: Penguin, 2005), 108–10.

45. William James, *The Varieties of Religious Experience* (New York: Random House, 1994), 272–73.

46. Christopher Deacy, "Salvation," in *The Routledge Companion to Religion and Film*, ed. John Lyden (Milton Park, UK: Routledge, 2009), 351.

47. Joseph W. Childers, "So, This Is Christmas," in *Contemporary Dickens*, ed. Eileen Gillooly and Deidre David (Columbus: Ohio State University Press, 2009), 125.

48. Ibid., 124–25.

49. Joseph Gold, "The Conversion of Scrooge," in *Readings on Charles Dickens' A Christmas Carol*, ed. Jill Karson (London: Greenhaven Press, 2000), 102.

50. Davis, *Lives and Times,* 15.

51. Mark Connelly, *Christmas: A Social History* (London: I.B. Tauris, 1999), 169.

52. Fred Guida, *A Christmas Carol and Its Adaptations* (Jefferson, NC: McFarland, 2000), 97.

53. Davis, *Lives and Times,* 174.

54. Ibid., 202.

55. Ibid., 292–93.

56. Ibid., 203.

57. Ibid.

58. Ibid.

59. Ibid., 296.

60. Chapman, "God Bless Us," 28.

61. Ibid.

62. Davis, *Lives and Times,* 234.

63. Chapman, "God Bless Us," 31.

64. Ibid.

65. Alistair Harkness, "Shane Black on His Love of Writing, Superheroes and Iron Man 3," *The Scotsman*, April 25, 2013.

66. Forrest Wickman, "The Dickensian Aspect of Iron Man 3," *Slate*, May 3, 2013.

67. Ibid.

CHAPTER FOUR: Scroogelike Characters: Grinches, Skeletons, and Surrogate Santas

68. Dr. Seuss, *How the Grinch Stole Christmas 50th Anniversary Edition* (New York: Random House, 2007, originally published 1957), 60.

69. Ibid. 54.

70. Thomas A. Burns, "Dr. Seuss' *How the Grinch Stole Christmas*: Its Recent Acceptance into the American Popular Christmas Tradition," *New York Folklore* 2, nos. 3–4 (Fall–Winter 1976): 200.

71. Ibid., 198.

72. Ibid.

73. Ibid., 199.

74. Ibid.

75. Paul Flesher and Robert Torry, *Film & Religion* (Nashville: Abingdon Press, 2007), 31.

76. Ibid., 32.

77. Burns, "Dr. Seuss' *How the Grinch*," 199.

78. Judith and Neil Morgan, *Dr. Seuss & Mr. Geisel* (New York: Da Capo Press, 1995), 191.

79. Burns, "Dr. Seuss' *How the Grinch*," 196.

80. Phillip Nel, *Dr. Seuss: American Icon* (New York: Continuum, 2004), 133.

81. Gloria Goodale, "How Grinch Leaped Off the Pages and Onto the Screen," *Christian Science Monitor* 92, no. 251 (Nov. 17, 2000).

82. Ibid.

83. Vinette K. Pryce, "Bigotry Made the Grinch Steal Christmas," *New York Amsterdam News* 91, no. 46 (Nov. 16, 2000): 26.

84. Ibid.

85. Jonah Goldberg, "Hollywood's Grinch," *National Review* 53, no.1 (Jan. 22, 2001): 26–27.

86. Flesher and Torry, *Film and Religion*, 32.

87. Ibid., 33.

88. Lee DeVito, "'The Nightmare Before Christmas'—Tim Burton's Lesson of Cultural Appropriation Gone Awry," *Detroit Metro Times*, Dec. 17, 2014.

89. Viktor Frankl, *Man's Search for Meaning* (New York: Touchstone, 1959), 108.

90. Ibid., 112.

91. Ibid., 114.

92. A. O. Scott, "The Death of Adulthood in American Culture," *New York Times*, Sept. 11, 2014.

93. Ibid.

94. Anthony Balducci, *I Won't Grow Up: The Comic Man-Child in Film from 1901 to the Present* (Jefferson, NC: McFarland, 2016), 138.

CHAPTER FIVE: The First Wave

95. Mark Glancy, "Dreaming of Christmas: Hollywood and the Second World War," in Connelly, *Christmas at the Movies*, 59.

96. Eugenia Kaledin, *Daily Life in the United States 1940–1959: Shifting Worlds* (London: Greenwood Press, 2000), 9.

97. Ibid.

98. Dorothy Rabinowitz, "American Masters: Bing Crosby Rediscovered," *Wall Street Journal*, Nov. 28, 2014.

99. Glancy, "Dreaming of Christmas," 65.

100. Ibid., 70.

101. Carolyn Sigler, "I'll Be Home for Christmas: Misrule and the Paradox of Genre in World War II–Era Christmas Films," *Journal of American Culture* 28, no. 4 (Dec. 2005): 350–51.

102. Ibid., 347.

103. Ibid., 349.

104. Ibid., 351.

105. Judith Weisenfeld, "The Silent Social Problem Film," *Catholics in the Movies,* ed. Colleen McDannell (New York: Oxford University Press, 2008), 42.

106. Frederick C. Szebin, "Hammett Rewritten," *Films in Review* 45, no. 7/8 (Jul./Aug. 1994).

107. William Paul, *Ernst Lubitsch's American Comedy* (New York: Columbia University Press, 1983), 176.

108. Ibid., 187.

109. Ibid.

110. Ibid.

111. Daniel Miller, *Unwrapping Christmas* (Oxford: Clarendon Press, 1995), 6.

112. Glancy, "Dreaming of Christmas," 61.

113. Andrew Dickos, *Intrepid Laughter: Preston Sturges and the Movies* (Metuchen, NJ: Scarecrow Press, 1985), 65–67.

114. Ibid., 72.

115. Ibid.

116. Ibid.

117. Ibid., 71.

118. Schrader, "Notes on Film Noir," 56–57.

119. Ibid., 57.

120. Ibid., 56.

121. Aljean Harmetz, "Deanna Durbin, Plucky Teenage Star of the Depression Era, Is Dead at 91," *New York Times,* May 1, 2013, B20.

122. Andrew Spicer, *Film Noir* (New York: Pearson, 2002), 114.

123. Alain Silver and Elizabeth Ward, *Film Noir: An Encyclopedic Reference to the American Style* (New York: Overlook Press, 1979), 167.

124. Robert B. Ray, *A Certain Tendency of the American Cinema 1930–1980* (Princeton, NJ: Princeton University Press, 1985), 84.

125. Ibid., 83.

126. James Naramore, *The Films of Vincente Minnelli* (New York: Cambridge University Press, 1993), 88.

127. Ibid.

128. Glancy, "Dreaming of Christmas," 69–70.

129. Ray, *Certain Tendency*, 84.

130. Robert L. McLaughlin, and Sally E. Perry, *We'll Always Have the Movies: American Cinema During World War II* (Lexington: University Press of Kentucky, 2006), 271.

CHAPTER SIX: George Bailey as a Modern-Day Job: The Suffering of an American Dreamer

131. Daniel J. Sullivan, "Sentimental Hogwash? On Capra's *It's a Wonderful Life,*" *Humanitas* 18, no. 1–2 (2005): 121–22.

132. Ibid., 121.

133. Robert B. Ray, *A Certain Tendency of the Hollywood Cinema 1930–1980* (Princeton, NJ: Princeton University Press, 1985), 186.

134. Ray Carney, *American Vision: The Films of Frank Capra* (Middletown, CT: Wesleyan University Press, 1986), 399, 410.

135. Lorraine Mortimer, "The Grim Enchantment of *It's a Wonderful Life*," *The Massachusetts Review* 36, no. 4 (Winter 1995): 658.

136. Genesis 37:19.

137. Ray, *Certain Tendency of Hollywood Cinema*, 198–99.

138. Carney, *American Vision*, 381.

139. Jeanine Basinger, *It's a Wonderful Life Book* (New York: Alfred A. Knopf, 1986), 75.

140. Robin Wood, "Ideology, Genre, Auteur," *Film Comment* 13, no. 1 (Jan. 1, 1977): 48–49.

141. Basinger, *Wonderful Life Book*, 75.

142. Basinger's *It's a Wonderful Life Book* contains some tantalizing script excerpts and information about plotlines from earlier scripts of the film. Unfortunately, no early scripts have been published in their entirety. Basinger's book includes a few scenes and plot overviews, including an early script that included two versions of George Bailey.

143. Jonathan Mundy, *A Hollywood Carol's Wonderful Life*, in Connelly, *Christmas at the Movies*, 45.

144. Basinger, *Wonderful Life Book*, 54.

145. Frank Capra, *The Name Above the Title: An Autobiography* (New York: Macmillan, 1971), 382–83.

146. Jimmy Hawkins, *It's a Wonderful Life: The Fiftieth Anniversary Scrapbook* (Philadelphia: Courage Books, 1996), 40.

147. Ibid., 42.

148. Ibid., 40.

149. Mundy, *Hollywood Carol's Wonderful Life*, 48.

150. Sullivan, "Sentimental Hogwash?" 132.

151. Carney, *American Vision*, 410.

152. Ibid.

153. Basinger, *Wonderful Life Book*, 75.

154. John 8:11.

155. Randall Fallows, "George Bailey in the Vital Center: Postwar Liberal Politics and *It's a Wonderful Life*," *Journal of Popular Film and Television* 25, no. 2 (1997): 54.

156. Ibid., 52.

157. Greg Asimakoupoulos, *Finding God in* It's a Wonderful Life (Escondido, CA: eChristian, 2012), 47–48.

158. John Noakes, "Bankers and Common Men in Bedford Falls," *Film History* 10 (1988): 316.

159. Carney, *American Vision*, 382.

160. Wood, "Ideology, Genre, Auteur," 49.

161. Sullivan, "Sentimental Hogwash?," 137.

162. Ray, *Certain Tendency of Hollywood Cinema*, 198–99.

163. Emmanuel Levy, *Small Town America in Film: The Decline and Fall of Community* (New York: Continuum, 1991), 25.

164. Ibid., 107.

165. Jeffrey Richards, "Frank Capra and the Cinema of Populism," *Movies and Methods*, ed. Bill Nichols (Berkeley: University of California, 1976), 77.

166. Susan Mackey-Kallis, *The Hero and the Perennial Journey Home in American Film* (Philadelphia: University of Pennsylvania Press, 2001), 1, 7.

CHAPTER SEVEN: The Christmas Film at Its Most Probing: The Postwar Years

167. Schrader, "Notes on Film Noir," 55.

168. Kaledin, *Daily Life in the United States*, 70.

169. Ibid., 69.

170. R. Barton Palmer, *Hollywood's Dark Cinema: The American Film Noir* (Woodbridge, CT: Twayne, 1994), 6.

171. Connelly, *Christmas at the Movies*, 6.

172. Russell Belk, "Materialism and the Making of the Modern American Christmas," in Miller, *Unwrapping Christmas*, 91.

173. Ibid., 92.

174. Leigh Eric Schmidt, *Consumer Rites: The Buying and Selling of American Holidays* (Princeton, NJ: Princeton University Press, 1997), 173.

175. See John 2:15.

176. See Matthew 27:15–26; Mark 15:6–15; Luke 23:13–25, and John 18:38–40 and 19:1–16.

177. See Matthew 26:57–68.

178. Schmidt, *Consumer Rites*, 173.

179. Mark Connelly, "Santa Claus: The Movie," in Connelly, *Christmas at the Movies*, 120.

180. Ibid., 121.

181. Matthew 16:15.

182. Proverbs 31:28.

183. Matthew 10:29.

184. James Pearl, "History and Masculinity in F. Scott Fitzgerald's *This Side of Paradise*," *Modern Fiction Studies* 51, no. 1 (2005): 1–33.

185. Joseph McBride, *Frank Capra, the Catastrophe of Success* (New York: Simon & Schuster, 1992), 509.

186. Palmer, *Hollywood's Dark Cinema*, 19.

187. John David Rhodes, "White Christmas, or Modernism," *Modernism/Modernity* 13, no. 2 (2006): 300.

188. Ibid., 292–93.

189. Linda Mizejewski, "Minstrelsy and Wartime Buddies: Racial and Sexual Histories in White Christmas," *Journal of Popular Film & Television* 36, no. 1 (2008): 24.

190. Andre Breton, *Anthology of Black Humor* (San Francisco: City Lights, 2001), xix.

191. Kaledin, *Daily Life in the United States*, 121.

192. Ibid., 121.

193. Ibid., 122.

194. Freedom of Information and Privacy Acts, "Communist Infiltration—Motion Picture Industry" (COMPIC) (Excerpts), File #100-138754, https://ia801003.us.archive.org/29/items/FBI_File_Communist_Infiltration_Motion_Picture_Industry_COMPIC_ALL_EXCERPTS/compic9a.pdf.

195. Ian Brookes, "The Eye of Power: Postwar Fordism and the Panoptic Corporation in the 1950s," *Journal of Management History* 37, no. 4 (2009): 153.

196. Ibid.

197. Nora Henry, *Ethics and Social Criticism in the Hollywood Films of Erich von Stroheim, Ernst Lubitsch, and Billy Wilder* (Westport, CT: Praeger, 2001), 162.

198. A common translation of the Yiddish "mensch" would be "a person of integrity."

199. Henry, *Ethics and Social Criticism*, 160.

200. Ibid., 169.

201. Bert Spector, "The Man in the Gray Flannel Suit in the Executive Suite: American Corporate Movies in the 1950s," *Journal of Management History* 14 (January 11, 2008).

CHAPTER EIGHT: Rankin-Bass and the Second Wave

202. Chris Welch, "'Rudolph the Red-Nosed Reindeer Figurines Get a Second Life,'" CNN.com, Dec., 23 2015, www.cnn.com/2015/12/23/living/rudolph-red-nose-reindeer-figurine-feat/index.html.

203. Television Academy Foundation, Arthur Rankin Jr. interview, 2005, interviews.televisionacademy.com/interviews/arthur-rankin-jr.

204. Ronald D. Lankford, *Rudolph the Red-Nosed Reindeer: An American Hero* (Lebanon, NH: University Press of New England, 2017), 128–29.

CHAPTER NINE: Rankin and Bass: The Auteurs of the Second Wave

205. Matthew 5:8.

206. Lucy Rollin and Mark West, "Pinocchio's Journey from the Pleasure Principle to the Reality Principle," in *Psychoanalytic Responses to Children's Literature* (Jefferson, NC: McFarland, 1999), 65.

CHAPTER TEN: The Third Wave

207. Douglas Keay, "Interview for Woman's Own," Margaret Thatcher Foundation, Sept. 23, 1987, https://www.margaretthatcher.org/document/106689.

208. Daniel Miller, "A Theory of Christmas," in Miller, *Unwrapping Christmas*, 15, 32.

209. *This Christmas*, directed by Preston A. Whitmore II, performances by Delroy Lindo, Loretta Devine, and Idris Elba, 2007, Rainforest Films, DVD extra interview.

210. *The Wizard of Oz* characters and a *Boy's Life* magazine suggest the film takes place in 1939; the calendar, radio show, and decoder ring indicate 1940; the football game

1941; and the Bing Crosby song "Santa Claus Is Coming to Town" suggests 1943, the year of the song's release. Less overt references including cars, clothes, and toys suggest an even wider range of dates.

211. Naomi Klein, *No Logo: Taking Aim at the Brand Bullies* (New York: Picador, 2002), 4.

212. Eugene B. Bergmann, "Christmas Revisited: Minor Disasters and Happy Endings," in *A Christmas Story: Behind the Scenes of a Holiday Classic*, ed. Caseen Gaines (Toronto: ECW Press, 2013), xviii.

213. Ibid., xvi.

214. James Poniewozik, "Generation X-mas: The Rise of 'A Christmas Story,'" *Time,* Dec. 24, 2011, entertainment.time.com/2011/12/24/generation-x-mas-the-rise-of-a-christmas-story.

215. Ibid.

216. Erin Haire and Douglas Nelson, "Crummy Commercials and BB Guns," in *Christmas Philosophy for Everyone: Better Than Coal*, ed. Scott C. Lowe (Oxford: Oxford University Press, 2010), 84.

217. Ibid., 89.

218. Janet Maslin, "On Vacation Once Again," *New York Times*, Dec. 1, 1989, C12.

219. Marc Horton, "Christmas Vacation Ho-Ho-Ho Ho-rrible!" *Edmonton Journal*, Dec. 1, 1989, E1.

220. Bruce Rolfsen, "Sentimentality Softens 'Christmas Vacation's' Bite," *Northwest Florida Daily News*, Dec. 8, 1989, http://search.proquest.com.ezproxy.hacc.edu/docview/379321959?accountid=11302.

221. See Luke 23:34.

222. Hal Lipper, "Christmas Isn't Gifted: Low Humor Wraps Lampoon's Film Series," *St. Petersburg Times*, Dec. 1, 1989, 7.

223. Anthony Balducci, *I Won't Grow Up! The Comic Man-Child in Film from 1901 to the Present* (Jefferson, NC: McFarland, 2016), 9.

224. Gina Kim, "You thought irony was dead? What a joke," *Sacramento Bee*, Jan. 2007.

225. Ibid.

226. Simon Thompson, "The 25 Highest-Grossing Christmas Movies of All Time at the U.S. Box Office," *Forbes*, Nov. 27, 2016, www.forbes.com/sites/simonthompson/2016/11/27/the-25-highest-grossing-christmas-movies-of-all-time-at-the-u-s-box-office/#408903c913b3.

227. Rowana Agajanian, "Peace on Earth, Goodwill to All Men: The Depiction of Christmas in Modern Hollywood Films," in Connelly, *Christmas at the Movies*, 150.

228. Ibid., 151.

229. Ibid., 150.

230. Ibid.

231. Larry Rohter, "John Hughes in Macaulay Culkin is 'Home Alone' at the Top," *Worcester Telegram & Gazette*, Dec. 16, 1990, 4.

232. Several popular YouTube videos, including "Doctors Diagnose the Injuries in Home Alone," outline how the villains Harry and Marv would not have survived many of the injuries they underwent in the films.

CHAPTER ELEVEN: Christmas and the Family under Siege

233. Ana Swanson, "144 Years of Marriage and Divorce in the United States, in One Chart," *The Washington Post*, June 23, 2015, www.washingtonpost.com/news/wonk/wp/2015/06/23/144-years-of-marriage-and-divorce-in-the-united-states-in-one-chart/?utm_term=.252220d6ca37.

234. Thomas D. Snyder, ed., "120 Years of American Education: A Statistical Portrait," National Center for Education Statistics, 1993, 67.

235. Gretchen Livingston, "Fewer Than Half of U.S. Kids Today Live in a 'Traditional' Family," Pew Research Center, Dec. 22, 2014, www.pewresearch.org/fact-tank/2014/12/22/less-than-half-of-u-s-kids-today-live-in-a-traditional-family/.

236. Kim Parker and Wendy Wang, "Modern Parenthood: Roles of Moms and Dads Converge as They Balance Work and Family," Pew Research Center, March 14, 2013, www.pewsocialtrends.org/2013/03/14/modern-parenthood-roles-of-moms-and-dads-converge-as-they-balance-work-and-family/.

237. Russell Belk, "Materialism and the Making of the Modern U.S. Christmas," in Miller, *Unwrapping Christmas*, 87.

238. David Peterson del Mar, *The American Family: From Obligation to Freedom* (New York: Palgrave MacMillan, 2011), 3.

239. Richard F. Selcer, "Home Sweet Movies," *Journal of Popular Film and Television* 18, no. 2 (Summer 1990), 56.

240. Peter F. Parshall, "'Die Hard' and the American Mythos," *Journal of Popular Film and Television* 18 (Winter 1991): 137.

241. Susan Jeffords, *Hard Bodies: Hollywood Masculinity in the Reagan Era* (New Brunswick, NJ: Rutgers University Press, 1994), 19.

242. Yvonne Tasker, *Spectacular Bodies: Gender, Genre, and the Action Cinema* (New York: Routledge, 1993), 64.

243. John Lyden, *Film and Religion: Myths, Morals, and Rituals* (New York: NYU Press, 2003), 151.

244. Adam Sternbergh, "On the Enduring Appeal of 'Die Hard,'" *New York Times*, Feb. 21, 2013, www.nytimes.com/2013/02/24/magazine/on-the-enduring-appeal-of-john-mcclane-and-die-hard.html. moved.

245. Parshall, "'Die Hard' and the American Mythos," 137.

246. Ibid.

247. Ibid., 136.

248. Rowana Agajanian, "Peace on Earth, Goodwill to All Men: The Depiction of Christmas in Modern Hollywood Films," in Connelly, *Christmas at the Movies*, 158.

249. Parshall, "'Die Hard' and the American Mythos," 136.

250. The Bobbie Wygant Archive, "Classic Interview: Bruce Willis for 'Die Hard' 1988," bobbiewygant.blogspot.com/2012/06/classic-interview-bruce-willis-for-die.html.

251. Lyden, *Film and Religion*, 149.

252. Agajanian, "Peace on Earth," 157.

253. Lyden, *Film and Religion*, 151.

254. Agajanian, "Peace on Earth," 156.

255. John Mundy, "Christmas and the Movies: Frames of Mind," in *Christmas, Ideology and Popular Culture* (Edinburgh, UK: Edinburgh University Press, 2008), 154.

256. Ibid., 176.

257. Christopher Orr, "'Love Actually' Is the Least Romantic Film of All Time," *The Atlantic*, Dec. 6, 2013, www.theatlantic.com/entertainment/archive/2013/12/-em-love-actually-em-is-the-least-romantic-film-of-all-time/282091/.

CHAPTER TWELVE: I'm Dreaming of a Dark Christmas

258. Andre Breton, *Anthology of Black Humor* (San Francisco: City Lights Publishers, 2001), xix.

259. Harold Ramis, *The Ice Harvest*, 2005, Universal, director commentary.

260. Ibid.

261. Bob Strauss, "Harold Ramis Discusses Religion, 'Ice Harvest' in 2005 Interview," *The Los Angeles Daily News*, Nov. 25, 2005, republished Feb. 24, 2014, https://www.dailynews.com/2014/02/24/harold-ramis-discusses-religion-ice-harvest-in-2005-interview/.

262. Kim Newman, "You Better Watch Out: Christmas in the Horror Film," in Connelly, *Christmas at the Movies*, 139.

263. Carol J. Clover, "Her Body, Himself: Gender in the Slasher Film," in *The Dread of Difference: Gender and the Horror Film*, ed. Barry Keith Grant (Austin: University of Texas Press, 1996), 77, 81, 84.

264. Ibid., 92.

265. Stephen Thrower, "Ringing the Changes: Bob Clark's *Black Christmas*," in *Yuletide Terror: Christmas Horror on Film and Television*, ed. Paul Corupe and Kier-La Janisse (Canada: Spectacular Optical, 2017), 19.

266. Jim Knipfel, "'Christmas Evil—You Better Watch Out' Is the 'Taxi Driver' of Christmas Movies," Den of Geek, Dec. 9, 2017, http://www.denofgeek.com/us /movies /santa-claus/34766/christmas-evil-you-better-watch-out-is-the-taxi-driver-of-christmas-movies.

267. Amanda Reyes, "You Better Watch Out: A Talk with *Christmas Evil* director Lewis Jackson," in Corupe and Janisse, *Yuletide Terror*, 63.

268. Julie Scharper, "You Better Watch Out: Krampus Is Coming to Town," TCA Regional News, Dec. 9, 2014, https://search.proquest.com/wire-feeds/you-better-watch-out-krampus-is-coming-town/docview/1635055146/se-2?accountid=3588.

269. Al Ridenour, *The Krampus and the Old Dark Christmas: Roots and Rebirth of the Folkloric Devil* (Port Townsend, WA: Feral House, 2016), 10.

270. Paul Corupe, "Horns for the Holidays: The Krampus Conquers North American Horror Films," in Corupe and Janisse, *Yuletide Terror*, 314.

271. Susan Bernardo, "Recycling Victims and Villains in *Batman Returns*," *Literature Film Quarterly* 22, no. 1 (Jan. 1994): 16.

272. Alessandro Giovannelli, "Cognitive Value and Imaginative Identification: The Case of Kubrick's Eyes Wide Shut," *The Journal of Aesthetics and Art Criticism* 68 (Fall 2010): 356.

273. Thomas Allen Nelson, *Kubrick: Inside a Film Artist's Maze* (Bloomington: Indiana University Press, 2000), 289.

274. Richard Schickel, "Eyes Wide Shut: All Eyes on Them," *Time*, July 5, 1999, http://content.time.com/time/subscriber/article/0,33009,991414-1,00.html.

275. Raleigh Whitinger and Susan Ingram, "Schnitzler, Kubrick, and 'Fidelio,'" *Mosaic: A Journal for the Interdisciplinary Study of Literature* 36, no. 3 (2003): 63.

276. Charles H. Helmetag, "Dream Odysseys: Schnitzler's Traumnovelle and Kubrick's Eyes Wide Shut," *Literature/Film Quarterly* 31, no. 4 (2003): 281.

277. Mattias Frey, "Fidelio: Love, Adaptation, and Eyes Wide Shut," *Literature/Film Quarterly* 34, no. 1 (2006): 39.

278. Schickel, "Eyes Wide Shut."

279. Amy J. Ransom, "Opening 'Eyes Wide Shut': Genre, Reception, and Kubrick's Last Film," *Journal of Film and Video* 62, no. 4 (2010): 43.

280. Nelson, *Kubrick: Inside,* 286.

281. Giovannelli, "Cognitive Value," 360.

282. Ibid.

CHAPTER THIRTEEN: The Minority Report: A Return to Transcendentalism

283. Bradley Herling, "The Horror of Playing God: Job's Nightmare and Michael Haneke's Funny Games," *Journal of Religion and Popular Culture* 24 (Summer 2012): 234.

284. Job 1:1.

285. Job 1:11.

286. Louis Giannetti, *Understanding Movies*, 3rd ed. (Upper Saddle River, NJ: Prentice-Hall, 1982), 139.

287. Newman, "You Better Watch Out: Christmas in the Horror Film," in Connelly, *Christmas at the Movies,* 138.

288. Shaila K. Dewan, "Do Horror Films Filter the Horrors of History?" *New York Times,* Oct. 14, 2000.

289. Dave Canfield, "Silent Night, Holy Sh*t: Holy Terror and the Dark Side of the Nativity," in Corupe and Janisse, *Yuletide Terror*, 234.

290. Filipa Antunes, "Rethinking PG-13: Ratings and the Boundaries of Childhood and Horror," *Journal of Film and Video* 69 (Spring 2017): 36.

291. Ibid., 37.

292. John D. Denne, "Society and the Monster," in *Focus on the Horror Film*, ed. Roy Huss and T. J. Ross (Upper Saddle River, NJ: Prentice-Hall, 1972), 125.

293. Angus McFadzean, "The Suburban Fantastic: A Semantic and Synactic Grouping in Contemporary Hollywood Cinema," *Science Fiction Film and Television* 10 (2017): 1.

294. Ibid., 4.

295. Ibid., 8.

296. Ross Murfin and Supryia M. Ray, *The Bedford Glossary of Critical and Literary Terms* (New York: Bedford/St. Martin's, 2003), 252.

297. Amy Longsdorf, "Ferrell's 'Cotton-Headed Ninnymuggins' Kicks Off Holiday Film Fare," *The Morning Call*, Nov. 6, 2003, E3.

298. Steven Heller, "Chris Van Allsburg, *Creator: The Polar Express*," *Print* 58, no. 6 (Nov./Dec. 2004): 52.

299. Sheryl O'Sullivan, "The Invisible Being: Finding Images of God in Secular Children's Literature," *Christian Education Journal* 3, no. 1 (2006): 52.